Understanding and Responding to Homeless Experiences, Identities and Cultures

Edited by

Mike Seal

Russell House Publishing

First published in 2007 by:
Russell House Publishing Ltd.
4 St. George's House
Uplyme Road
Lyme Regis
Dorset DT7 3LS

Tel: 01297-443948
Fax: 01297-442722
e-mail: help@russellhouse.co.uk
www.russellhouse.co.uk

British Library Cataloguing-in-publication Data:
A catalogue record for this book is available from the British Library.

ISBN: 978-1-905541-06-5

Typeset by TW Typesetting, Plymouth, Devon
Printed by Biddles Ltd, King's Lynn

About Russell House Publishing

Russell House Publishing aims to publish innovative and valuable materials to help
managers, practitioners, trainers, educators and students.

Our full catalogue covers: social policy, working with young people, helping children and
families, care of older people, social care, combating social exclusion, revitalising
communities and working with offenders.

Full details can be found at www.russellhouse.co.uk and we are pleased to send out
information to you by post. Our contact details are on this page.

We are always keen to receive feedback on publications and new ideas
for future projects.

Contents

Preface v

About the Contributors vi

Dedication and Acknowledgements viii

Introduction: Homelessness and identity 1
Mike Seal

Section One: Homeless people making sense of their experiences

Chapter 1: Identities of Rough sleepers in Oxford 10
Chantal Butchinsky

Chapter 2: Homelessness and the denial of sexual identity 27
Phillip Flynn

Chapter 3: Love on the streets: the denial of homeless people's
relationships 43
Tony Dodson (edited by Mike Seal)

Section Two: Organisational constructions of homeless experiences and identities

Chapter 4: Understanding the refugee experience 58
Jennie Geddes

Chapter 5: Difficult people? – Unresponsive services! Working with
homeless people with multiple needs 74
Pip Bevan

Chapter 6: Contesting and working with challenging behaviour 93
John Ames

Section Three: Identities and cultures in the homeless sector and societal and personal reactions to homelessness

Chapter 7: Homelessness and its impact on our personal and societal
identities 112
Mike Seal

Chapter 8: Homeless sector culture   126
           Andrew Van Doorn and Mick Kain

Chapter 9: Workers in the homelessness industry: towards an
           identity   142
           Mike Seal

Chapter 10: Conclusion: lessons to be learnt and actions to be taken   160
           Mike Seal

References   170

Index   181

Preface

There is a tendency to categorise homeless people into various stereotypes and to make assumptions about their lives. Only by understanding how we thereby construct homeless people's identities for them, can we guard against continuing this unhelpful practice and instead get to know them as they really are. By exploring how they cope with their environments, and make sense of their experiences, we can instead work effectively with them and support them.

In a previous work (Seal, 2005) I looked at how for many people homelessness is more than having no access to housing. Effective resettlement for many involves cognitive, emotional and practical changes on behalf of the homeless person. However, a number of homeless people have been through the 'homeless system', or rather different 'systems', many times. For some these experiences become a part of their identity. This book is concerned with understanding the nature of various homeless identities, how they are formed and what are the implications of them.

This is important for two reasons. Firstly, we need to understand particular identities, and the experiences and processes that are linked with these identities, because the process of change the person will need to undertake in addressing their homelessness will differ, as will the appropriate responses from agencies and practitioners. Secondly, in taking a particular stance on homeless identities, that they are social constructions subject to forces from both within the sector and from wider society, agencies need to acknowledge that homeless people create identities within and through those agencies' services. The book takes the view that forces of social construction should not bind homeless people. Rather the identities that are foisted on them are contested and negotiated by homeless people, and others, at the local and the political level. How the various identities are received, and contested, will form part of the exploration. The book therefore seeks to create an agenda for action for homeless people, practitioners, organisations and the homelessness sector as a whole.

The book features contributions from leading academics, practitioners, and people who are or have been homeless and work in relevant contexts. The book is topical and valuable to anyone working in the homelessness field, as well as those in social services, the probation service and the wider housing sector.

About the Contributors

John Ames has worked or studied in the social work and caring sector for 23 years and for the last ten years in the field of homelessness; currently he is the training officer for Thames Reach Bondway. Previous to this he managed homeless hostels and worked in a specialist mental health project with the homeless. He is also a freelance trainer and an associate tutor at YMCA George William College in East London. He has a Diploma in Social Work, a degree in Applied Social Studies from Sheffield Hallam University and a Postgraduate Certificate in Management from the Open University.

Pip Bevan has worked for 30 years in the field of homelessness and mental health. He was initially a priest and encountered homelessness in pastoral work in parishes and as a chaplain to mental hospitals and prisons. He then worked for organisations like the Richmond Fellowship, the Patchwork Community and St. Mungo's. He was seconded to the National Homeless Alliance to research and write the *Resettlement Handbook*. Three years ago he returned to Homeless Link, to co-ordinate work on homeless people with Multiple Needs. He is also the lead for health and homelessness at Homeless Link, and co-ordinates the Health Inclusion Project funded by the Department of Health.

Dr Chantal Butchinsky is a part-time Lecturer at Oxford Brookes University. She was recently awarded her doctoral degree in Social Anthropology, looking at the serial nature of street homelessness in Oxford. She has been a worker in night shelters for the homeless. Her current research interests include: the 'junkie' identity; rough sleepers' transition to indoor places; and processes of forming identities.

Tony Dodson has lived the homeless experience for over 30 years since being moved into temporary accommodation at the age of seven. He has lived in squats, shelters, hostels, communes and with the travelling community. In recent years he has been involved in many research projects for Crisis, Shelter and the Office of the Deputy Prime Minister to name a few. He has been pioneering peer-led and narrative research in the field. He has sustained a relationship with another rough sleeper for 15 years.

Andrew Van Doorn has worked in and with the homelessness sector for nearly 15 years as a frontline worker, researcher, policy analyst, and development worker across the UK and Europe. He has published research in the fields of voluntary sector development, homelessness, multiple needs and housing. He was awarded the Tony Denison Award for Homelessness Research in 2004 for his *Good Practice Companion* to *Emergency Accommodation* for homeless people. He currently works as the Head of Programmes at the Housing Associations' Charitable Trust (HACT). With Mick Kain, he co-authored a paper to the 2003 Housing Studies Association conference on the transformation required in the homelessness sector.

Phillip Flynn is currently working at an LGBT youth project (see p. 27) working with homeless young people and has previous experience of working in 'wet' homeless hostels. He recently graduated from the YMCA George Williams College with a degree in Informal and Community Education. He has experienced being street homeless and stayed in various hostels between 1990–2001. In the past, he was labelled by others as 'Lesbian' and tried to fit in with this identity. Since going back into education he has found his own identity and is in the process of gender reassignment surgery to be a transsexual man.

Jennie Geddes manages a project providing support to people living with and affected by HIV in Liverpool. She is also a counsellor in Manchester providing counselling to survivors of torture and is a part-time trainer. Jennie Geddes has worked in the care field for 15 years as a frontline worker with homeless people, has managed a project for street sex workers and more recently, has been supporting the development of refugee community organisations. She has a BA in Psychology and a Postgraduate Diploma in Counselling from John Moores University.

Mick Kain is an Organisational Facilitator supporting the development of third sector organisations. He comes from a background of specialist housing provision in the mental health sector offering support across a range of client and housing needs. He has ten years of management experience and, as a full-time trainer, developed frontline and managerial training programmes for national and local organisations. He offers organisational events, coach-mentoring and consultancy for senior management teams and boards. He also offers skills training in one-to-one work, group work, and training for front-line workers and service users.

Mike Seal is a Senior Lecturer in Informal and Community Education at the YMCA George Williams College in East London. He is the Programme Director for the Advanced Professional Certificate in Working with Homeless People. He has worked in the homelessness field for 16 years as a front-line worker, trainer and development worker in a variety of settings. He has an MA in Applied Anthropology and Community and Youth Work from Goldsmiths College, and is undertaking a doctorate at Kings College London. He is the author of *Resettling Homeless People: Theory and Practice* (2005) and *Working with Homeless People: A Training Manual* (2006), published by Russell House Publishing.

Dedication

This book is dedicated to all who have been homeless, still are homeless or who have come to the UK after much hardship. You shared your experiences with dignity and strength.

'Hold to the light' your strength in adversity. Be true to yourself

(Tony D)

Acknowledgements

We would like to thank, in no particular order: Jeremy Swain, Alice Evans, Lesley Dewhurst, Emma Daniel, Sarah Johnsen, John Hamblin, Jacqui and Cath Lewis, Adam Marshall and all at Homeless Link for their comments and thoughts at various stages; The Wingate Foundation, the Royal Anthropological Institute and the Satusoma award, who's scholarships contributed to making Chantal's research in Oxford possible; all those workers who responded to Mike Seal's Worker survey and Jack Ames for all the encouragement he gave John when he was alive and for the strength that this has given him since he's been gone. Finally I would like to give a big thanks to Caroline Gerrard for her thoughts, comments, proof reading and for generally putting up with the editor.

Also by Mike Seal:

Resettling Homeless People: Theory and Practice
2005   978-903855-65-2

Working with Homeless People: A Training Manual
2006   978-903855-71-3

Both published by Russell House Publishing Ltd
www.russellhouse.co.uk

Introduction: Homelessness and identity

Mike Seal

Homes are an inseparable element of our human identity. Deprived of all the aspects of his home, man would be deprived of himself, of his humanity.

(Havel, 1992)

Home is sometimes a place inside of me.

(Mise, 2000)

Home is where I return to myself.

(Jenkins, A., 2000)

Introduction

For many homeless people the experience of homelessness is an episode they live through, a temporary state of being, whose solution is access to housing. In a previous work (Seal, 2005) I explored how for many it can be more complex than this, and that often resettlement involves cognitive, emotional and practical changes on behalf of the individual. There are a number of homeless people who have been through the system, or rather different systems and experiences, many times, and for whom these experiences become a part of their sense of who they are. This phenomenon is the prime subject of this book: Identity. A legitimate question immediately arises as to why attention should be given to questions of identity in addressing a person's homelessness. Practitioners have challenged me in the past for such concerns, arguing that we should concentrate on meeting people's basic needs; and there can be nothing more basic than the need for shelter (Seal, 2005).

However, in making these challenges, people are implicitly embracing a humanistic viewpoint and invoking Maslow's (1962) 'hierarchy of needs'. Within this paradigm, self-actualisation and identity are 'higher needs' to be met after 'primary needs' have been satisfied. This position is understandable and I would argue that the meeting of Maslow's primary needs is the basis of much homelessness provision. However, the humanist paradigm is contested by many (Pearson and Podeschi, 1997). One criticism is that Maslow privileges middle class perspectives, implying that if you are poor you cannot fulfil 'higher needs' such as spirituality or having a coherent identity, or even have the need to conceptualise. One could counter-argue that a high self-esteem and a positive identity are just as essential to poor people, if not more so. Znaniecki (1934) thought that people's need to create identities is perhaps the defining aspect of humanity.

In this book we are concerned with the natures of various homeless identities and how they are formed. In particular we are interested in the part the homeless industry plays in constructing homelessness. This is in the belief that if people adopt particular identities, the process of change the person will need to undertake in addressing their homelessness will differ, as will appropriate responses from agencies and practitioners. The majority of cultural and social identities use 'place' as an important component (Brah, 1996): we need to ask how people who lack this, who are homeless, construct a sense of who they are as individuals and as a group.

The book will also take the view that, from being a rational and objective label, 'homelessness' is a socially constructed one that is a result of a broad combination of cultural meanings and values (Hutson and Liddiard, 1994; Hutson, 1999). However, I would contend that while homeless people's identities are subject to forces of social construction, from both within the sector and from wider society, they are not bound by them. Rather they are contested and negotiated by homeless people, and others, at the local and the political level. They are not simply victims; all individuals have some agency even when they seem totally powerless (Foucault and Gordon, 1986). Through the homeless provision they are subject to and in their encounters with the public, people who are homeless battle to make sense of their lives and part of this is through the identities they adopt, adapt and reject. It is for this reason that grappling with issues of identity is important for agencies and workers as they are a part of the process of identity formation. Once agencies acknowledge that people who are homeless create identities within and through their services, they can start to address how this process operates and the part they play in it. The book will therefore seek to create an agenda for action for homeless people, practitioners, organisations and the sector itself.

This introductory chapter aims to do two things. Firstly, it will examine the existing literature concerning homeless people and identity construction, building primarily on the work of Snow and Anderson, Daly and other American authors, exploring their applicability to the UK. Secondly it introduces subsequent chapters, which will explore different manifestations of homeless people's experiences and identities.

The literature on homeless identities

Some authors (Neale, 1997; Daly, 1996) say that while homeless peoples' actions seem illogical, contradictory and even self-destructive, this is a result of these competing dialogues and the social constraints that they are facing. People create an order, and a logic of their own according to their circumstances and life plans. Daly contends that most people seek 'rationality, coherence and predictability'. Many homeless people lose all three. They do not get rational responses from people and play up to this irrationality, sometimes to make a living. Coherence and predictability are again outside of their control – they could be made to leave a hostel with no notice, move on from a street 'pitch' or be thrust into their own flat at any moment. Consequently their lives are often characterised by 'immediate comfort, short-term satisfaction and long-term survival' (Daly, 1996). Change is almost always outside their sphere of control, chance is a major factor in their existence, they are rarely in equilibrium, and small changes become amplified. Nevertheless they do create coping strategies and a sense of order in isolation, anxiety, frustration and rejection.

People's behaviour in hostels is an example of how people do not think about the future because it is blurred with the past and present. Perpetual fatalistic uncertainty means the idea of future is quite incomprehensible. Behaviour in hostels is also an example of how agencies are assuming that people are not autonomous, adapting to their circumstances. As said before, they are assuming that people will just be held in a bubble until their permanent housing is sorted out. In fact they do adapt and meet other 'needs' but in often self-destructive ways.

I talked in a previous book about a model of needs held by Brandon (1998) that holds that in any situation people will seek four things:

- Some sense of control.
- Ways of using their skills.
- Ways of experiencing pain and joy.
- Ways of having contact.

The observed phenomena from my research is that drug and alcohol use in hostels rises to that of the highest user and that if people go in with a small marijuana habit they will often come out with a raging heroin habit. According to Daly the fact that the behaviour is destructive is not relevant to people, as they do not have a sense of the future. Alternatively, and given that a sense of future is often seen as an essential part of identity (Snow and Anderson, 1987), it may be that denied a future, people start to create a myth of one. One of the earliest pieces of work on homeless identities was in an ethnographic study by Snow and Anderson (1987). They identify three progressive stages of identification amongst homeless people, which I think echoes some of these ideas:

1. **Distancing:** either from the *association* of themselves from other homeless people ('I'm not like so and so'); from the *role* of the homeless person ('I'm not a typical homeless person'); or from the *institutional* that is meant to serve them ('they're all out to make money').
2. **Embracing:** again of *association* with other homeless people ('we're all in it together'); with the *role* of a homeless person ('I'm a bum') or of an *ideology* (taking on religious, spiritual beliefs). This happens either as an *explanation* of their situation ('I'm on a mission of salvation') or as *protection* ('I have nothing to fear, I'm a Christian').

3. **Fictive story telling:** either *embellishment* (typically of the past, saying they used to be a mercenary, when in fact they were a private in the army) or *outright fantasising*, typically of the future ('I've got this bloke whose going to set me up') or ('I've just got this feeling that I'm going to be a millionaire').

Patterns of identity are seen as fluid, moving from associational distancing and future fantasising to associational embracement and embellishment of the past. Importantly Snow and Anderson talk about how these identities are formed. They see a tension between the roles that homeless people are obliged to play, i.e. homeless people, and their 'self-identities', whether they are imagined or not. Self-identity and social role can be 'congruent' where the self implied by the latter is 'positive' or 'incongruent' where the self implied by the role is negative. It is in the latter case that *imagined* identities, the storytelling, will be formed.

Apart from the inherent problems with any staged models, most notably their positivistic nature (Ingleman, 1991), later authors found some of these roles, and the underpinning constructions of homeless people behind them, overly negative (Butchinsky, 2003; Boydell et al., 2000). Sommerville (1992) explains how 'the cultural milieu of life on the street becomes a means of redefining home': the camaraderie experienced on the street being a surrogate family they never had anywhere else. Zufferey and Kerr (2004), talk about a 'street norm' of reciprocity and a connection with other people experiencing homelessness, something Dodson will return to in his chapter on couples.

Returning to Snow and Anderson, what I find interesting about this last identified stage, fictional storytelling, is that while they explore the content of these stories to a degree, they do not explore their source. If we examine Snow and Anderson's analysis of how homeless people create their identities we find that they leave four questions unanswered:

- What factors influence how roles are constructed for homeless people?
- What is the dynamic between these constructions and people's personal identities?
- What part do agencies and practitioners play in this dynamic?
- What are the implications of these for practice and policy?

Hopefully some of these gaps will be filled by some of the chapters in this book.

Content and structure of this book

In the chapters that follow we will be concerned with understanding the nature of various homeless identities, how they are formed and their implications for the homeless sector. Three dimensions of this construction will be explored, in three sections of the book.

Section One: Homeless people making sense of their experiences

Section One will examine those identities that are at least partly 'owned' by the individual, sometimes as a form of resistance.

In Chapter 1 Butchinsky explores the conflict between discourses of dependency and independence that shapes or frames many of the processes leading rough sleepers to repeatedly depart from accommodation and return to the streets. She maintains that identities of neediness, though derived from empirical reality, are, in many contexts, rejected by rough sleepers whose survival in the harsh circumstances of street life provides evidence instead of strength. The account is based on ethnographic material obtained through participant observation, undertaken with rough sleepers, and is drawn on to show many different examples of this clash. The chapter raises questions about categories of 'deservingness' and 'needs', as well as a neglect of resources that rough sleepers create for themselves.

In Chapter 2 Flynn looks at why lesbian, gay, bisexual and transgendered (LGBT) people come to the West End of London every year, often to seek acceptance, but instead end up homeless. It explores and analyses why many LGBT homeless people are made to feel that they have to hide their sexuality or gender whilst on the street or in some hostels. The author will reflect on his own experiences and those of others in identifying as LGBT homeless. He examines how it feels when 'homelessness' becomes your identity and your sexuality or gender often has to be suppressed in order to survive. Here, the author highlights the impact this has on homeless LGBT people's identities.

In Chapter 3 Dodson explores the nature and importance of personal relationships on the streets. He takes the view that, while the formation of loving relationships is seen as a human and natural thing to do, it is a right that is systematically denied to homeless people by the services that are meant to meet their needs. The chapter explores these obstacles in the light of *Supporting People* and the St Mungo's report *Double Blind* as well as examining how the acknowledgement of people's relationships can be a key to building self-esteem and responsibility, and to breaking isolation. It again takes a narrative approach, cataloguing the experience of several couples, and drawing out general lessons to be learnt.

Section Two: Organisational contructions of homeless experiences and identities

Section Two will examine identities where the homelessness sector, and the care industry in general, have both played a major part in the construction of that identity. In Chapter 4 Geddes explores the particular resettlement issues faced by people granted leave to remain in the UK. It covers how people adjust to the UK system of housing and benefits and to their changes in status from asylum seeker to refugee with a right to remain but not yet a citizen. It explores the impact of 'pre-flight' and dispersal experiences on the resettlement process. It does this within the contexts of individual refugees, refugee communities and agencies concerned with resettlement and the provision of related support.

In Chapter 5 Bevan outlines how multiple health needs are prevalent in the lives of many single homeless people and how they are one of the most vulnerable groups in our society. He outlines recent research that shows how homeless people with multiple needs are becoming the majority of the people agencies work with. However, Bevan will contend that in reality, this group has a number of simple needs: a home, friends, income, meaningful daily activities, health needs and so on, which necessitate co-ordinated responses from several agencies. It is in realising this co-ordination that the complexity lies. This chapter therefore looks at the definition of multiple needs and examines who homeless people with multiple needs are; the prevalence of homeless people with multiple needs; the challenge of this client group for health services; and recommendations for ways forward.

In Chapter 6 Ames explores how we as 'professionals' contribute to the concept of 'challenging behaviour', through exploring ideas of labelling and stereotyping our clients. He looks at how this affects the way we work with the people who fall within this definition, and outlines some examples of good practice from both the author's own experience and from research. Within this he looks at what challenging behaviour is and what it means, and will question it as a term.

Section Three: Identities and cultures in the homeless sector and societal and personal reactions to homelessness

Section Three looks at identities within the sector itself, exploring the culture and character of the homelessness sector and of the workers within it. Van Doorn and Kain's Chapter 8 invites the reader to explore the nature and character of the culture of the homelessness sector. They show how culture drives the sector's problem-identification and decision-making which ultimately drives the thinking behind the models of service and support for homeless people. They explore how the culture defines the nature of the relationships with service users, other agencies, commissioners and funders and how the history of the sector has produced its cultural anchor points. They ask practitioners, managers, policy makers and commissioners to consider how these may help and enable, but also limit and block creative responses to the current changes in policy and the needs of homeless people. The authors draw upon their own and others' experience and analysis of the homelessness and other sectors, relating it to models and current thinking of culture and transitions in organisations. This is rooted in their analysis of the current drivers of change in the homelessness and wider social care sectors.

In Chapter 7 Seal seeks to address the fact that while much has been written about the characteristics of homeless people (this book continues that project), little attention has been given to the characteristics of those that work in the field. In this chapter he will try to develop a profile of workers in the field, including their backgrounds, experiences and attitudes towards their working conditions and the work itself. It will build on research he has conducted with over 200 workers in the previous year. It will seek to identify common trends and issues that need to be addressed both in the structures that are meant to support workers and in the culture of workers themselves.

This is developed through to Chapter 9 where I attempt to examine the impact homelessness has on our own senses of self, both as individuals and as a society, and how this impacts on how we construct homelessness.

Chapter 10, the conclusion, tries to draw together some common threads from the preceding chapters. This will not necessarily be characteristics these identities have in common; but what common issues arise in their formation, how they manifest, and what responsibilities they place on practitioners and academics to address.

A note on style and content

I thought a word was needed on the choice of chapters in the book, and the styles the reader will encounter in reading it. To do so will also fit into my vision of what the book is trying to do. These identities and experiences were chosen because, in my view, they have hitherto been largely neglected both in terms of academic consideration and practice, something I shall explore further below. For that reason, identities and experiences such as those of homeless women, young people, drug users and black and ethnic minorities have not been covered. I would not deny that work is still needed on them as issues, and would support any initiative that attempts to do so. However, I feel that they have had a degree of attention elsewhere, by people more qualified than me to expand on the issues. The authors in this volume are a mix of academics, practitioners, homeless and ex-homeless people, and this is for a purpose. I believe that for these issues to move forward it takes an alliance of these stakeholders. The starting point is people's experiences and their interpretations of the significance of those experiences. However, to progress we need to analyse and theorise these experiences in the context of the wider care sector and dominating paradigms of our times. We also need to build alliances with those who deliver services to homeless people and examine the interface between them. For, as I will show in my chapters on the experiences of workers, there is potential to have some powerful alliances but also to strengthen organisational resistance to engagement with the issues.

There are consequences from having such an approach. As the reader will see, when the variety of backgrounds of the authors is compounded with their variety of interpretations of what is meant by experiences and identities, and what their significance is to the sector, it makes for quite an eclectic collection of chapters. For instance, my consideration of the impact of homelessness on the identities of other members of society is quite 'academic' and theoretical, whereas Geddes has firmly concentrated on what workers should think about when working with refugees. Flynn is different again, having taken a far more confessional approach, while Dodson has concentrated on reporting the experiences of members of his community and tracing the development of policy in response to it. However, I would like to present these differences as both positive and necessary, for two reasons. Firstly, as many authors have referred to, homeless people are not a homogeneous group: why therefore should our interpretations of their significance be any more so, particularly where we are dealing with issues of identity, which in the recent literature is largely concerned with, and celebrates, subjectivities? Secondly, the spirit of this book is about starting and continuing debates rather than attempting to give definitive positions on them.

The genesis of the third section was a conversation with Andrew Van Doorn on a train journey where we discussed our experiences of the homelessness sector. I remember our being in earnest agreement that 'someone' needed to write something about this area because it was important. Fast forward six months and I remember sitting in Pip Bevan's back garden with Andrew and Mick, discussing their chapters. We had brought together people we knew who had been involved in the sector for years to discuss our ideas. We were aware that this was not terribly scientific, nor that we, as a group, were totally representative, and this had been a big concern for us initially. However, we were all agreed about starting a debate, and to be overly worried about getting it right was not the point at this stage. What was important was to get the issues onto the agenda. I think it would be fair to say that this was a common concern amongst the authors. One of the reasons I approached the people I did to contribute, was an awareness that they had perspectives that they felt needed to be heard, and that they had hitherto been neglected 'voices'. I was also assured that they would be balanced in their accounts, but knew that their style, approach and even conclusions would vary, as indeed they should, for any 'new' debate. I hope the reader will approach the book with this spirit in mind; if you see us on your travels, please come up to us and carry on the debate.

Action points for stakeholders

As I said, an alliance is needed of various stakeholders and my conclusion outlines a vision of how the issues raised in this book can start to move forwards, and the part the different stakeholders should play in this. I hope that the starting points for the debate will be my Action Points, and this is their intention.

Section One:

Homeless people making sense of their experiences

Chapter 1

Identities of Rough sleepers in Oxford

Chantal Butchinsky

Introduction

This chapter is about the processes of engagement and disengagement undertaken by those sleeping rough: about the expectations and images of them, held by non-homeless individuals and parties. Whether in fleeting encounters with passers-by, or in long-term professional relationships with services providers, the accommodation status of the rough sleepers formed the basis of their characterisation, as their street – homeless condition seemed to invoke images of addiction, aggressiveness, crazy and uncontrolled ('chaotic') behaviour in those who looked upon them. Rough sleepers themselves made fine distinctions regarding such 'identities' and their 'sense of self' is shown here in an ambiguous relationship towards diagnoses and practices. Whilst these may accurately have described a condition (of need, addiction, anti-social behaviour, etc.) and rough sleepers could legitimately accept them, their capacities to 'play the game of identity' were practical evidence, to rough sleepers, of their skill, independence and personal ability. The subtle, tactical uses of 'identity' made by rough sleepers can be shown to have important implications in relation to the repeated nature of many rough sleeper's homelessness; in clashes between rough sleepers and others, individuals or parties (such as residents living near homeless accommodation, or staff members supervising homeless people's behaviour inside accommodation). Interpretations of 'identities' can lead to renewed homelessness, and the chapter ends with a consideration of various situations in which this has been found to occur.

There is a focus, in this chapter, on events and processes as I interpreted them whilst undertaking participant observation with 200 rough sleepers on the streets of Oxford. Over a three year period (2000–2003) I interviewed rough sleepers and 'part-time homeless' people, a term used by rough sleepers to mean people who had obtained some form of accommodation, but still partook in the routines of street life to a degree. Most of the data used in this chapter comes from in-depth interviews, both structured and semi-structured, with 42 research participants (35 men and 7 women) as well as chats with, observations of, and participation in the daily routines of many sleeping on the streets. These people fell into three categories: street dwellers, part-time homeless people, and individuals recently become homeless and new to street life. This is particularly important to state at this point, because in the text that follows I have tried to honour the atmosphere of struggle that I sensed and still sense, in my encounters with these people. (In this chapter there is sometimes a mixture of tense because the data I have used is from my fieldwork.) It is the anthropologist's way – to try to understand other people's worlds from other people's perspectives – but their claims to scientific accuracy are fraught with creative possibilities rather than solely empirical fact. Whilst further analysis of anthropologists' truth-claims is beyond the scope of this chapter, it is important to mention that there were other possible perspectives that I could have represented here. These perspectives, such as the views of workers currently in the system of services provision or those of policy makers, might well have yielded very different and even, at times, contradictory accounts to the ones I have offered here.

Many of the rough sleepers who participated in the research were intravenous drug users or heavy drinkers, and the narratives of people such as these are often thought to be unreliable. This belief in the unreliability of drug users' and drinkers' stories is a part of the very processes of 'discursively narrating' their identities (or projecting an image) in the wider social domain and forms a part of the analysis presented here. I believe the viewpoints explored here, though, are likely to be familiar, in an informal sense, to many, especially workers providing services. Spending time with rough sleepers and participating in their routines eventually led me to see how they are constantly and routinely transforming the meanings of things through their skills in using spaces creatively, though fleetingly, and also through their control over how they presented themselves to domiciled parties and individuals.

Nevertheless, despite the arguable benefit of conveying the opinions of rough sleepers about their situation, the overarching reason to offer this account is to demonstrate what I believe to be a dichotomy between the fairly hegemonic views of street dwellers and their public identity. The contention in this text is that the public perception, and the prevailing practice of professionals, is to associate street dwellers with models of need and pathology – including illness and 'bad character'. In contrast, the rough sleepers in my study seemed not to match these models but demonstrated talents, resourcefulness and aspirations to freedom. Ways of talking about street homeless people invoke a number of identity-type images; these images are rooted in meanings about homelessness – a lack of shelter, privacy, retreat and warmth; there are further images of criminality and anti-social behaviour – people who steal things, are threatening to others, are aggressive, are part of a group. Additionally, a notion of 'dependence' is constantly present in discourses about the street homeless – lonely and dangerously mad people, addicts, drunkards – all of these images can be conjured up. For example, one worker I interviewed said that young drug-using rough sleepers were 'feral'; another worker told me that there were many paedophiles amidst the rough sleeper population. Even New Labour politicians such as Jack Straw, have made negative remarks about rough sleepers as 'squeegee merchants, winos and addicts' (cited in Humphreys, 1999). The approach adopted towards 'identity' in this chapter is not comprehensive – of course, people's personal biographies were pretty significant in relation to their 'identities', which is not represented in this chapter, and the sources of individual's self-image are widespread, continual and multifarious. Instead I focus here on how relations between homeless people and other members of society also contribute to notions of homeless identities, in ways that are public and shared collectively in society.

The chapter is organised into five sections. The first four are about particular aspects of 'the homeless identity which rough sleepers had to negotiate whilst living on the streets; they are presented under the broad headings of: 'being homeless', 'being criminal', 'being dependent', and 'being self-reliant or free'. In the conclusion I briefly examine how these factors form a part of the processes of repeated homelessness.

1. Being 'homeless'

In Oxford, street living was 'a battle'. Shaun said: 'It's like this: you're fighting to sell the Issue [*The Big Issue*, a magazine that homeless people sell on the streets] to score [to buy drugs] to trek about the place, to find somewhere to dig [to 'dig' here means to find a vein to inject oneself with drugs]. Then the fight stops for a little while.' The hardships rough sleepers experienced in their daily lives were multi-dimensional; chronic lack of sleep, irregular diet and often a continuous mobility made life on the streets exhausting; physical ill health was another factor rough sleepers frequently had to contend with. The friendships they had were very supportive in many ways, but they were also volatile and often plagued by mistrust. Rough sleepers had to fend off competing territorial claims; they had to learn how to avoid trouble, sometimes even at the expense of their dignity and they had to forego their privacy each time a form about them was filled in. They also endured low social status and its consequence: of never feeling safe, feeling threatened by potential and actual attacks from members of the general public as well as (some claimed) the police. These factors can be seen as some of the reasons to leave the streets, and rough sleepers cited them when they expressed the desire to obtain accommodation.

Mobile and institutionalised homelessness

Identification with the different categories of homelessness ('homeless rough sleeper', 'roofless', or 'street homeless') was ambiguous. Rough sleepers rarely used these terms internally but did use them to describe themselves to domiciled parties when undertaking certain activities (for example, begging, vending *The Big Issue*, applying for a place to live). 'Part-time homeless' was a term used, in a joking way, to 'diss' (put down) someone who managed to get a room (either in a hostel or a bed-sit, or even a bed at the Night Shelter, if it was for more than a few nights), but who still 'worked' on the streets. Some people were considered to be 'homeless' but not 'rough sleepers' or 'part-time homeless'. Rough sleepers saw those who stayed at the Night Shelter on a permanent basis or who lived in hostels over long periods of time as institutionalised people whose homelessness was qualitatively different. Whilst length of time was a factor, it was the institutionalised nature of their lifestyles that was highlighted in their classification, rather than their longer experience of homelessness. This institutionalisation was associated, by many street dwellers, with mental illness and an inability to cope with life on the streets.

Spatial and temporal organisation on the streets

The importance attached to the dichotomy between indoors and outdoors can perhaps be understood better by a closer look at the spatial and temporal structures rough sleepers developed on the streets. Circumstances on the street were unpredictable, changeable and contingent. Rough sleepers had to endure difficult situations (for example, inclement weather, aggressive passers-by, and also their own emotional states and the exposure to others which they could not avoid); and they needed to be mobile, have ideas of where to go when it was no longer possible to occupy one place, and thus they needed to know the streets fairly intimately. In their own words they had to be 'streetwise' so as to be able to predict, to varying degrees, the unpredictable. 'Place-making' for rough sleepers was a difficult endeavour that required them to oppose other rough sleepers as well as to employ ruses to appeal to passers-by and thus to 'earn' money. Their control over space was highly unstable but, whilst knowing they were viewed with disdain and likely to be moved on, they also learnt how to predict, and at times to overcome, the circumstances that might lead to their eviction. I think the key to understanding how rough sleepers used space, is their ability to transform places, to reinterpret seemingly mundane, almost non-places (doorways, small stretches of pavement, a ledge on the outside of a shop, a bin area, for example) as sleeping places, socialising places, living places where talking, smoking, drinking, drug taking, eating, take place.

Figure 1 shows the variety of spaces that 42 rough sleepers occupied over the duration of my fieldwork. Raymond obtained a flat in the social rented sector and managed to keep it going for two years. He then moved into another council flat. Despite relapses in his efforts to give up drinking, he has managed to sustain his tenancy so far. Only two other participants obtained flats in the social rented sector – they both reached their fiftieth birthdays during that time and believed their age was a factor in their obtaining such accommodation. Although both kept up their links with rough sleepers they had known, neither of them kept up their 'work' pitches or other street activities. Both were drinkers and, whilst living indoors helped them to regulate their drinking, neither of them gave up. Over the three-year period of fieldwork, only one rough sleeper, Nick, did not use the hostels and housing association accommodation provided for rough sleepers. Instead Nick obtained a

1. Accommodation

1a. Self-contained accommodation
Council/socially rented accommodation – tenure: long-term, permanent accommodation
Shorthold assured tenancies (bedsit accommodation) – tenure: six months, can be renewed

1b. License accommodation – tenure: 'reasonable notice' (can be less than a day)
Someone else's home (live-in landlord or landlady)
Housing association supervised accommodation (houses of multiple occupation)
Supported accommodation in hostels
High care accommodation in hostels
Detoxification hostel
Residential rehabilitation hostel

1c. 'Emergency' accommodation – no security of tenure
Friends' or relatives' floors/sofas
Being 'sneaked in' to hostel accommodation
Night shelter

2. Other indoor spaces

Doctors' surgery, Dept. of Social Security offices, job centre, police station, hospital – attending appointments

Day centres and evening facilities – for sandwiches, showering and laundering

2a. Indoor commercial spaces
Shops and Shopping malls – window shopping, making purchases, shoplifting, passing through
Chemists – picking up prescription heroin substitute (methadone)
Fast-food outlets – killing time, eating, drinking coffee/tea, using toilets (also for drugs' use)

3. Outdoor sites

'Pitches' 'sites' (spots along streets) – vending, begging
Derelict or empty houses – sleeping
Public toilets – sleeping, using substances
Car parks – sleeping, using substances, scavenging
Parks and fields – sleeping, purchasing and using substances
Fronts, backs and sides of buildings – sleeping, scavenging, using substances
Benches – sleeping, killing time
Church porches – sleeping, begging
Covered market lanes – sleeping, begging
Shop and college doorways – sleeping, begging
Underneath bridges – sleeping
Railway stations – sleeping
Wheelie bin areas – sleeping, scavenging
Phone boxes – ringing dealers, meeting other homeless people

4. Routes

Streets in city centre – vending, begging, selling commodities
Streets between city centre and residential areas – purchasing substances, waiting for dealers

Figure 1.1   Spaces: indoors and outdoors

room, effectively on a license agreement, and managed to stay living there permanently, getting a proper tenancy agreement in the end. All the other rough sleepers had, often on various occasions, used the hostels, Night Shelter, and the housing association rooms that agency workers referred them to. All of these either left voluntarily or were evicted. The most successful tenancies other than in the social rented sector were those that rough sleepers undertook in the private rented sector, often occupying bed-sits in houses where the other rooms were let out to ex-rough sleepers, drinkers or drug-users. The various forms of accommodation rough sleepers inhabited and vacated are considered again below, when processes of repeated homelessness are explored.

Whereas in the urban landscapes of the 1980s and early 1990s there were wastelands of derelict and abandoned sites, in the early 2000s there were very few such sites in Oxford. Instead, it was within the same spaces as the domiciled that rough sleepers sought to meet their needs. It was by transforming the meaning of a place that street dwellers were able to make shared spaces into their own places. Their occupation of spaces often depended on their being 'streetwise', discovering where their presence was authorised and unauthorised, working out ways of entering forbidden sites, or making illegal uses of sites. Making a tactical use of spaces sometimes required negotiating, down to the last inch, over sites. This was commonly the case, for example, with pitches located outside shops. Managers of shops often accepted the presence of *The Big Issue* vendors outside their shops, whereas beggars were usually not welcome. Vendors though, were required to place themselves at precise distances and angles specified by the manager or shop assistant, in order not to 'block the way', 'intimidate customers', 'scare children', or other such reasons. Such negotiations could at times become confrontational as vendors learnt in their training that they had a right to occupy public space, a right they might invoke if they felt managers were treating them unfairly. For the most part vendors and, on a few occasions, beggars, tried to establish friendly relations with shop assistants and managers, an approach that was reciprocated to a large degree.

A consideration of what could be thought of as rough sleepers' 'spatial relations' requires one to think how they are subjected to public scrutiny by virtue of their presence. Rough sleepers are expected to make progress in their plans to leave the streets. This is something they are aware of (for example, Eammon, who used to vend *The Big Issue* in the city centre, moved his pitch to a small village in Oxfordshire as he became increasingly unable to justify his continued homelessness to regular passers-by who enquired about his 'progress' in leaving the streets) and, whilst such practices do have a disciplinary effect upon their behaviour, they are also able, by presenting themselves as 'disciplined' homeless people (in other words 'deserving'), to gain the confidence of passers-by and the favour of traders. This helps them to establish themselves in a spatial niche. Interestingly, a person's long-standing occupation of a pitch can lead to a reversal of attitudes from members of the general public and traders. Once a vendor has 'proven' that they are not 'taking advantage of the goodwill' of others, such people may even defend 'their' vendor against unfair accusations or encroachments by less friendly rough sleepers.

Killing time on the streets

Lars Eighner wrote an autobiographical account of the two years he and his dog Lizbeth spent homeless in the USA. Introducing his work he said: 'Day after day I could aspire, within reason, to nothing more than survival . . . the identical barrenness of existence was exposed to me, day in and day out. I do not think I could write a narrative that would quite capture the unrelenting ennui of homelessness . . . Every life has trivial occurrences, pointless episodes, and unresolved mysteries, but a homeless life has these and virtually nothing else' (Eighner, 1993). Whilst Lovell (1992) has explored a temporal category of 'marginal time' (which is not ordered by regular sequences of events and which lacks a conventional division of everyday life into the work or leisure dichotomy), findings in Oxford were slightly different because most rough sleepers found ways to work, albeit in informal and at times illegal ways, and thus to organise their time. From the very beginning of fieldwork, most rough sleepers emphasised a particular category of very negative time, which they would refer to as 'empty' time they had to 'kill'. This category I have labelled 'empty time'.

Rough sleepers described many different instances and experiences of 'empty time' but they all seemed characterised by how empty time brought up negative thoughts, emotions and memories. The gist of this temporal problem was the exclusion rough sleepers felt from structuring conditions, such as 'home' and conventional work, their very low status and precarious grip within the quotidian. Variously, empty time was experienced as boredom, fear, anguish, excruciating loneliness and dread. People had vivid memories of periods of time characterised by nothing but their own wandering around and sitting in places, until being moved on.

'Pacing yourself' was a common way of tackling a stretch of empty time. Gerry used to walk into town, from a derelict house where he stayed, just after the rush hour. Once in town, at around 9am, he had an hour or so to 'kill' as the office where he could buy *The Big Issue* only opened at 10am. Most days Gerry would sit in a fast-food outlet, nursing a cup of coffee and making it last until he could go to the office for his magazines. On the other hand, going about things at a very high speed, as Glen did, appeared to have a similar 'time-busting' effect. Glen used crack cocaine, more than any other rough sleeper I met. He would 'score' many times a day – sometimes ten times, and he would stay up very late, until all the dealers had gone to bed. This may account for not only the haste with which he undertook activities, but also the intensity with which he went about it; he hardly ate, rarely washed, threw his clothes away when they got too dirty (as washing them took too long), and spent most of his time begging, 'scoring' and using his drugs – and he was very short of time.

'Making raises' – getting money, working – was the main structuring force in the daily routines of many rough sleepers. The streets presented many opportunities to those most able and willing, whether begging or vending *The Big Issue*, hunting round skips for food, informally selling used (but not expired) parking tickets to motorists, shoplifting or 'tricking'. Tricking involves making a purchase and seeming to pay with a high denomination note (such as a twenty pound note) then handing over a low note (such as a fiver) and getting away with it. Only one man had the expertise required to live solely by this means, but Double Diamond, a rough sleeper, linked up with this man and learnt how to do it too, though not as well. Some rough sleepers, however, were not very good at establishing themselves on the streets and instead found themselves wandering for long periods of time, with absolutely nothing to do but wait until the next homeless agency opened its doors.

Dom, a drinker, was frequently without work. This was often because he had been drinking. His problems, as he explained, although ostensibly caused by his drinking, in fact were really caused by 'empty time'; this was because he was so 'miserable' when wandering around with nothing to do, that drinking helped him to pass the time and to feel less unhappy. Furthermore, drinking was sociable and by drinking more, Dom made more friends. Prior to becoming homeless Dom claimed he had not had a 'problem' with drink – he had become an alcoholic because he was unable to cope with street life and the long stretches of empty time. The fact that he was often unable to make raises was less of a problem when he was drinking. This was because, rather than trying to earn enough money to pay for a deposit on a room, or travel to another town and make a new start (options he had tried before), Dom worked until he made just enough each day to buy some drink to share with his friends.

On a day-to-day basis, empty time may or may not plague someone. The determining factor here was how a rough sleeper was fairing generally. 'Good' times tended to be stable times when a person could establish regular patterns. A permanence of sorts could develop remarkably quickly – friendships, relations with passers-by and traders, and so forth – and it was often at such times that many rough sleepers started unaided 'detox' (coming off drink or drugs), using a variety of individually developed 'systems' (cutting down, alternating between heroin and methadone, stopping crack, using only crack and not heroin, and so on). Some people started saving money at such times – often asking trusted workers or friends to bank their money. Vending *The Big Issue* could be helpful to those 'cleaning up their act' because a person can claim they are 'working' rather than 'begging'. The domiciled give money to beggars in exchange for nothing and therefore do not see it as work; rough sleepers however, do see begging as work because it is physically tiring and cold, involving exposure to insults and arrest. People also cleaned up their personal appearance, clothes and personal grooming. At bad times people neglected themselves, often allowing beards to grow, wounds to go untreated and ignoring other physical complaints. Christmas was often a bad time, likewise sudden family visits or the death of a friend, a not infrequent occurrence – such events stirred up emotional reactions that could throw someone's routine into disarray. At such times some rough sleepers resolved to 'clean up their act' but the turmoil they were undergoing invariably made this harder.

'Part-time homeless'

For the most part rough sleepers appeared to consider part-time homeless people as part of the same social circuit as themselves. The division between these two groups was highlighted only in specific situations – namely, when disputes over a person's right to a pitch arose, rough sleepers would invoke their more pressing needs to trump a part-time homeless person's claim. The blurring of the division between rough sleepers and part-time homeless people was important because the rooms that part-time homeless people obtained often became part of rough sleepers' valued resources. Access to a warm place, out of the way of the 'gaze' on the streets that came from CCTV cameras, passers-by, the police, services providers and others, was very attractive and rough sleepers tried, though often failed, to moderate their use of other people's places, in order to extend their welcome as long as possible. Likewise, part-time homeless people kept up their links with street life and, in particular, access to work pitches, through sharing their rooms with their rough sleeper friends.

To the domiciled however, the differences between rough sleepers and part-time homeless people were not visible; these two groups of people shared the same locations, the same dress codes and applied the same identity techniques (humble bearing, looking downwards, speaking very quietly and politely, etc.). The category of 'part-time homeless' has developed on the streets because when rough sleepers obtain accommodation, it does not seem to meet their needs (for safety, for example, or privacy, or freedom to have friends to visit) and they return to the streets. Visible street homelessness can be visualised in terms of the difference between front and back stage in the theatre – except that what is being 'shown' on the front stage is not a deceitful lie, but a simplified and palatable version of homelessness that rough sleepers hope will prevent the domiciled seeing 'criminal' or 'dependent' images and tempt them instead into parting with some 'spare change'. If the domiciled could distinguish between rough sleepers and part-time homeless people, it is reckoned on the street that they would give preferential treatment to rough sleepers whose needs they would assess higher. But it is widely known among rough sleepers that all accommodation they may be offered is temporary, likely to come to an end soon enough, and that part-time homeless people have the same needs as they do and share their accommodation with rough sleepers. Protection, companionship and pooled resources were much stronger markers of their shared identities than their more public 'accommodation status'.

2. Being 'criminal' and 'anti-social'

Criminal images are frequently invoked and accusations of anti-social behaviour often made about rough sleepers and part-time homeless people. Rough sleepers were routinely woken by the police and, on many occasions, searched as well; they were moved on from places where they begged, given warnings and often arrested. Many of the accusations made by members of the general public against rough sleepers seemed to be largely concerned with what was perceived as aggression, whereas part-time homeless people were faced with a wider variety of concerns expressed by local residents. In this respect members of the general public seem to feel very empowered and vocal, as there were usually witnesses against rough sleepers and often collective action taken against part-time homeless people.

Aggression

Street dwellers were acutely aware of how easily their behaviour could be thought of as aggressive by the domiciled. In reality, there were only a few who were guilty of aggressive behaviour. Mostly they were older drinkers whose aggression was often more playful than real but who nevertheless scared people who did not understand. There was one rough sleeper who used somewhat aggressive techniques, on occasions swearing and threatening those who did not give money to him, approaching people without humility. Other rough sleepers disapproved of this – partly because they saw no need for it but also because they worried about how it added confirmation to the notion that all beggars are aggressive. Rough sleepers also felt they did not stand a chance against an accusation of aggressive behaviour, as any domiciled person had more credibility than a rough sleeper simply by virtue of a 'home'. Shortly after fieldwork ended, various ASBOs were introduced and many rough sleepers were threatened with them. ASBOs expressed, if not reinforced, public perceptions of rough sleepers' anti-social behaviours.

More than anything it was my overwhelming impression that rough sleepers were usually acquiescent and humble; when they were argumentative it was by virtue of being stubborn and feeling a need to 'stand up for their rights'. 'Being argumentative could be perceived as 'being aggressive' because it involves raising one's voice, gesticulating, having a contrary point of view, but what is an admittedly loud, slightly defiant and rude but logical quibbling over the rules, is, I believe, too readily interpreted as aggressiveness.

Problems with neighbours

People who obtained accommodation were aware of their low social status in the neighbourhood. Double Diamond received a letter from the Residents' Association, when he first moved in to a bed-sit, warning him that they would take action if any signs of drug use or dealing were noticed. On a wider scale, the East Oxford Parliament members have argued that East Oxford, an area that traditionally welcomed many different kinds of short-term renting populations, should be designated an 'area of restraint', which means there should be a limit to the amount of rented properties in the area. The local newspaper reported that 'long-term residents . . . claim communities are being destroyed because too many properties are let to short-term tenants' (Oxford Mail, 30.03.02: 1). Councillor Ellise Benjamin, chairman of the Parliament, was quoted as saying 'It's not that we don't want students or vulnerable people in Oxford, but that the burden for housing them should be shared across the city' (ibid.: 2). David Barton, from the Iffley Road Residents' Association, voiced the complaint that 'anti-social behaviour had increased' (Oxford Mail, 20.09.03: 5). Drug dealing and prostitution were increasing, residents claimed, as a result of a property being used for homeless people. Bill Baker, representing the protests of local residents, said 'the spread of HMOs [houses of multiple occupation] is . . . making it difficult for people to live in the community. It's causing a lot of unrest, a lot of violence and a lot of resentment' (ibid.).

It was noticeable during fieldwork that many rough sleepers sustained black eyes and other signs of violence. Dom had a swollen face, broken jaw and two black eyes after taking a beating; Hayley had been gang-raped whilst sleeping rough in Birmingham when she was only 15 years old; Shanks required hospitalisation after being found unconscious from a beating from three drunken club-leavers. Perhaps they are less sensitive to the impact their presence has in residential areas partly because their experiences of crime have been so much more intense than local residents' experience of them.

Many rough sleepers had also been to prison and some found this had been of positive value. Jack (32 years old), a rough sleeper and homeless from the age of 15, told me that when he was first in prison he was befriended and he worked out in the gym and gained self-esteem, which helped him a great deal, as he had been bullied at school. Prison could provide a relief from life on the streets, as Bobby B, a heroin-using rough sleeper in his twenties told me. Bobby B had stolen from his dealer, was unable to find a friend and failed to raise enough money for a hit of heroin. As he became increasingly sick, from withdrawals, he decided to get himself arrested and taken care of by the prison doctor instead. He went to a supermarket and shoplifted in a very obvious manner.

3. Being 'dependent'

To conform with the prevailing 'homeless' identity, to fit the public perception, rough sleepers must 'act' homeless. Passers-by and others judge their 'act', as genuine or fake (and they as deserving or undeserving, see McIntosh and Erskine, 2000). Because the 'act' is a simplified and palatable 'user-friendly' version of the truth of rough sleepers' homelessness it omits aspects of their lives. In particular, any passer-by may see images of welfare dependency, mental incapacity and addictions to drink or drugs in their views of rough sleepers. One factor, which I am sure has contributed to current feelings like this, is the promotion, by central government and also by the founder of *The Big Issue*, Sir John Birt, of the notion that giving to beggars is bad, and *promotes* street living rather than end it. The desire to stop rough sleepers' ability to gain resources from members of the general public simultaneously encourages the idea that rough sleepers pose a social problem that should be dealt with by specific staff from agencies providing welfare and public order. Some passers-by, however, do establish long-term relations with particular beggars. These people become known as 'regulars'. Feelings of friendship can flourish quickly on the part of a rough sleeper towards a 'regular' because often a regular can become trusted with the less palatable aspects of being a rough sleeper, such as being addicted to drugs. Many rough sleepers are perfectly aware of their 'dependence' (on welfare, on charity, on drugs, on drink) but this does not mean that they are not able to control and determine, to an important extent, the effects of these processes.

Many of the comments and observations made about services provision and accommodation for the homeless were negative, but rough sleepers were still in a precarious situation. The cycles of addiction, which they were caught up in sometimes, could lead to all manner of related problems, such as committing crimes, suddenly having no heroin and no possibility of obtaining it, and such like. Physical injuries often become worse on the streets as rough sleepers showed a reluctance to keep visiting a GP; simultaneously they might be ripped off by or steal from their friends; suffer all manner of difficulties and feelings of 'blown it, there's no return'. These factors – an accumulation of events that have gone wrong somehow, plans that have gone awry – run together and when that person crashes, it can be fairly drastic – life-threatening in truth. For this reason the agencies are vital even if, on a good day, they symbolise the disenfranchisement rough sleepers sometimes feel.

Welfare

The highly visible nature of vending *The Big Issue* and begging could be considered as confirming the dependent status of homeless people. Many passers-by were angry with beggars, shouting at them to 'get a bloody job', appearing to voice what may be a widespread resentment in the relationship between 'tax payers' and welfare claimants. Government policies, since New Labour's electoral successes, have expanded provision to rough sleepers, introducing new, centrally funded, outreach teams and making it possible to charge extremely high rents under the 'Supporting People' programme, designed to enable hostels to take more rough sleepers.

Rough sleepers returning to the streets after eviction or voluntarily leaving hostels complained that, in addition to claiming housing benefits to pay the rent, they also had to hand over most of their Job Seekers Allowance, leaving them with very little cash and little choice over what to spend their money on; 'treating them like children', they complained. Likewise, when renting rooms in Housing Association properties for homeless people, they were charged high rents, but not allowed to have friends to visit, which they complained was discriminatory, making homeless people feel like children. Giving in kind (giving goods and services rather than money) has been promoted in local schemes such as 'Oxpat' and also encourages the belief that rough sleepers' autonomy cannot be trusted. Oxpat was an organisation that placed collection spots in a variety of shops where people who wanted to give to the homeless, but felt giving them money might not be a good idea, could deposit goods, such as clothes, books, toiletries and so on, for homeless people.

Rough sleepers had very ambiguous feelings about their 'welfare' status. On the one hand there were times – such as when barred from selling *The Big Issue*, or unable to find a pitch to beg on – when the fortnightly giro was literally the only income a person could look forward to. But they also felt the kind of exhaustion that comes from hard work, and felt that the words 'charity' and 'welfare dependency' did not accurately describe their experiences.

Mental health

Many domiciled people imagine homeless people to suffer mental illness. Rough sleepers, however, were very reluctant indeed to accept that label of mental illness. The meanings of the term 'mental health' varied according to context and as to who was using the term. Though doctors considered addictions to be a form of mental illness, rough sleepers who used drugs or drink claimed it was a matter of personal resolve, will and intention. Raymond, an alcoholic, was once referred, by his 'Key Worker', to a team of support workers who helped people with 'multiple needs'. For Raymond this meant they thought he was mentally ill, which had very negative connotations. For him, as for many rough sleepers, mental illness was a demeaning condition, the taint of which could last for years. More than anything, it appeared to be demeaning because it implied that he was unable to care for himself.

Being homeless required not only physical but also enormous mental effort. A person in the most pressing of circumstances had to be ever ready to interpret events and respond to situations: to stay alert enough to benefit from passing good fortune; to notice and avoid threatening sequences of events. Sometimes people 'gave up' – overwhelmed by too many problems and not enough solutions – owing money, losing 'face' and friends, suffering increasingly severe addiction (or relapse), losing a pitch, taking a beating. At such times a person may turn for help from the agencies, they may deliberately get themselves arrested or they may temporarily accept diagnoses of 'depression' and accept medication for their 'nerves' or 'anger'. Quite a few rough sleepers told me they had experienced 'paranoia, anxiety, panic attacks, depression and anger'. Some had been hospitalised in psychiatric wards in the past, many had attempted suicide at some time and the deaths of two of the participants in this project may be explained as semi-deliberate overdoses.

Drink and drugs

In the face of the many mental and physical challenges of street life there are some positive uses that rough sleepers found for substance use – for example, dealing with empty time by transforming it into relaxing oblivion with heroin. The business of creating structures and orders that constantly fall apart within an unpredictable context is exhausting. Many rough sleepers, even drug users, would drink at night in order to fall asleep; and most of the available drugs (illegal street drugs but also alcohol and a range of prescribed drugs, especially valium) were important means of escape and pain relief. Using drink or drugs was, additionally, a social activity – frequently people would partner up to earn enough money for drink or drugs and then they would spend their money, sharing the substances they bought.

Addictions had a cyclical nature, and both drinkers and drug users experienced repetitive cycles of increasing use of substances to a point of severe addiction; this in turn would lead to a breakdown (sometimes cumulatively, other times abruptly) of social relationships, economic structures and physical and mental well-being, which in turn could lead to emergency help from the agencies and, possibly, detoxification on a short-term basis. The influence of cyclical routines gave people the feeling of 'it's the same old story' – going round in tiresome circles.

4. Being 'self-reliant' or 'free'

Rough sleepers displayed a great deal of inventiveness and a capacity to seize good fortune, however tiny, in their survival tactics. The absence of prevailing structuring conditions, especially that of 'home', can be represented by the temporal category of 'empty time', and it often invoked, for rough sleepers, incoherence and fear as they were exposed to life-threatening conditions about which they could do nothing or almost nothing. Collectively, through working and consuming together, they created meaningful events and sequences of linked events out of the resources available to them and so safeguarded themselves against the physical and mental dangers of the street.

This aspect of rough sleepers' identities is perhaps the closest to their personal biographies, because it is in their own histories of survival that they most clearly see their capacities to endure. The image they render to the public is a 'sad' one – rough sleepers are 'down on their luck'. The real point is, as Kite said, 'the truth is much worse'. The individual biographies of the 42 rough sleepers I interviewed revealed histories of great suffering and resilience in survival. Rough sleepers, prior to becoming street homeless, reported a catalogue of abuse inflicted upon them in many different ways. For some of these people, the streets were a more friendly and trustworthy place to be than the family or marital homes they had left behind, even though they might have been attacked there, at times severely, by total strangers.

For rough sleepers and part-time homeless people, there was more fear of becoming institutionalised than there was of returning to the streets. Long-term residents of shelters and hostels displayed, to them, signs of mental weakness in being cared for entirely by others; of surrendering their rightful place in the wider society. What looks like a problem of repeated homelessness contains, even so, positive elements. By avoiding being cast in models of pathology, in the role of 'damaged victim', people asserted their autonomy. It is important to bear in mind how the long-term residents of shelters and hostels are viewed – rough sleepers dread 'becoming like them'.

If a rough sleeper largely avoids the 'help' offered by support agencies, sticking to signing on and attending independent charitable groups (such as The Gatehouse) and their GP (who seems to remain out of the fray of naming and circulating information), they can, ironically, retain their own self-created spatial and temporal structures and gradually change them to suit their changing needs. Robbie succeeded in accomplishing this – his two stints in the hostel had come to bad ends and he slept rough in a meadow for a few months, staying on a friend's floor very occasionally. He eventually found a place to live and has since worked at cutting down his heroin and methadone.

Double Diamond rejected the approaches of outreach workers and became embroiled in an argument that eventually led the city council to issue him with a warning against his aggressive behaviour; this letter was circulated through all the homeless agencies in the 'network'. After this series of events, and despite some very difficult times, Double Diamond never again turned to the outreach teams or stayed in the hostels or Night Shelter. He slept rough and stayed with friends and with a girlfriend at times. Although there were times when he got into trouble – including stints in prison, continued heroin addiction and a developing drinking problem – he limited his contact with welfare services to claiming Job Seekers' Allowance and seeking medical care.

This was also the case for Nick who, once he found a room to live in, stayed there for some years while he stayed working on the streets; until he had established for himself more security (of tenure, more domiciled friends, the habits that domiciled people enjoy; such as shopping, cooking, drinking in local pubs, etc.) and saved enough money to make finally coming off the streets a smoother transition.

Conclusion

From my experiences of participating in the everyday routines street dwellers developed, I found that whilst rough sleepers are often thought of as both dangerous and vulnerable, being aware of these images about them, they engaged with the domiciled in a tactical, creative way, keeping from view, if possible, what might be thought of as frightening or disgusting and emphasising their needs. The spaces they inhabited, though imbued with public meanings, they were able to transform, albeit briefly, into something with other kinds of meanings. This 'doubling' of reality helped rough sleepers in their survival, both physically and mentally. The fact that rough sleepers created, and had to maintain, their own spatial and temporal structures was important evidence of their strength and independence, and in their capacities to develop wisdom and to make good choices.

This self-sufficiency, not perceived by those in the wider social domain where 'criminal' and 'sick' images of street homeless dwellers prevail, is not *surrendered* when rough sleepers enter accommodation – it is automatically *removed* from them (when they sign the form agreeing to abide by the rules). Rough sleepers' autonomy is constantly assumed not to be an issue.

Leaving or eviction from accommodation	21
Leaving or eviction from hostel	19
Leaving or eviction from night shelter	12
Leaving prison	12
Picking area arbitrarily	5
Moving to come off drugs unaided	10
Going to rehabilitation	8
Leaving/eviction from detoxification	9
Leaving/eviction from rehabilitation	3
Leaving hospital	9
Going to festivals	3
Picking up dog	4
Leaving traveller site	4
Visiting friends/family	19
Getting or losing a job	5
Buying drugs in other part of country	2
Fleeing violence	7
Fleeing debts	6
Accompanying friends	13

Figure 2.1   **Some reasons for repeated homelessness for 42 respondents 2000–2003**

Repeated homelessness

These issues are of some importance when considering the problem some rough sleepers had of sustaining their tenancies or progressing into more secure tenancies. In Figure 2.1 I have listed the reasons for moving out of accommodation that were given to me by 42 homeless respondents over a three-year period.

Obtaining a place seemed attractive when on the street – here rough sleepers talked of lying around watching television, cooking for themselves, sleeping when they want, having friends to visit – but part-time homeless people complained to me about countless problems that arose when they moved into various forms of accommodation. In hostels, safety was sometimes a big problem and some people were intimidated into handing over their money or drugs. Lethargy could also be a problem, as Mary explained when, having a warm place to stay, Mary found she couldn't seem to get out of bed. Raymond lived in an isolated flat, far from the city centre where many of his friends stayed. He frequently felt bewildered, sleeping on the floor because he could not get used to being indoors. In bed-sit accommodation, Double Diamond was the only heroin user in the house, whereas the other occupants were drinkers, and they would frighten him by chanting 'junkie, junkie' and swearing at him in the stairwell. At times there were very sharp divisions between street homeless drinkers and drug users, and arguments that led to violence sometimes broke out between sets of drinkers and drug users. However, this division was certainly not absolute, as many drinkers used drugs occasionally and many drug users also drank. Sometimes friendships did develop between drinkers and drug users.

Repeated homelessness seemed to happen most of all with those rough sleepers or part-time homeless people who had the strongest sense of independence. Although they desired accommodation, they found they could not adapt to the rules and wished to reassert their own lifestyle as soon as they felt strong enough. For them, becoming street homeless was a way of returning to social inclusion, rather than of being socially excluded. The fact that street homelessness was endured in public places meant rough sleepers were constantly facing their own degraded position in society, as it was reflected back to them by members of the general public through the meanings of the spaces they inhabited, in their relationships with services providers, legal and penal authorities and others, and in their lack of entitlement to occupy spaces for very long. But on the streets there was the company of other homeless people and a capacity for independence.

Not only did rough sleepers have experience of a variety of different homeless facilities, they also had intricate knowledge of the rules that constrained their actions in all these places, and how these rules were always broken. They mitigated the powers of the institutions by routinely breaking the rules and thus appropriating for themselves a measure of self-sufficiency within a structure designed to take control over their care. When homeless people left accommodation they often commented on how the only route through accommodation would involve allowing other people to take over parts of their lives – the route involves giving up ones autonomy on buying into the idea of being institutionalised by other people; accepting the idea that someone else is more qualified to make decisions for the homeless.

The creativity of homeless street dwellers, and their capacities for independence and for seizing passing opportunities, suggests the possibility of exploring less institutionally oriented forms of support for rough sleepers in all of their housing and medical problems. It seems important to not demand that rough sleepers change their way of thinking when they have proven themselves adept at surviving the odds by a tactical use of their knowledge. Likewise, it seems imprudent to demand rough sleepers give up all their friendships, even if these are with drinkers or drug users. Rough sleepers have ties of loyalty and bonds of friendship which, though struck up in unpromising circumstances, are significant. Ways of acknowledging the resourcefulness rough sleepers show in the face of difficult choices could be explored and maybe incorporated into practices, in particular in the relations between workers and rough sleepers.

Chapter 2

Homelessness and the denial of sexual identity

Phillip Flynn

Introduction

Identity refers to the sense that someone has of who they are, of what is most important about them. Important sources of identity are likely to include nationality, ethnicity, sexuality (homosexual, heterosexual, bisexual) gender and class. Although it is individuals who have identities, identity is related to the social groups to which the individual belongs and with which they identify. However, there is not always a perfect match between how a person thinks of themselves and how others see them. Personal identity may be different from social identity . . . a person perceived by others as male may see themselves as female with the physical characteristics of a man.

(Haralambos and Holborn, 2000)

Historically, in the UK, the development of Lesbian, Gay, Bisexual and Transgender (LGBT) identities has been often ignored, overlooked or downplayed by academics, professionals and institutions. Jackson and Sullivan (1994) say:

There has been little systematic longitudinal study of the adjustment of lesbian and gay adolescents . . . and that void is itself reflective of the marginality of these youths.

(cited in DeCrescenzo, 1994)

When applied to the homelessness field this is compounded as the issues concerning gay, lesbian, bisexual and transgendered homelessness are still largely under-researched and misunderstood (Homeless Pages, 2005; Stonewall, 2005).

In this chapter I hope to achieve two things. Firstly, to develop awareness in the reader of the plight of LGBT homeless people, focusing on what it means to develop an identity as a homeless person and the conflicts involved in identifying as LGBT at the same time. In doing this, I will develop a model arguing that there are three cycles of reinforcement in the creation of a LGBT homeless identity, with rejection being the driving force behind each of these cycles. These are:

- The initial feelings of rejection that all LGBT people experience.
- The confirmation of rejection through the experience of becoming homeless.

- The reactions of other homeless people and of homelessness agencies leading to the development of a double identity as means of negotiating this homeless experience.

I will be focusing on London's LGBT homeless, mainly in order to manage the vast nature of the subject area, and because I can draw upon my own experience of being homeless and of working with young, homeless, LGBT people. I will be reflecting on personal experiences of being street homeless, being in hostels and identifying as LGBT and having a homeless identity. These experiences cover a span of over twelve years.

Secondly, I would like to argue that British research and provision has failed to adequately address the issues involved in being LGBT and homeless, and, in the case of being transgendered and homeless, it is uncharted territory. I will redress some of this imbalance by drawing on literature and research that has been carried out in America. Consequently, I would like to highlight the need for a 'research agenda' in relation to LGBT homelessness. In the light of all this I will finish by developing a similar agenda for action for the homelessness sector and the workers in it. I will be listing points for professionals to consider.

I shall start by looking at the term 'identity', and examining theories of human development which give an insight into the difficulties often faced in the early development of LGBT identities. In doing this I will try and cover the differences and commonalities of LGBT experiences. I think it is important to create a common understanding of the subject area from which I have developed my ideas and to clear up any confusion, both for the reader and for myself.

The development of lesbian, gay and bisexual identities (LGB): the first cycle of rejection

Studies of gender concept provide a model for the understanding of how and when young people absorb knowledge of gender roles and stereotypes. It is possible that awareness of these roles also informs what behaviour is acceptable through play in the exploration of sexuality and sexual identity (Kohlberg, 1984). In the process of the development of gender identity, sex-role stereotypes and sex-typical behaviour appears to be clearly absorbed by young people by the age of seven or eight. At this age they are recognising and beginning to form sexual identities. By this age too, young people are very aware that open exploration, through play, of non-heterosexual roles or behaviour is likely to incur negative reactions.

From an examination of theorists from different traditions (Kohlberg, 1984; Piaget, 1926; Erikson, 1950) it is possible to provide a synopsis of the development of gender identity. Most human development models say that young people place themselves in a basic gender category in early childhood. Gender identity is commonly understood to have been acquired by the age of three, with gender stability by about four years old (Erikson, 1950). By the age of seven or eight, young people have knowledge of sex-role stereotypes and sex-typical behaviour, that is, how boys and girls are 'supposed' to behave. This is expressed through play, through the taking on of roles and use of certain 'gender specific' toys.

I can relate this to my experience when I was a child of receiving a 'doll' for Christmas. I was extremely upset and confused to get such a toy, and this led to me ripping the doll's head off and throwing it away as I related to, and enjoyed playing with, 'boys' toys. Many LGB young people develop at an early age an attraction to the same sex. In cases where the young person has confided in others, such as professionals, their inclinations have sometimes been put down to the fact that they are just 'going through a phase':

> *Homophobia and heterosexism impinge on the developmental tasks associated with developmental stages of gay, lesbian and bisexual youth. Young people are socialised to hide their sexual orientation if it is not heterosexual.*
>
> (Mallon, G., cited in Appleby and Anastas, 1998)

In terms of identity concerning sexuality, feelings of attraction and sensuality are also explored at a young age. Through interviewing LGBT young people my findings show that their sexual identity is often explored through play with others, though mostly as a 'discreet' or hidden activity. Strategies are developed to keep this identity exploration as hidden as possible. As a female child I can vividly remember playing in a toy house and wanting to take the role of the 'daddy' but ending up in a female role. I remember this because I wanted to play with the tools, not the pots and pans. I can relate this experience when working with young people aged eleven to twenty-five years old who identify as lesbian, gay or bisexual. The majority of them revealed that they knew or felt different from other young people at a young age and began to discreetly explore their identity between the ages of five to twelve years old.

These dates fall within Freud's (1923) **latency stage** in which development of the **ego** is a central element. It is during this period that Erikson (1963) argues that individuals become more aware of cultural and societal norms. Here, it is unsurprising that having become aware of others' feelings and normative values attached to non-heterosexual identity, the Lesbian, Gay or Bisexual individual's self-identity (ego) must explore discretely in order to live up to what Kohlberg (1984) describes as the morals or expectations held by the family or other groups (Bee, 2000).

I can relate to this too from my experience with one of my devoutly religious parents. As a young person I naively confided in them (maybe to check if such feelings were normal) that I was attracted to another girl at school. The reaction from my parent was one of disgust and dismissal. The message sent to me was that these feelings of attraction I had were a bad thing, and reinforced in me the need to keep these feelings secret and hidden from others. DeCrescenzo (1994) notes '. . . the exploration of these possible identities is thwarted by devaluation. Therefore mastery of these roles is diminished'. These beginnings of a double identity, as with early explorations of sexual identity, would be a fruitful area for research.

Where the development of heterosexual identity is explored (and expected) through play, young people who do not feel that they are, in themselves, heterosexual, realise that exploration needs to be hidden – and devise methods through play to ensure that this is the case. Despite being the thrust of some developmental theories, the view that homosexual feelings and activity are 'just a phase' that people go through in their teenage years, is not borne out. Erikson (1963), in his work on the development of the ego, identifies the ages of thirteen to eighteen as the period at which the development of sexual identity is most relevant. My findings show that the development of sexual identity occurs and is explored through play, one stage earlier than he suggests.

Understanding the development of Transgender identity

The document that the homelessness organisation Shelter produced is inclusive of bisexuals as well as lesbian and gay people, but mentions nothing about Homeless Transgender people. This does little to raise awareness into why transgender young people find themselves homeless. Is it that they assume that the reasons for becoming homeless are not very different to LGB youth? This would be another fruitful area for future research.

Transgender is an umbrella term which includes all variants of dress, manner and attitudes that are excluded from the traditional stereotypes of male and female (Hopkins, 2000). In its wider sense, the term 'transgender' includes anyone whose identity or behaviour falls outside stereotypical gender expectations (Mottet and Ohle, 2003). Quite often sex and gender are categorised or confused as one and the same thing. However, there are of course distinct differences and meanings to the words 'sex' and 'gender'. In order to clearly separate the issues we can note that the term sex describes the physical differences between males and females. Gender on the other hand refers to the socially constructed roles given to each sex, masculine and feminine. Giddens (2000) says:

> . . . *sociologists use the term sex to refer to the anatomical and physiological differences that define male and female bodies. Gender by contrast, concerns the psychological, social and cultural differences between males and females.*
>
> (Giddens, 2001)

Here Giddens argues that gender is socially constructed as opposed to being mainly determined by biological differences. In many cultures, stereotypical roles imply or dictate, for example, that men are strong and aggressive whereas women are caring and passive. In looking at various perceptions by the media and society at large of the LGBT community in relation to transsexuals, there is evidence that there are specific gender stereotypes that are relevant to gay men. Here gay men are often perceived as being effeminate and taking on female characteristics such as feminine voice tone and mannerisms.

Lesbians, conversely, are often thought of as exhibiting male traits such as short hair, masculine mannerisms and coarse voices. Bisexuals are often perceived as wanting the 'best of both worlds' sexually. Transsexual young people are seen as going to the extremes of trying to be and live as the other sex. Here the similarities in experience can be compared to those issues faced by LGB young people. Mottet and Ohle (2003) note:

> ... many people are confused about the difference between sexual orientation and gender identity or gender expression. Some people believe that all LGB people are transgendered, or vice versa.

However, these images are largely based on stereotypes constructed by the media and society at large. The reality is very different. Many LGB young people do not fit into these predetermined stereotyped boxes. Consequently, family and friends make the assumption that their children are heterosexual.

Transsexual young people are uncomfortable with their assigned sex from birth. Brown and Rounsey (1996) note that transsexuals:

> ... have a mind/body conflict; they self identify as one sex but have the body of the opposite sex ... at some point most transsexuals feel compelled to do something to resolve their conflict so as to live full and satisfying lives.

Whilst doing research and conducting interviews for my dissertation (2003) into how LGB youth groups could work with transgender youth it became apparent that transsexual people see having surgery as a corrective procedure. Transsexual young people have very different issues from LGB young people. Along with feeling out of sync. with their assigned sex from birth, these young people are still seen as having a medical condition that needs to be cured or fixed. This is no longer the case for LGB people.

I believe that all LGBT people do suffer from similar prejudices, discrimination and assumptions. However, the oppressive nature of the stereotyping is often coming from different angles and is not one and the same thing. An example would be that because a young person is transsexual this does not automatically make them heterosexual. There are many transsexual people who also identify as LGB (Mollett and Ohle, 2003).

There have also been views put forward by members of the LGB community which are excluding of transgender and transsexual people. One of these is that transpeople:

> ... hold back the LGB movement for civil rights, because it is difficult for people to talk about lesbian and gay issues, let alone complicating the discussion with transgender issues.

(Cross, 2001)

Cross (2001) argues that some people believe that transgender issues are not related to LGB issues, saying '... transgender people are defined by their gender expression and not their sexual orientation as are LGB people' (ibid.). My findings show that these claims prove groundless. I have found that some transsexual people identify as lesbian, gay, or bisexual.

In the 21st century, some lesbian, gay, bisexual and transgender people and organisations have to some extent moved mountains in terms of better legislation. This legislation is a marked improvement from the previous century where LGB people had no legal standing in terms of employment, partnership rights and homophobic abuse. LGB people can now be legal partners through civil ceremonies. Stonewall Housing Association notes '. . . same sex couples can be 'registered civil partners' and will acquire a package of rights and responsibilities in the same way as married couples' (www.stonewall.org.uk). This law came into effect from December 2005 and is known as the Civil Partnership Registration Scheme.

Section 28 of the historical Local Government Act 1986 prohibited local authorities in England and Wales from promoting homosexuality. It also labelled homosexual relationships as pretend family relationships. On 18 September 2003 section 28 was finally repealed. Stonewall Housing Association notes:

If Section 28 and the attitudes behind it remain then society will still believe that gay people are second class citizens and that it is right that they should be treated as second class citizens.

(www.stonewall.org.uk)

Despite such advances, many arenas in which young people explore their identity retain negative and confused approaches to LGBT. The repeal of Section 28 had very little media attention and as a consequence mentioning the subject in schools is still avoided. At the LGBT youth project we are still working with young people who identify as LGBT and who are exposed to homophobic attitudes from both teachers and other pupils, attitudes which still remain because they are generally not being challenged within schools. Transgender is also not mentioned even though there is no legislation to stop local authorities or schools from mentioning this subject – thus it remains a taboo subject that is largely misunderstood by the general population.

However, there is current legislation intended to help. Transgender people can now be recognised in their 'true' gender through the Gender Recognition Act 2003, and be issued with a new birth certificate. This is whether or not surgery has been sought. However, there still persists a homophobic and trans-phobic attitude in the general populace. The culture of most schools in the UK has historically condoned, either explicitly or implicitly, the use of the term 'gay' in a negative and deragoratory fashion. This is a term of abuse, and unlike other terms of abuse, goes unchallenged by staff in too many schools (NUT, 2006).

At school I can distinctly remember other children suspecting I was 'gay' or 'weird' because I did not fit into a stereotypical gender role. I remember at secondary school being asked by another pupil to meet their friend in the toilets only to find when I entered the school toilets that my name was written on the door claiming I was a 'lezy'; I immediately felt hurt, fear, panic and wanted to kill myself. Thus, this reinforced to me how important it was for my survival to keep my identity hidden. Many of the young people I now work with confirm being bullied at school and then being told by school heads that they brought such bullying upon themselves or that they 'provoked' the bully because of the way that they talk, walk or express themselves. These people found themselves socially isolated, ignored in the hope that they will go away or, at the very least, patronised.

Many LGBT young people are fearful of 'coming out' within their school environment. Herek and Berrill (1992) wrote a report based on bias-related crime and found that:

> ... adolescents who are open about their sexual orientation, who are suspected of being lesbian or gay, or who behave in ways associated with lesbian or gay stereotypes are the most frequent victims of abuse not just at home, but also in schools and community settings.

> (Pilkington, 1995, cited in Ryan and Futterman, 1998)

Also, many parents still dread and fear that their offspring might identify as LGBT. The initial reaction from parents or carers can be extreme, with many 'throwing away' their children. This is fairly well documented and represents the initial cycle of rejection that most LGBT people experience. However, it is in the next stage that homeless people start to differ, for they are the ones where this 'throwing away' sticks.

The known causes of LGBT homelessness: confirming rejection the first time

In 1999 The National Housing Federation published a report on equality for housing for LGB people (www.shelter.org.uk). The report stated that limited research has been done about LGB people's housing needs (Rogers and McVeigh, 1999). Stonewall Housing Association conducted research into LGBT homelessness in 2001 and 2005. Stonewall works with homeless LGB young people aged 16–25 years, providing long-term temporary housing and resettlement. The 2001 research looked at homelessness amongst young lesbians and gay men in a variety of cities across the UK. They found (2001) that lesbian and gay young people's experiences of becoming homeless included reasons both related and unrelated to their sexuality.

In practice, I found that workers and agencies tend to concentrate on the unrelated issues, viewing LGBT young people in a similar way to young homeless people who do not identify as LGBT. While this is understandable, being one interpretation of equality, it can be another smokescreen and become another reason for not addressing the needs of LGBT homeless people. I therefore want to focus on the causes that are related to sexuality.

It is the extremities of the experiences of rejection that many LGBT homeless people have that marks them out (though I accept not uniquely). They are rejected to such an extent that they are disowned and thrown out, or feel they cannot come back home. They can be subject to any number of types of (sometimes quite violent) homophobic and transphobic rejection. Homeless LGBT people have described to me in my work their leaving home to escape physical, sexual or mental violence, or being kicked out, locked out or thrown out after a period of mental stress. Personally, one of my parents constantly reminded me throughout my childhood and adolescent years that I was not 'normal' and that I was an abomination against 'God'.

Crisis notes that:

There is a long standing association between homelessness and the everyday lives of LGBT. For young people intolerance may originate with family members and be openly promoted within the wider social context (i.e. in schools or other institutional settings) ... Homelessness may emerge due to the pervasiveness of homophobia ... The loss of home for LGBT youth, as a runaway or as a result of being thrown out of their home, is an all too common experience.

(www.crisis.org.uk)

Stonewall similarly found that lesbian and gay men experienced an intolerance both directly and indirectly at home; or young people had an expectation that there would be such intolerance. They also found that young people were being bullied by their peers in school or in the vicinity where they lived. Young people who have had difficulty coming to terms with their sexuality have found that their behaviour and emotional health has been affected in a negative way. Lastly, they found that young people had a desire for independence, to explore their sexuality away from the family home.

The Office of the Deputy Prime Minister (ODPM) published a report highlighting the need for local authorities to investigate homelessness amongst lesbians and gay men (ODPM, 2002). In 2003 the ODPM stressed the need for monitoring of sexuality within the homeless sector. However, where Stonewall and Shelter have largely ignored writing about transgender homeless young people, Crisis has included LGBT in their document, but their main focus is on issues of sexuality and sexual identity. There is no mention of gender in terms of transgender people. Transgendered homelessness remains untouched.

This will have an impact on the formation of their identity. Where well-being, happiness, affirmation and confidence are essential to the formation of a positive identity (Kohlberg, 1984), the absence of these factors for LGBT homeless young can easily be internalised. It feels like a rejection of oneself as a person even when one refuses to identify as 'immoral', 'sick', 'perverted', 'unnatural or 'confused'.

It is no surprise, then, that young LGBT people spend as much time and effort as is necessary to 'hide' their sexuality in the best ways that they know how. What is very seriously damaging about having to live a lie, deny one's true being and adopt a double protective identity is that people have to do so in the very places where they should be experiencing well-being, positive affirmation, love and confidence. Instead, in their families, homes, schools, places of religious worship and neighbourhoods they are very often experiencing rejection, oppression and abuse. Robinson (1997) noted how, with the development of identity with excluded groups, after the crisis of rejection and recognition of one's own difference, many people go into a period of immersion in their own culture. Shelter notes that many LGBT young people move to urban areas to be able to associate with what they perceive to be a more visible LGBT community. However, as I will contend in the next section, in contrast to other LGBT experiences, homeless people often encounter a second level of rejection, through the experience of being homeless.

Encounters with homelessness agencies; a second confirmation of rejection

Shelter highlights that many homelessness services overlook sexual identity. There is no mention within legislation that recognises LGBT people as being in priority housing need. There is no 'official' recognition, then, that the rejected and the oppressed in this way might conceivably need somewhere safe to live. In my experience, many young LGBT people have been let down and damaged by 'unofficial' personal attitudes or personal moralities expressed by Social Services or Housing Services staff. Despite the training courses that Housing and Social Services staff will inevitably attend concerning equal opportunities, prejudices remain. Homophobia and Transphobia are still seen by some to be 'acceptable prejudices' sometimes fuelled and legitimised by religion, faith, or other beliefs.

A young person can be seen as too young to identify as LGBT (though never too young to identify as heterosexual). In my professional practice I encounter many young LGBT homeless people who are patronised and not taken seriously by professionals. One example concerned a young lesbian who was 'thrown out' of the family home by her mother for bringing disgrace upon the family. When the young woman turned up at her local Homeless Persons Unit, the professional worker suggested to her that she had only pretended to be lesbian in order to get back at her mother after a family argument and that she did not require emergency accommodation at all. The worker suggested that the young woman go home, apologise and promise to be good.

Professional intervention has been denied to homeless people because the professional involved is of the opinion that the young LGBT person in front of them is merely the result of 'a little family argument' that can be sorted out with a quick phone-call to the parents or carers. In none of the cases that I am aware of was the rejection, oppression and physical and mental violence experienced by young LGBT runaways and throwaways capable of being 'solved' by a magic phone call.

Another example from my professional practice concerned a young gay man aged 15 years who was ejected from the family home, once again for bringing disgrace upon the family. Efforts by the project staff to get social services or housing services to take his situation seriously fell upon deaf ears. All the worker was prepared to do was telephone the parents to ask them to pick up their son. When informed that the young man was likely to face violence if he returned home, the professional worker said that he was aware of that as it had been documented in the young man's social services file.

Other examples have involved HPU staff demanding written confirmation from parents stating why they had thrown their children out before action can be taken. In most cases where 'disgrace' concerning sexuality and gender is involved they know too well that the parent 'out of shame' will not co-operate with their children or the HPU. In too many instances, then, professionals have failed to recognise that young LGBT runaways or 'throwaways' are 'in need' or that their welfare is likely to be seriously prejudiced if they are not provided with safe accommodation. With the exception of cases where young LGBT people have approached specific LGBT organisations such as Stonewall Housing Association or the Albert Kennedy Trust, they find that their needs are seldom recognised or met. In my own initial experience of direct access and short stay hostels I found these environments, and the majority of staff, to be cold, regimented, uncaring and indirectly and covertly suspicious of why I was homeless. Based on this experience I was not prepared to disclose anything truthful about why I had become homeless.

I stayed in one hostel in later years and found a voluntary support worker who was kind, caring, and warm. Here, after a period of informal chats with the worker, sufficient trust and confidence was built up which made me feel comfortable enough to confide in the worker, and to face my fear of the worker's possible negative reaction. The worker was very positive towards me and discussed with me areas of support and assisted me by putting me in touch with and helping me to arrange my first visit to an LGBT youth group. However, in the absence of any obvious policies to make LGBT people welcome, this worker's reaction, that made a significant difference to my future, was by chance.

Generally I found it was always safer to disclose as little about why I had become homeless for fear that I would not be re-housed or given a bed for the night. Had it been the case that homeless services were more open and welcoming to all ideas and reasons for becoming homeless, I feel I would have been better served by these agencies. I was made homeless because of my own confusion over sexuality and gender – not fitting into the stereotypical role – and growing tensions between my family and myself at home became intolerable and I was asked to leave. For all these reasons, LGBT runaways or 'throwaways' are often reluctant to enter emergency or short stay accommodation because they fear the risk of further rejection, oppression or harassment. Here the street seems somehow safer, leading to a third re-enforcing experience.

LGBT identity with the homeless community: a third reason to keep one's mouth shut

Here, I want to highlight the impact that homophobia in the 'homeless community' has on LGBT identities. We have already established that homophobia (and trans-phobia) can be direct causes of homelessness and difficulties with housing. We have also seen that the effects of such oppressions often cause young people to run away to a perceived safe haven, usually large cities such as London. The question before us now is: what is that experience like?

The stress and anxiety that young people who find themselves homeless can feel cannot be underestimated. My own experience of the first night, knowing that I would have to sleep rough on the streets, can only be explained as a slow building of panic. I walked around the West End trying to look like I had a place to go to, whilst inside knowing this was not the case. Much time was spent discreetly looking for a safe hidden-away place where I could sleep, and where hopefully no one would see me. As with LGBT identity, my safety would depend on how 'invisible' I was. I would spend a lot of time searching for a back alley and a door way – sitting down and patiently staying awake, watching, listening to see if people frequent the alleyway. All the time I would be double-checking that I was as camouflaged as possible.

I can also clearly remember finally lying down in a foetal position to try and keep the cold at bay, dozing off but not fully asleep in case I was spotted. At various times through the night the cold took hold of my body, a deep inner cold, the only warmth coming from uncontrollable shivering. Although this description focuses on isolation during street homelessness, I did meet and form social bonds with other homeless young and older people. Here the sense of belonging to a group becomes a coping mechanism for living relatively safely on the street. However, there are inherent dangers encompassed in this situation. Most of the people I socialised with were volatile, dishonest and extremely displaced. Despite the positive sense of belonging to a group, I was always well aware that possible negative views may be held by this group about gender and sexuality, which would present a danger to me.

Becoming a part of a group can provide comfort, friendship and a sense of belonging. The social isolation from the rest of society is somewhat alleviated. You become part of a minority of people who suffer similar prejudice, discrimination and oppression by the majority of society because of your homeless status. However, having found comfort in a group you do not want to risk rejection from it.

In my experience of being street homeless there are many cultural expectations, both positive and negative, which in some cases are a mirror image, and a romanticised view, of society's attitudes. Certain expectations and norms are reinforced. These include: not hitting women; honour among thieves; and a distorted and chaotic type of looking out for each other (though not always the case in reality). An example of this would be having giro money to buy and share beer and cigarettes. Another homeless person would share with you quite freely with no strings but the following day or another time would expect and demand that you either pay them back or share what you have. Here, to spend more time with them without giving back is frowned upon and the fact that you may have nothing is seen as not relevant.

Negative and hateful attitudes are also often expressed, among the homeless society at large, towards certain groups such as ethnic minorities, homosexuals and transsexuals, paedophiles, those scavenging or ripping off other homeless people, homeless people who take illicit drugs and those who drink. Many of these attitudes are borne out of a desire to transfer blame for their situation, their mental health, frustration, anger, hate, and lack of understanding, onto certain groups; they embodied too an unspoken 'code of honour' amongst the established homeless community.

So, identifying openly as LGBT can attract negative and hateful attitudes. In my experience homophobia is very visible within the homeless population, both on the street and in many hostels. Here, many LGBT young people feel they have to deny their LGBT identity often in order to protect themselves from homophobic abuse. This means that they have to make up other reasons, or omit information, with regard to the causes of them being homeless. The positive side to this was the culture on the street that usually your business is your own. In general, other homeless people were inherently not that concerned with specific details and past experiences of others.

Experiences that *are* disclosed to others are often downplayed. This will all have an impact on the individual. Freud's (1901) **motivated-forgetting theory** highlights that 'people who suffer trauma often have to internalise or discriminately try to forget in order to cope' (Gross et al., 2000). The process of internalising an LGBT identity can sometimes manifest itself as 'internalised homophobia or transphobia' so that a LGBT young person may be homophobic or transphobic towards other young people who identify as LGBT or are suspected as such. This is again exacerbated in the case of being transgender, as it is an identity that is often misunderstood and distrusted in the LGB community itself. In my own experience of being homeless and going to homeless centres and hostels, there were only two, opposing, types of sexuality: you were either 'gay' or 'straight'. For years I did not know of the term 'transgender' or suspect that this would form an important part of my identity later in life.

Attending LGBT youth groups I was labelled lesbian. In my naivety I went along with this and assumed this was why I had felt different to other young people. However, I learnt that to be lesbian you first have to like being female. I was never 100 per cent comfortable with this fact, though I tried to fit in with the gay community. I found that most other lesbians saw me as a man so were not physically, emotionally or sexually attracted to me, though I did have plenty of offers from gay men and a few bisexual women.

Brown and Rounsley (1996), when discussing initial assessment of people who formally go to a therapist for diagnosis in relation to gender dysphoria, highlighted that some people had causes that made these people think that they may be transsexual when they were not. Some gay men and lesbians, in denial of their sexuality or in a state of confusion about the differences between sexual orientation and gender identity, had thought they might be transsexual. Here, we can see that the confusion is also reversed with transsexual young people, who identify as heterosexual, being labelled gay or lesbian, adding to their stress and confusion about who they are and how they feel about themselves.

Cochran et al. (2002) found that LGBT young people left home more regularly than heterosexual young people. LGBT young people suffered more from bullying, were more likely to use illicit drugs and were more susceptible to suffering from mental health issues. Through experiencing abuse, neglect and homelessness, I succumbed to using alcohol and illicit drugs. I developed a crack habit, which, at the time, gave me a sense of coping and inner confidence. On reflection I feel the hopelessness and desperate situation that I found myself in whilst being on the street meant that my mental, physical and emotional health suffered in regard to stress, trauma and excessive tiredness, and needing something to get me through from day to day.

The development of a double identity

As already mentioned, Shelter and Crisis have acknowledged that LGB has not been taken fully into consideration by homeless agencies. They recommend equal opportunities monitoring forms for collecting data on how many homeless people identify as LGB. My concern is that this misses the point I have been making about the dynamics of a LGBT identity in the homeless community. Where a young person has not experienced a history of love, acceptance, equality and positive nurturing concerning their homosexual or transgender being, they are very unlikely to be 'open' about their sexuality or true gender when seeking shelter, emergency housing, a hostel or even a room in a B and B. They will conceal their identity to prevent the cycle of rejection and oppression starting again. Monitoring forms could easily often be a rehash of a procedure that has not worked in the past. They will also not reveal accurate statistics about people's identity, as LGB people need to conceal their identity and fear ticking an LGB box.

Many young LGBT people, by this point, do not trust forms and are unconvinced of confidentiality being kept. The fear for many LGBT young people is that they identify with a social group of people who are often stigmatised and treated with contempt by certain factions in society. To ask them to disclose that they are LGBT to staff there needs to be an open door policy that completely reassures LGBT people that they are welcome and valued. I have certainly not dared to tick such a box in the past. The fact that there seems to be no significant research or findings about LGBT homelessness shows that this minority of the population is largely ignored or forgotten by the homeless sector in London and around the UK. I feel that hostels need to not just train staff but also have a zero tolerance of homophobic and transphobic attitudes. Equal opportunities forms should not be just signed and used as a cushion in case of complaint, but should be seen to be put into practice by both staff and other residents.

In some cases, for young people who come from small towns or villages where there is no noticeable LGBT community around them, where support is very limited and the nearest LGBT group is maybe 30–40 miles away, coming to big urban cities such as London is often their only means of finding appropriate support and a way of mixing with other LGBT young people. In my experience of running away to London, back in the early 1990s, I felt hostility towards being LGBT in most direct access hostels I went in. In one such hostel there were posters on the wall in the reception, one about racial equality and another with a helpline number for lesbians and gays. However, I still felt that I needed to hide my LGBT status from staff for fear they would judge me negatively as had happened with my family.

Shelter notes that in terms of best practice many housing staff have little if any understanding of the often multiple needs of people who identify as LGB. Shelter also notes that school, family and negative reactions to LGB can be in itself a direct cause of homelessness. Here, Shelter recommends that staff should be offered training on the issues surrounding sexuality. In my experience I think this training should be mandatory, and resistance towards such training from staff should be seen as misconduct.

A further factor to consider in the development of a double identity, the LGBT side being hidden, is the suspicion LGBT people hold of the fact that many homeless organisations were either founded by or have links with religious institutions, organisations or representatives. Many churches and church organisations have a history of difficulties with people who identify as LGBT. Trying to uphold true equality in hostels and other homeless facilities may be hard, as there is a clear conflict between some Christian values and LGBT issues and needs. These potential difficulties can manifest in three ways.

Firstly, some organisations have declared outright antagonism towards LGBT identities, both in terms of workers and clients. The Salvation Army is very clear about its Christian values and are open about its views on sexuality. Their positional statement on homosexuality includes: 'The Bible thus teaches that God's intention for mankind is that society should be ordered on basis of . . . heterosexual unions. Scripture opposes homosexual practices by direct comment (Leviticus 18: 22). The Bible treats such practices as self evidently abnormal' (www.salvationarmy.org.uk). The Salvation Army is a leading homeless charity. Another example that has been documented by the lesbian and gay Christian movement is St George's Crypt Centre, a church-run homelessness charity in Leeds. A job applicant who was gay ran up against an equal opportunities policy declaring active homosexuals – together with adulterers and those involved in occult practices – to be contrary to its 'Christian ethos'.

On another level it can mean that LGBT issues become invisible, marginalised or not given sufficient priority, whether in a conscious or unconscious way. For instance, a recent piece of research by a major provider of youth homeless services, into the complex needs of their clients, mentions nothing about sexuality or transgender issues being one of these complex issues. The focus is summed up in a broad sphere of family breakdowns, abuse, leaving or being in care, unemployment and socio-economic marginalisation. This is despite the fact that other research has found that 42 per cent of homeless youth identify as lesbian, gay or bisexual (Orion Center, Survey of Street Youth, 1996).

On a third level the fear of homophobia may be unfounded, but still real. As an example, Church Action on Homelessness in London (UNLEASH) has a list of organisations that includes St Mungo's, Connections at St Martins, Simon Community and Providence Row. Others, like Centrepoint, were founded by a curate and initially started up in 1969 in St Ann's church in Soho, London. Many of these organisations have actively fought homophobia, their view of Christianity being one that accommodates LGBT identities, or their Christian association being largely historical. However, their names retain religious connotations and the fear and suspicion that these organisations might be homophobic or transphobic because they are religion-based is real for many clients, and will determine how some LGBT young people behave and conceptualise those organisations.

Conclusion

If organisations and institutions continue to ignore the fact that some people's negative reactions to LGBT identity can be a cause of homelessness there will continue to be a detachment from a full understanding of homelessness itself. LGBT identity is not a 'phase' that can be safely ignored or a 'blip' on the 'normal' causes of homelessness. People's negative reactions to LGBT identity can be not only causes of homelessness, but reasons why LGBT young people seek safety in the anonymity of the street rather than risk suffering more abuse in homeless shelters.

Where the need for socialisation on the street takes hold, LGBT identity remains hidden. The homeless population are mostly perceived as 'unacceptable' social constructs and LGBT homeless are perceived as not just 'unacceptable' but, in most cases, as immoral or unnatural. As a society we have gone some way to understanding reactions to LGB identity as a cause of homelessness, but we need to go even further to understand the position of transgender homeless people.

In terms of the development of a double or denied identity we need to acknowledge the process people have been through before we meet them. By the time they have become our client they are likely to have denied their identities, making our monitoring forms largely redundant: to undo some of these processes is going to take a lot of proactive behaviour on our part.

Professionals and institutions working with homeless people need to consider collating and displaying information about LGBT youth groups, support groups and advice centres that are located outside of the West End of London (such as Hackney, Tower Hamlets etc.). Also, direct access hostels need to be promoting organisations such as the Albert Kennedy Trust and Stonewall Housing Association as possible housing options for young people who identify as LGBT. Training on LGBT issues should be mandatory for staff, and other residents should be fully aware that there is a zero tolerance of bullying, harassment and violent homophobic behaviour. Institutional homophobia and transphobia should be challenged. Where it is not challenged, it is in effect condoned.

On a wider level, individual organisations need to revisit their overall ethos. If organisations were to make overt and emphasise their following of value bases such as the Human Rights Act, rather than religious ones, people might actively feel that they will be treated as individuals who deserve to feel warmth, love and care. They will start to feel that organisations have a genuine interest in working with them. It is only then that the negative experiences LGBT people have in terms of accessing hostels and homeless provision would be significantly reduced.

LGBT identity should be made a priority need under the Housing Act 1996 and the Homelessness Act 2002. Lastly, homeless organisations should realise that if there is a culture of homophobia (whether it be directly or indirectly) in their facilities, there is little hope of young LGBT people ticking boxes on questionnaires or equal opportunity forms. LGBT young people will remain the hidden homeless because of their instilled fear of further stigma and abuse, or as a result of their lack of trust in confidentiality.

Chapter 3

Love on the streets: the denial of homeless people's relationships

Tony Dodson (edited by Mike Seal)

Introduction

Single homelessness is defined as individuals and couples, without dependent children, under 60 years of age.

(OED; 2004)

Two people live cheaper than one
Two people live better than one
We don't want to part
This can only break our hearts

(Bradford Homeless People's Charter, 2005)

Definitions are semantic; but they are nonetheless important as words can sometimes determine the way we think. I explored this issue in 2001, in Homeless Link's response to the development of homeless strategies, written with Andrew Van Doorn. The term 'single homeless' was coined to distinguish between two conceptual groups of homeless people: those who were in priority need, as defined by homeless legislation as being households with children, or vulnerable adults; and those who were not. An assumption was made that all those who were in the latter category were single. On top of this traditional hostels, and nightshelters, provided only single-sex dormitory-style accommodation and were unable to provide services for couples. Single homelessness in reality has been used as a shorthand for non-statutory homelessness. This has had a negative consequence and is based on false assumptions. Many homeless people, albeit a smaller proportion, but no less important, are actually couples.

In this chapter I will argue that homeless couples have for many years had problems gaining access to both temporary and permanent accommodation. There are hostels in the UK available to couples, but there seems to be a culture of either prevention or discouragement towards couples. It would seem that the structure of single homeless services can let them down on the very thing they are looking for in services; stability. While this is particularly important when they are on the street, where they are at their most visible and vulnerable, this is equally so for hostels and other forms of temporary accommodation, which in London alone accounts for about 10,000 bed spaces (Crisis, 2003).

Practically, the majority of direct access hostels in the UK are for single homeless people, and by this they mean solitary homeless people. While the rolling shelter set up by the Rough Sleepers Unit has recently made some space and beds available for couples, moving on from there is an issue. Average move-on from rolling shelters is three weeks (Crisis); however, for couples there are usually many obstacles to face to progress to the next stage (a direct access centre) and even more so if they want to move onto any form of second stage housing.

As an example, one couple recently described in a focus group the discrimination they encountered going through the hostel system (Groundswell, 2006). They went through the rolling shelter system seven times in London before they managed to secure accommodation together in a St Mungo's Hostel (rolling shelters normally operate for three months in the winter, during which time attempts will be made to resettle residents). They are now at the stage of moving on to semi-supported accommodation, but will have to be separated again, as the organisation had no such provision for couples. Positively, the organisation is at least trying to find them space in the same project together.

The chapter will begin with some case studies to illustrate the issues that exist for couples. I will then examine why relationships are important for homeless people, moving on to an exploration of why discrimination might exist and finish by tracing how services are, and are not, reacting to the situation. In doing this I would like to thank Jon Cox, hostel manager in Newbury, Oxfordshire, for his personal thoughts on services' responses to couples. I will finish with some recommendations for both services and professionals in the sector on what we need to do to work effectively with couples.

Case studies

Example one

On 17th November 2005 the East End Advertiser published a story called 'Homeless Find Cold Comfort on the Streets'. The story was related to the reader through an outreach worker from Thames Reach Bondway, which is, as the name suggests, part of the street rescue service, a scheme whose aim is to 'rescue' people off the streets.

> The gentleman is a Sikh and the woman is a Muslim. The couple met before they became street homeless, but their families rejected them because of religious reasons, particularly when the woman became pregnant and subsequently had a child.
>
> *Because we are a couple, I think couples are more vulnerable. We have to look after each other, but most of the time we are bored. There's nothing to do, nowhere to go.*
>
> (East End Advertiser)

The article goes on to describe how when they hit the streets the issues associated with the lifestyle, not chosen by them, were drugs, boredom and bullies. They also encountered predators, looking for vulnerable girls to procure, though not necessarily from the homeless community itself. That they had each other was useful in protecting themselves against these elements. The man said he could have been off the streets long ago, and gone into a hostel, but obviously he did not want to leave his partner alone out there.

Example two

This was an example from the late nineties, but it would appear that quite a few of the same problems for couples are still around.

This couple met on the streets, being service users of day centres. They got together when the woman was trying to self-refer into a hostel, not knowing that it was a referral-only hostel. Consequently, she was refused admission and the man, in passing, stopped to ask if she was OK as she seemed quite distressed. On hearing her problems, he told her he knew a project where she could stay the night, be fed etc. The woman walked to the shelter with him, as she felt she could trust him. This being a winter shelter, their relationship developed over a short space of time. This is a characteristic of many relationships on the street. It is not unusual for relationships to develop quickly, as the tendency is for a couple to be together 24/7, and to get to know each other, their background, problems, and what they want from the future, quite quickly.

Unexpectedly, they also found their problems had only just begun. They had to contend with numerous verbal attacks on their relationship. Some were from other residents, who were often jealous, but others were from staff and volunteers who felt that their relationship was inappropriate. It was not uncommon for staff to encourage one or the other partner to end the relationship. Services were also reluctant to undertake assessments of them as a couple, preferring to treat them as individuals, sometimes by having separate housing interviews, or having two resettlement pro-grammes which paid no attention to the nature of the partnership.

Feeling aggrieved by this treatment they decided to leave together, street-bound. On hitting the streets, both knew it was not going to be easy, as both had encountered street homelessness before. The man had serious drink problems and was a 'jake' drinker (surgical spirit) and the woman had mental health as well as literacy issues. The woman had also developed an ongoing physical health problem. However, finding they had a common goal, they were starting to help and fend for each other. They became known by the outreach teams who, though the woman's health problems were recognised by the teams as a significant factor, did not feel able to help because of their relationship. Some options were not open to them: help could only be given to them as individuals, not together. The solutions offered them were either separate hostels, or the same hostel but on different floors. As far as they were concerned they had no choice but to stay out on the streets. However the woman's health problem became worse, and after a few months reached the stage where she was becoming a fixture at the local hospital outpatients.

Eventually the woman was admitted, when the problem had reached a crisis point, leading to her needing a full hysterectomy. She was told to take it easy for the next six weeks and not to lift any heavy loads. Six days before being released from hospital she was asked if she was returning back to the streets. However, the discharge protocols only looked at her health issue and did not take account of her housing. The partner managed to solve the short-term housing problem by getting a former homeless person to put them up until she had regained her strength and mobility. This only lasted for three months and they then reached a decision that if they were going to solve their housing problem they had to look elsewhere. It was the desire to look after his partner that made the man act as an advocate for them both. At that time persistence and single mindedness was able to get them re-housed into their own flat.

Example three

This was recorded in March 2006.

The man is forty years old, with a history of homelessness for twenty four of those years. His partner is Lithuanian and not entitled to benefits. I think this story is best related in the person's own words as they seem to encapsulate admirably the issues they are facing:

Yeah you know, streets, hostels, christmas shelters, cold weather shelters and more, I've done the lot. I have a drink problem, but I've got that under control now – want to know why? I've got myself a responsibility. I'd been back on the streets for fourteen months, walking around, doing the day centres, handouts, etc, when I met a girl one day on the street, same position as me, the circuit that we know. We just got talking, found somewhere to stay quiet on the streets, safe, and it just happened. Just the same, people meet in pubs, clubs you know, that was it – we are now inseparable since then, now I have got someone to look after; got me eyes everywhere. My partner comes from Lithuania, she is twenty-six years old, and as long as I've got her I don't care about being on the streets. I am with the person I love and who loves me, we support each other, all the time. Isn't that the way it should be? Her problem is now she gets no benefits at all, been here 13 months, look, I get forty-six pounds a week and I give her twenty-six of that, that's my drinking money gone, ok, have a can every now and then to keep me on the level but that's it, got better things to spend my money on – to look after her.

How we spend our time sort of goes like this: day centres, food, clothes, handouts and just sometimes she does a bit of begging – if we have no money. We both smoke fags, dog ends are OK. We've been seen by outreach workers and they can find a place for her but not for me; no couples see? The other problem is because she gets no benefits at the moment if we find a hostel that will take us together, how is she going to pay the rent, my money will not cover it? But there is no way I'm going into a hostel and leave her behind on the streets.

The importance of relationships on the street

We place great importance on the formation of a trusting relationship and see it as the single most important factor in ensuring a formerly homeless person makes a successful transition to permanent housing.

(Director of Wintringham, a service for older homeless people in Melbourne)

Perhaps the overarching theme that I came across in the accounts of homeless people was that of a complete break in trust with others, an obliteration of any remaining shred of a social contract between them and others.

(Rowe, 1999: 82)

Something acknowledged by various pieces of research as being an essential pattern in street culture is the need to create a supportive unit, either embodied in a drinking school or some other loose collective (Snow and Anderson, 1993; Rowe, 1998). In terms of couples this supportive unit can often be each other. At the same time the couple may have both taken routes in life that have been damaging emotionally and, as illustrated above, a relationship is important in working through this and other experiences associated with homelessness. MacKnee and Mervyn (2002) investigated what factors in people 'escaping' (his words) the street lifestyle are. They outline the five most significant:

1. Establishing supportive relationships.
2. Discovering some measure of self-esteem.
3. Accepting a level of personal responsibility.
4. Accomplishing mainstream lifestyle goals.
5. Changing perceptions.

Several aspects of relationships seem significant here, particularly regarding the first three factors, and they resonate with the examples I have outlined above: the importance of people finding a network to support and protect them, discovering that they can trust again and having to take responsibility for another person.

Supportive relationships: the importance of the street network and protection

What seems significant about the first example is the value people put on the street network. Indeed, when the worker finally found them a hostel space together and wanted to get news to them, it was through the informal street network that she contacted them, i.e. daycentres, soup runs, etc. As well as being part of the survival techniques of people on the street, it becomes a source of strength, a way of connecting with other people in the 'houseless community'. The couple described how, being out of touch with their family and their respective communities, the street 'was a source of community, similar to belonging to a family or a local community'.

The first example also mentions the importance of each partner protecting the other. In their case this was against perceived predators. However, the protective element can extend to protection from passersby and the general public. Kendra Inman and Alison Benjamin, writing an article on homeless couples (Inman, 2003), give an account of another partnership where the man protected his girlfriend from the spit and abuse dished out by passersby, doing his best to make a frightening situation easier. 'It can be really dangerous on the street', Darren says, 'I know people who have been set on fire and even pissed on. If Katrina hadn't been with me, she'd be dead.'

Relationships and self-esteem

Relationships can be a source of self-esteem. Positively, some service providers acknowledge this. Jon Cox feels that relationships can promote support, confidence, self-esteem, chances of timely re-housing and sustainable and fulfilling lives. The acknowledgement of homeless person's rights to develop relationships is an important part of ensuring service users' human rights are not impinged and that individuals feel valued as human beings deserving of equality. While writing *The Big Issue* survey in 2002, I noted that 'there is no deeper human emotion than attachment. It gives us a sense of identity, a common shared history and culture. It helps develop openness, generosity and realism' (Cockson et al., 2002).

In this sense it goes beyond self-esteem into the realism and support that helps develop this kind of self-belief.

Taking responsibility for others

It seems, as in the third case, that having responsibility for others has a significant effect on people's behaviour. MacKnee and Mervyn (2002) see this as taking personal responsibility, but it seems that people were finding having to take responsibility for another as a significant factor here. To draw a parallel, Clare Kivlehan, Dogs Trust outreach manager, explains the importance of pets to homeless people: 'The stability, love, responsibility and companionship brought about from looking after a pet is essential for their eventual resettlement and a life of independence.' If this is true of a pet then it will be equally so of another human being, if not more so.

Changing perceptions: the importance of trust in another person

Significant in the second example are the issues of trust. As Rowe says, a significant factor in the homeless experience is loss of trust in others. He also says that a significant sign of someone coming to terms with their experience is regaining trust in another person. In another context, Laub (2005) found that the most significant single factor in people changing long-term offending behaviour was in forming a lasting and loving relationship. While I would not want to equate homelessness with criminality, the factor in common here is the place relationships have in changing entrenched behaviour and lifestyles.

People's experience of being in hostels, and agency rationales

Outcomes are not healthy for relationships [between those] who happen to be homeless as well.

(Crane et al., 2005)

In many supported housing settings for single people, for example, those who form relationships and sleep together are evicted. Nor are they helped to plan a joint future together by, for instance, being jointly re housed.

(Lemos, 2006)

Crane's comment is interesting because it has two interpretations, which belie the differing attitudes towards homeless relationships. On the one hand there is the attitude that relationships make individuals worse; and the other, that I would propound and Lemos illustrates, is that couples are in for a hard ride going through agencies. Groundswell recently conducted a series of focus groups for the ODPM that seem to dovetail neatly with the experiences of the couples in our examples. They found that discrimination against couples in hostels seemed to take three dimensions: rules that actively discouraged or punished people for having relationships; a lack of understanding about the importance and potentially positive impact of having a relationship; and structural discrimination against couples. The following quotes illustrate these dimensions and positively demonstrate that homeless people recognise both the dimensions and the importance of a relationship:

Yeah, I was in XXXX, and I got kicked out because there was a complaint made that I was kissing my partner outside, someone complained, they didn't like it, they said if you want to leave we'll make you leave.

Some people draw strength from their relationship, and if you're in a constructive relationship, the last thing you want to do is lose that support. And I think it should be taken into consideration when people are assessed and communicated with.

Me and my other half have got mental problems and we want to be moved together but they will not . . . we are being split up – there has to be a place that takes couples, there has to be?

In terms of structural discrimination, as we saw from the second example, what often happens is that the couple find themselves separated or segregated by hostel management either into separate hostels or in different areas. Crisis research backs this up, finding that:

Many hostels restrict visits of the opposite sex and rough sleepers have little opportunity for intimacy. While some people believe that being in an intimate relationship helps them cope with homelessness, others say that having a relationship while homeless causes more problems; as one man responds 'it's twice as hard'.

(Crane, 2003)

Some of the reasons for this discrimination are monetary. For homeless couples, a double room comes at a price. Councils have discretion when deciding housing benefit claims. In the Inman and Benjamin article mentioned above, David Devoy, a senior manager from the largest homeless agency in London, St Mungo's, admitted that a couple's joint housing benefit claim is worth £153.50 a week, two-thirds less than if they were claiming separately. This shortfall is one reason why so few organisations are willing to take in couples, says Devoy:

> *We are having to pay for the privilege of getting homeless couples off the street. On the one hand, we are obliged to reduce rough sleeping, but the housing benefit obstacle is making this difficult to achieve.*

> (Inman and Benjamin, 2003)

However, these issues are not insurmountable. Jon Cox feels that many couples do not want to claim as such, particularly in the early days, as this reduces the amount of benefit payable and can lead to financial arguments. He believes the issue can be addressed, in part, by allowing people residing in a hostel who have relationships to have 'overnight stays'. This 'in theory' could mean a service user in a relationship could overnight in their partner's room for three nights and the partner could overnight in their room for a further three nights and still not breach HB regulations. The only downside to this, Jon feels, is that this is sometimes hard to justify when there is a waiting list. However, if you are at agreed capacity, you are at agreed capacity and this should not be a problem for long, as these are short-term services seeking to move people on swiftly. This approach would also overcome the difficulty that arises if the couple splits up, as each still have their own rooms to go back to.

A second reason is a lack of understanding of relationships. This can take two dimensions, a lack of appreciation of their value, and a lack of appreciation of their dynamics as well as a lack of skills base in this area. Lemos examines the first dimension of this lack of understanding:

> *Professionals too readily assume that relationships involving vulnerable people are doomed not to get off the ground, or, if they do, are bound not to last. Many would even assume that they are actively harmful, re-activating suppressed disquiets and disturbances in the smooth surface of day-to-day stability.*

> (Lemos, 2006)

There seems to be a general culture of seeing relationships as negative, or of at least seeking out the negative aspects of relationships, rather than the positives. Practitioners would do well to dwell on some of the positives as explored in the last section. A linked issue is that workers do not understand the particular dynamics of homeless relationships as illustrated by our second example. They may develop more quickly because of their 24/7 nature and the extent of their co-dependence. Homeless relationships rarely have the luxury of a dating process. This may explain some of the suspicions of workers about the transitory nature of street relationships, especially when they may not have existed for very long. However, this can be misunderstanding the dynamics involved. As Jon Cox says, this is just one of the things we need to take account of in how we manage the communities in hostels:

> *It's true to say that at times some relationships can create tensions in hostels. For those in relationships when things are tough, for those who don't have them and when secondary relationships form. It's also true, and more common amongst younger service users, that dynamics change when members of the opposite sex are present. Not always for the worse though, I feel. Quite simply, robust housing management expectations and remedial action can alleviate this problem and soon help to engender and maintain a reasonably respectful culture. Again, the involvement of service users in the creation of such agreements cannot be over stated.*

The third factor is that lack of experience in working with couples could explain people's reluctance to take them on and, as we saw in the second example, to try and split them up. Workers tend to be trained in how to work with individuals rather than couples or groups. Structures such as action plans and support plans are individualised and hard to adapt. It then follows that workers will not have the skills to do the work or the structures to support the skills even if they had them. This can then lead to couples being labelled as difficult or harder to work with, rather than just being different. The already mentioned St Mungo's report found that more than three-quarters of clients in couples had drugs problems, compared with just over half of those who were single. It goes on to say that it is harder to treat couples because if one partner is not ready to give up drugs, they can hinder the other's progress. 'We undoubtedly have less success helping couples come off drugs', he says. However, this may be, again, because they are approaching them as individuals. Indeed there is research that shows that you are more likely to have success with drug-using couples, if you treat them as a couple rather than individuals (Kelly and Fals-Sewart, 2000).

Reactions to services

> *While homeless hostels might not seem the most romantic of places, many homeless people are in relationships, but finding accommodation together proves a difficult task.*

> (Crane et al., 2003)

We can see from the examples that as a result of their treatment, with couples refusing to be separated, they often stay longer on the streets; or by way of using their own informal networks become part of the hidden homeless population by sleeping on friend's floors; or many choose to go squatting. David Devoy, head of services at St Mungo's, again speaking in *The Guardian*, said:

Couples are staying out on the streets longer than single homeless people because most refuse to live apart. As a result, their health deteriorates, they are exposed to danger and they become demotivated.

(David Devoy)

Given this recognition, you would think that provision would have moved on, and in some ways it has. I will finish by examining how the sector has reacted to the phenomenon of couples and giving some recommendations on what still needs to be done.

Recognition of the issue and the development of services

Vulnerable or homeless people should not be assumed to be single now and forever. On the contrary, many are already in relationships and many are busy starting them up. These relationships are sometimes longstanding and a profound source of well-being to the people involved.

(Lemos, 2006)

Jerry Ham conducted research into user perceptions of direct hostels for CHAR in 1996, published in a report called *Steps From the Street*. He highlighted the fact that homeless couples were being failed by the system. Jerry Ham went on to co-ordinate Groundswell, an organisation supporting the development of user-led initiatives. Streetlife, a group of homeless service users and ex-service users, conducted a pilot series of 'speakouts' in London, targeting refugees and asylum seekers, young people and the general hostel population, culminating with a 'superspeakout' on HMS *President* in 1996. The idea originated in Scotland with Edinburgh Speakout. Their aim was to be a bridge, and build trust and goodwill between other homeless people and decision and policy makers. They developed a model of speakout that facilitated this dialogue. A prominent call was coming through from homeless people about the importance of the relationships they formed with people, an example of a contribution being:

. . . *what about couples, the relationships we have with people, which we met along our travels, which we wish to continue with.*

(Speakout contribution)

In attendance at a subsequent forum of Groundswell members, where again the issue of couples was repeatedly raised from the whole of the Groundswell network, were the late Dr Mo Mowlam and Louise Casey (from the Rough Sleepers Unit). Dr Mo Mowlam famously replied that this was a serious issue and that 'the government was not opposed to shagging'. When attention was drawn to the lack of homeless provision Louise Casey commented that this highlighted where agencies seemed almost Dickensian in their approach.

The first report that explored the importance of companionship actually focused on pets, namely *Homeless People and Pets*, by the Blue Cross in 2001 (Baker). The report found that people with pets are treated differently, but not in a positive way. It opens by saying:

> *Some populations of homeless people have been highlighted more than others –*
> *often for good reason, such as those with mental health issues or drug problems*
> *etc. As with single homeless people who form relationships on the streets, those*
> *with dogs are not a recognised category within the homelessness sector.*

(Blue Cross, 2001)

It found that many service providers, even when they have the best intentions, do not allow pets into buildings and so, by implication, their owners are denied the use of services. They comment that this level of discrimination is almost unique in the homeless sector, the only other grouping coming near to it being single people who form relationships while homeless. It concluded that in these two cases the systems that have been set up to help homeless people are unable to accommodate their lifestyles.

In 2002 none of the 27 emergency winter shelters run by Crisis catered for couples. Positively, Shaks Ghosh, the charity's Chief Executive, admitted this and saw the benefit of having provision for couples:

> *We provide single rooms or dormitories because that's how the programme is*
> *funded. Homeless legislation divides the world into families and single people.*
> *Couples don't get a mention. One of the few generalisations you can make about*
> *single homeless people is that they are all incredibly lonely and isolated. What they*
> *tell us is that all they want is a flat and a relationship . . . There was an ex-homeless*
> *guy who volunteered at Crisis. When he got into a relationship and needed to help*
> *someone else, he started to get his life together. So we're missing a trick if we don't*
> *find ways of helping people to stay together.*

(Shaks Ghosh, *The Guardian*, 2003)

St Mungo's homeless organisation in London has been aware of this through their outreach work and conducted research, producing a report called *Double Bind* in 2003. Through further research they found that 10 per cent of their clients encountered through outreach were in couples, and that fewer than 1 per cent of bed spaces in the capital are for homeless couples. As a result of this they set aside 10 double bedrooms in two hostels. Of the couples who have lived in St Mungo's hostels, only one has split up. Others have gone on to have children and eventually set up home together. But the problem is not unique to London. Although no nationwide figures exist for the number of rough sleepers in a relationship, only 11 per cent of the 266 direct access hostels run by voluntary organisations in England, Scotland and Wales say they are able to accommodate couples. Thames Reach Bondway also now runs some accommodation for couples.

Moving on, another speakout was held at the Abbey Community Centre on 28 April 2004 in front of Westminster Council officers. Again, the issue of lack of suitable accommodation for couples was raised. In Bradford the holding of speakouts for three years resulted in the 'Bradford Speakout Charter of Rights' in 2005. This group consists of service users of housing and advice projects, staff from those projects and other community groups. The issue of relationships was raised and became part of their charter of rights. The first quote from this chapter is taken from this charter, it goes on to say:

> *People shouldn't have to separate from their partners, or family, because they are homeless and services can't accommodate them. In the end, people who have experienced homelessness should be afforded the same consideration that other people take for granted. People shouldn't be punished for being homeless.*
>
> (Bradford Homeless Charter, 2005)

More positively, the ODPM Hostel Capital Programme (a £90 million programme to be delivered over three years to improve existing, or develop new hostel accommodation) has issued guidelines about both pets and childless couples. However, a report for the Pan London Providers Group (Warnes et al., 2005) called *London's Hostels in the 21st Century* did not address the issue at all, except, as the Homeless Link website notes, for a somewhat misplaced comment that 'no one would force a husband to live apart from his wife'.

A finishing word is needed on same-sex couples. Since the passing of the law on same-sex Civil Partnership in 2006, this may be another area for service provision, as there do not appear to be any same-sex hostels with rooms for couples. Same-sex street homeless couples are not unknown, but are not well documented or researched. With the choice of being separated, many choose to stay on the streets or become hidden homeless, 'sofa surfing' or squatting. Much of this is true of the whole issue of homeless couples, as we have seen. Perhaps after reading this chapter, if nothing else it has given the reader some food for thought.

Conclusion

It seems, then, that the picture is still mixed and, at least in terms of understanding, we have a long way to go. A few providers are starting to recognise that these assumptions have led to a form of discrimination against homeless couples, whether of the opposite sex or the same sex. I visited a project recently, Dawn in Leicester, where, as well as having provision, it was seen as normal to be in a couple and something to be encouraged and celebrated. There are guidelines on pets and informal ones for couples. A worker says on the matter: 'It's a service they pay for, so why shouldn't they be allowed to have a relationship?' Sometimes people are referred as a couple and sometimes a relationship forms in the hostel. If a couple splits up, as will happen, they are offered single rooms and their joint resettlement plan becomes two separate ones. Again, this is seen as normal and just a change of circumstance.

Couples have always existed in the homeless community and, if we are honest, in hostels. It's just they were at best ignored and at worst excluded. Due to definitions of services as being for single homeless people, and through a set of real and perceived operational difficulties, couples have been debarred from entering hostels and discouraged, by prohibitive hostel rules and regulations, from forming. People sometimes present in partnerships, other relationships form within schemes.

To sum up, I would like to hand back to Jon Cox, giving his views on how services need to change with regard to couples:

> It is my contention that if we are to truly manage hostels as 'places of change' for service users we must change the way they are managed and perceived by service users. There will always be a certain amount of seemingly prohibitive rules due to the size of a scheme and the nature of the client group. The question is not one of getting rid of rules but ensuring unnecessary restrictions are not present, and that service users are aware of the rationale behind the operational running of a scheme. The best way to ensure this is via meaningful service user involvement. We must ask ourselves – are we empowering people and helping them prepare for independence by restricting the few freedoms we all enjoy regardless of status? It is hard enough to find a relationship if you are at a low ebb in your life without trying to do so in an environment which discourages. Anyway, love conquers all!! Ha ha!! I have personally found as many positives about relationships in hostels as I have problems.
>
> If this argument doesn't sway you then consider the requirements of the QAF [Quality Assessment Framework] S 3.2 which requires 'that there are no **unnecessary** arbitrary rules that restrict service users' freedoms'. Fundamental change is required in how we manage this issue in the longer term by commissioners and regulators as well as providers. However, it is a positive step forward from the complete segregation and curtailment of rights experienced in recent years.

(Jon Cox)

Recommendations

These recommendations are a bottom line, and starting place, for agencies and policy makers to respond appropriately to the needs of homeless couples. They are in no particular order:

- There needs to be more extensive research into the nature and dynamics of relationships between homeless people.
- Hostel regulations should acknowledge relationships between homeless people, recognise where they discriminate against them and seek ways to make relationships between homeless people possible in hostels.
- Personal relationships should be viewed as a positive thing for homeless people to engage in and workers should seek to understand their dynamics.
- The development of personal relationships should be seen as an appropriate area for support for workers.
- Workers should receive training in working with couples; and structures, such as action plans, should encompass the joint goals and aspirations of couples.

- There should be specific funding for supporting homeless couples, and working with couples should be in the Quality Assessment framework so that agencies cannot have arbitrary rules against couples.
- Local authorities should see provision of services for homeless couples as a specific area of concern within homeless strategies.

Section Two:

Organisational constructions of homeless experiences and identities

Chapter 4

Understanding the refugee experience

Jennie Geddes

Introduction

This chapter will aim to explore key issues relevant to refugees and the resettlement process.

'Resettlement' is a term often used to describe the process of a refugee settling in one country after fleeing another. For the purposes of this chapter, however, 'resettlement' refers to the process of moving into a tenancy. It is worth the reader being aware of the different meanings applied to this term, as it will be relevant when exploring further reading with regard to refugees and asylum seekers. At the time of writing, the asylum system remains a complex one. There have been several changes in the systems for people seeking asylum in the UK. The impact of these systems on people is in itself a subject which could fill several books, and is outside of the remit of this chapter.

Suffice to say, the asylum system does not lend itself to an auspicious start to a person or family's resettlement process. On arrival in the UK, a person seeking asylum is subjected to a number of processes prior to any decision being made on their right to reside in the country. During this period, an asylum seeker is not entitled to access the benefits system as it applies to UK citizens; instead they are able to access the National Asylum Support Service (NASS). This system is in two parts – one being *subsistence*, i.e., money, or tokens, or vouchers that are issued to provide the means to obtain basics – the other being *accommodation*. Currently those who are in need of the accommodation element of support will first receive 'emergency' accommodation, and are then usually 'dispersed' to any part of the UK on a 'no-choice' basis, with very limited exceptions.

This chapter will focus on the issues facing people who have been granted some form of leave to remain in the UK, following the decision on their asylum claim. At the time of writing, new legislation has recently come into force, which means that people will no longer be granted refugee status which entitles them to the right to stay indefinitely: rather they may given leave to remain for a maximum period of five years, during which time their case will be reviewed.

Whilst this chapter deals primarily with people who have been given some right to stay in the UK, housing or resettlement workers who work in the field of homelessness will be undoubtedly aware of the fact that destitution is on the increase amongst people who are still *asylum seekers*; that is people who have not yet been given a decision on their asylum claim. Workers will also encounter people who have had their claims for asylum refused, and who have either severely limited or no provision made for their housing or subsistence needs. This area is indeed one of importance, but is tied to the increasingly complex and frequently changing legal system. This chapter will not cover this issue in any depth, as it will inevitably be out of date quickly. Workers are advised to seek specialist advice and information when encountering people in this situation. Key sources of information can be obtained from local groups, and excellent information can be obtained from campaigning groups and bodies. The Refugee Council, for example, have provided accessible information that can be downloaded from their website, including advice packs for those advising people seeking asylum, or people who are 'failed asylum seekers'. For anyone without a right to remain in the UK with no existing asylum claim in process, or who has been refused asylum, it is essential that legal advice is obtained.

There is much written on the needs of refugees in relation to the resettlement and integration process, and many good examples of localised and regional initiatives. However, there are not enough specialist providers to cover the needs of all refugees, neither is there any one accepted model for working.

Broadly speaking, there are two types of **specific** initiatives relating to the support of refugees in Britain:

- Self-help groups; including refugee community organisations (RCOs).
- Refugee service provider organisations (RSOs).

RCOs are community organisations, usually growing from small groups of people from specific refugee community groups. Much funding has been made available for the start up and promotion of these (as with UK or 'host') community groups in recent years. Whilst this enables refugees themselves to develop and provide support packages, funding is often limited, both in the amounts available and in the length of time that funds can be granted. It is not difficult to see how RCOs alone cannot provide the support needed by all refugees in relation to their resettlement needs. In Merseyside alone at the time of writing, there are estimated to be in excess of 60 RCOs representing people from as many countries, languages and cultural backgrounds. To fund all groups adequately to provide the necessary housing and resettlement support is not possible. There are, however, some excellent examples of refugee-led housing and resettlement programmes, including ARHAG (African Refugee Housing Action Group) based in London and covering 13 boroughs. ARHAG operates as a housing association, and provides services to refugees and migrants from any country and continent. With specialist skills and a history of tailored provision, such organisations are invaluable, but again, they are not able to serve all refugees in need.

Similarly, RSOs are varied in both their funding and their provision. Certainly, at the time of writing, there are not sufficient providers to meet the needs of all refugees in terms of the resettlement process. Some mainstream statutory and voluntary sector housing providers have specific workers or sections for refugees, but many do not. Those that do will also be limited. This leaves a significant gap in meeting the needs of refugees when it comes to resettlement, a gap that can only be addressed through developing the skills and knowledge of all who work in a resettlement context.

This chapter aims to cover the basic areas that will be significantly different for a resettlement worker when working with refugees.

Adjustment to the UK system of housing and benefits

Currently, once granted some form of leave to remain, people are then able to access the same systems as UK nationals. This includes having the right to claim appropriate benefits, and the right to work. The majority of people seeking asylum have no right to work or to access public funds outside of NASS until this time.

Whilst in NASS accommodation, people will have had no experience of paying bills, with their subsistence money being lower than the equivalent Income Support payments, so fuel and water bills are covered by their accommodation provider. Once a person seeking asylum has received a positive decision on their asylum claim, they will be given 28 days to vacate their NASS accommodation, and to place a claim for Income Support, Job Seekers Allowance, or to find paid work. This is also the time period they have to find suitable accommodation. For many people, this will mean entering the local authority homelessness system.

It must be emphasised that for many people currently in the asylum system there will have been a period of many months, or even years, of living in the UK, but no time where there has been any appropriate opportunity to gain an understanding of the aspects of living in the UK that many UK nationals take for granted, such as the systems for buying fuel, of rental agreements, for seeking employment or getting help with housing related issues.

It is important for resettlement practitioners to understand that whilst many homeless people are unaware of their rights and entitlements on becoming homeless, the refugee is often doubly disadvantaged as they have a number of additional hurdles, both practical and social.

Obtaining a National Insurance number

This can take several weeks. Until an asylum seeking person has been granted refugee status or a form of leave to remain, they will not have a national insurance number. This can lead to delays in processing benefits and in registering for or seeking employment. Negotiating with benefits agencies can be difficult for anyone, and practical support in this area can be essential to avoid delays in receiving basic support. For someone who has no knowledge of this system, and who may have limited English, lack of support can lead to periods without accommodation, or food and a decline in mental health.

> Sadia received a positive decision on her asylum claim and left NASS accommodation to stay with a woman friend who also originally came from her country. Her friend took her to claim Job Seekers Allowance. Sadia had difficulty understanding what she had to do to have her claim processed, and instead of claiming benefits accepted a low-paid cash-in-hand job packing food at a local factory. Sadia only received £60 per week, and when her friend could no longer afford to accommodate her, she became homeless. It was several days before she was directed to the local authority homelessness department, where she was eventually supported in claiming benefits and accessing accommodation in her own right.

Lack of knowledge from other professionals in relation to refugees' rights

Don't assume that the local authority, housing association officer or private provider knows the entitlements of refugees. With increasingly confusing legislation, myths on entitlements are common. The writer encountered the following situation in 2004.

> A woman who had leave to remain and was in receipt of state benefits for herself and her child was refused accommodation in a hostel when she fled domestic violence because she did not have a British passport. This is clearly not correct, but the worker who dealt with the issue was insistent that without a British passport, the woman would not be entitled to housing benefit, even though she was already receiving it, and could prove this, for her existing tenancy.

Basic practical knowledge is key for a resettlement worker in this area. Good advice can be obtained from a local refugee support specialist, though this may be easier for a worker or resettlement agency to obtain than for an individual refugee. To argue with a provider who is convinced that they are right is not always easy!

Racism

That host populations often hold very strong negative views of refugees and asylum seekers will not be a surprise to most readers. *The Sun* newspaper ran a campaign in 2003 against asylum seekers, with the tagline 'End the asylum madness'. Words such as 'polluted', 'terrorism' and 'disease' were used to describe asylum seekers as a group, and they were portrayed as 'threatening our way of life'. Being granted a form of leave to remain in the UK does not necessarily protect a person who is often part of a visible minority. There are many recorded instances of overt racism towards refugees across the UK, with attacks on people and their families whilst at home being, in some areas, commonplace. This means that extra support is needed when seeking accommodation, both temporary and permanent, as a part of the resettlement process.

> Ahmed was rehoused in a block of flats where several single men from Iraq and other Middle Eastern countries were living. The block was targeted by local youths, and frequently graffiti including 'terrorists go home' and 'asylum seeking scum' were spray-painted onto the walls. Ahmed did not go out after dark unless he was with a group of friends, as he said he felt afraid. He and his friends were reported to the police for 'threatening behaviour' by other local residents, although no evidence was ever found to support these claims, and no one reported any attacks from them.

Availability of other support services

In areas of dispersal across the UK, asylum seekers and refugees have often been located in areas where there has previously been no requirement for culturally sensitive services, including GPs and medical services, schools, adult education, social services, mental health services and recreational provision. This, too, should be taken into account as a part of the resettlement process. For a black woman alone with young children, to placed in an area where the only school is 100 per cent white, and there are few public transport links, can impede the resettlement process, for example exacerbating any mental health issues, or compounding any behavioural issues for her children.

> Jamilla was rehoused with her young son, aged 10, who was enrolled at the local school in a predominantly white area. Her son was followed home from school, and the windows were frequently smashed late at night by groups of children. Jamilla kept her son from school for several weeks and rarely went out herself. Eventually Jamilla and her son were rehoused after truancy officers visited and enlisted support from the police and a project in a neighbouring borough supporting women and children who were victims of racial attacks.

It is not difficult to understand from the examples above how there are often specific differences for refugees in the resettlement process. However, it is of great importance to remember that refugees, as with other homeless people, are individuals. To assume that one person will have the same issues as another would be to move away from the general principles of good resettlement: it is important to listen to the experience and concerns of the individual. For refugees, there may also be key issues why they do not want to be housed in an area close to others from 'their community'. Their reasons for leaving their home country may include issues such as sexuality, gender and war between political factions. Some of these issues may have travelled with the people who have fled their home country or continent.

Changes to status from asylum seeker to refugee

Practical issues as touched on above will have a significant emotional impact on an individual working through the resettlement process. Resettlement workers will be aware of taking a person-centred approach to resettlement, and will take into account this impact. This chapter cannot provide a blueprint for working with 'any refugee', but hopefully it does provide a front-line worker with some food for thought when engaging with people from refugee backgrounds. For instance, it is important to explore the impact of change on refugees when they are granted some form of leave to remain.

Imagine that you have fled a situation of extreme danger, and that you have arrived in a foreign country. Imagine that in that country you are given basic subsistence and you have to wait for two years before you may be told either (a) you have a right to stay and to access the privileges of those who were born in that country, or (b) that you must return to your country of origin. During that time you are unable to work or to receive the same benefits as the host population, and you are seen as 'undesirable' by that host population. You are waiting and hoping that you will be allowed to stay, as you fear the consequences of deportation. You are finally given a positive decision; your story has been accepted as genuine, and you can now receive the privileges afforded to others. How do you feel?

At first, on hearing this news, there may be a feeling of elation, not untypical for a homeless person from the host community receiving news of their offer of permanent accommodation. Finally, there is a feeling of freedom and acceptance, and the achievement of a goal central to a person's existence; the fulfilment of a basic need. However, for a person newly granted refugee status, this is often the *beginning* of their homelessness.

Homelessness itself can often mark the loss of status, and can often be only a small part of a bigger loss: loss of family, loss of employment, loss of relationship and loss of place in the community. For someone who is homeless a tenancy can be part of the process of rebuilding a life. Resettlement work acknowledges that simply to provide a roof is not enough, and that often the resettlement will break down if associated issues are not worked with. Floating support schemes work on the premise that for many homeless people, additional support that comes from an understanding of the individual and their practical, emotional and social needs are taken into account (as other detailed texts on the resettlement process cover in depth). It is often the point at which a tenancy is offered, or shortly afterwards, that the reality dawns – that all previous problems and concerns have not gone away, and that the tenancy has not been the magic ticket to happiness. It is well-known that tenancies are most likely to fail within the first three months if appropriate support is not available or utilised.

These issues are also apparent for someone receiving the good news about their asylum application. At this point, the complexity of the UK benefits system, the housing system, job opportunities and restrictions in the recognition of overseas qualifications can hit home, as well as the realisation that not all of their issues are resolved. Aside from the practicalities, many, must again face the issues of why they left their country of origin. An asylum application involves providing information to enable a decision from the Home Office on whether or not a person has a 'well-founded fear of persecution' in their home country. Such information must be given quickly and in detail in order to be given a chance of success. Many cases involve providing evidence of torture, rape, persecution and murder of family members, political affiliation to a party opposing the government, female genital mutilation, and abuse due to sexuality or gender, to name but a few examples. Many refugees arrive in the UK alone, or without close family members, and may not know if their family or children are still alive. A positive decision and some form of refugee status can often bring back to the fore the very issues that the person has fled from. Yes, they are believed; yes, it really happened. Being believed can be a focal point for people during the asylum process, can take up energy, and provide a focus. When this has gone, however, the focus will often become the losses that are now accepted by the host country.

Having an asylum claim rejected also has a clear negative impact. A client I worked with recently said, 'At home they beat my body. Here they beat my soul.'

However, being granted refugee status, whilst clearly a preferable outcome, is still not easy. Another client I worked with, who had been granted leave to remain, said:

> At home I was someone. People listened to me. I had respect. I could get people together. Here I am no one. I have nothing and no one to listen. Children still throw stones and people still spit at me.

Some refugees have come from backgrounds of community activism, as with the client granted status above. Some may have held respected occupations, such as doctors, surgeons, university lecturers. For most, their qualifications will not be recognised in the UK, and employment opportunities will be very limited. This loss of status is compounded by the fact that the UK system of rights and entitlements may be quite alien to someone from a different continent with societies that may hold very different cultural and social norms.

A right to remain but not yet a citizen

For many UK nationals, since the inception of the Welfare State, it is understood that people have the right to basic benefits in order to prevent destitution. Being completely removed from this system, supported by NASS, many asylum seekers will not be aware of the principles and rights behind this system. Accepting NASS support when the right to work is withheld is one thing, but to receive money 'for nothing' to some people from some cultures is deeply shaming. Many refugees feel a keen desire to work and to earn money to support themselves, and people will often take low paid and insecure work rather than claim benefits. Whilst this is also a reality for many UK citizens, it is rare that those of us brought up with knowledge of benefit entitlements will forgo benefits available for low paid workers. This can be an issue for refugees who simply want to earn a living and pay their way. It is essential that resettlement workers ensure that refugees are aware of their rights, and that those rights are clearly explained as being available to all those who have a right to reside in the UK. It is also worth checking out any qualifications that refugees do possess, and whether these can be 'converted' via shorter tailored courses in the UK, for example PLAB 1 & 2 conversion courses for medics who have qualified overseas.

Many research studies into the resettlement and integration of refugees show that learning English is a key to integration and settlement. Many refugees pick up English quickly and there are good courses available in many larger cities. However, this can be an issue for some people:

- The 'dispersal' system (relocating asylum seekers from London and the South East to other cities and towns to receive NASS support) has meant that some people have been moved to areas where there are few non-UK-born people, or that are predominantly white-British. As a result, the availability of good quality courses for people learning English as another language is limited.
- For women from some cultures there may be barriers to accessing mixed classes. For women with babies or small children, there may be a lack of opportunity to access classes. It will be important to explore the availability of language options for people in this situation.
- For some people, their level of education in their home country may be extremely high, and classes may not recognise this. To be taught rudimentary English when you were once a consultant neurologist can be demoralising.
- Conversely, some people from refugee backgrounds may have little or no formal education in their mother tongue, and this can lead to difficulty in a learning environment.

Again the lesson here for resettlement workers is that it is important to listen to the individual you are working with and to be aware of such sensitivities.

Whilst a refugee is entitled to receive benefits and health care, and able to take employment in the UK, they do not receive the full recognition of a UK citizen. Most importantly, they do not have the right to vote, unless they are a Commonwealth citizen, or have become naturalised as a British citizen. In order for a refugee to apply to become a British citizen, they must have lived in the UK for five years, one of which holding settled status (i.e. received a positive decision on their asylum claim). To then be successful with their application, they must fulfil a number of key criteria, and citizenship will then be granted at the discretion of the Home Office. Given that the new legislation will grant leave to stay for up to five years only, it remains to be seen how this will impact on a refugee's ability to become a citizen. Again, it is important for a resettlement worker to be aware of the impact of this on the individual they are supporting. Campaigns to enable homeless people to vote will not be applicable to most refugees.

The impact of 'pre-flight' experiences on the resettlement process

As mentioned above, it is often at the point of receiving a positive decision on an asylum claim that the impact of a refugee's pre-flight experiences can hit home.

The impact of torture and targeted abuse is well documented in other publications. It is, however, necessary for a resettlement worker to be mindful of how this will affect a person from a refugee background at different times during the resettlement process. There will be some similarities with the experiences of UK nationals who have experienced abuse – resettlement workers may have worked with young people who have been abused, women fleeing domestic violence and others who have received poor treatment or care at some stage in their lives – and in working with people who have experienced multiple loss such as loss of relationship, children, parents and status. It is, however, arguable that few UK citizens have suffered such loss as a result of the actions of their government, community, army or rebels operating within their home country. This is often the norm for a refugee. For some, whole communities have been wiped out as a result of war or oppression, and the impact of this cannot be underestimated. It is not the job of a resettlement worker to act as a counsellor, but it does help if the worker is able to comprehend that these issues may have an impact on the resettlement process.

The effects of past trauma may be heightened by current anxiety: this is also well documented. Moving house and taking on board the practical and social issues as highlighted above can trigger physical and emotional difficulties related to the trauma previously experienced.

Aimee had been kidnapped and forced to fight with a rebel force. On escape from the camp, where she had been raped and physically abused, she found her way home. Her father feared for her safety, so, aged 15, she was given over to an agent to be transported to safety. She ended up in the UK. She heard on arrival that her father had been shot. Her mother had been killed previously. After three years in the UK, Aimee was granted leave to remain. She had initially suffered severe nightmares whilst in care in the UK, but long-term counselling and community support helped her. She was given her own flat, but at this point her nightmares and flashbacks started again, and she felt afraid to be on her own in the flat. Every time she heard a neighbour coming in late at night she would be terrified, and unable to sleep any more that night.

Patrick was forced to leave his family home at night, when his parents were warned that soldiers were coming to take him away for execution. He left in fear with few belongings, and never regained contact with his family. In the UK he had to leave his NASS accommodation to move to a flat. He had adapted well to NASS accommodation after two years of support from fellow asylum seekers and had made friends. Moving to a flat brought back his fear and recurrent nightmares, and he became isolated and depressed, refusing to go out. Whilst he had received a positive decision on his asylum application, the move away from what had become familiar triggered his fear and anxiety about leaving behind what had felt safe.

It is easy to see from these examples how the impact of moving to new independent accommodation can create issues that could lead to the failure of the tenancy. Whilst resettlement workers are not counsellors, to ignore this issue would not support the resettlement process. There are, in some areas of the country, specific counselling services for survivors of torture, and some counselling services that can provide specialist support. A resettlement worker can refer to such services, liaise with GPs and social services, and listen and 'normalise' the anxiety that often happens when people move house.

Whilst it is not often possible to take account of every need someone may have when looking at the allocation of available temporary or permanent accommodation, it is important to be aware of the impact of issues relating to trauma that may be present. For example, a young man who experiences vivid nightmares and frequently wakes screaming may have problems in HMOs. One client the writer worked with recently fled his hostel accommodation to the streets, as he was frequently bullied by other residents who were woken up by him and who considered his behaviour bizarre. He was eventually accommodated in mental health specialist accommodation; although it was acknowledged that his primary needs were not those relating to 'severe and enduring mental health diagnoses'. Whilst perfect options may not be available in every area, it is often the resettlement worker who has an ongoing relationship with a client, and who can help to advocate on his or her behalf as a part of the re-housing process.

Pre-flight experiences will also include issues relating to health. As mentioned above, different areas will have differing levels of available services. As resettlement workers will be aware, the health needs of homeless people in general are often overlooked, and it can make a difference if appropriate services, including responsive GPs and health centres, are local to clients. For example, if you are working with a drug-user, it can make a positive difference if the individual has an experienced and sympathetic GP, and can get access to a local responsive drug support service. The same principle applies to refugees. A resettlement worker can investigate the availability of services through specialist refugee agencies and information from local primary care trusts. In some areas there will be specialist voluntary and statutory health workers providing tailored care and support to refugees and asylum seekers. If such services are not available, as can be the case, some services out of the area may be prepared to offer advice and signposting either to the client or a local service provider. Where referral is difficult, it is useful to ensure that your client is aware of the reasons for this, as when working with any person in a resettlement context, it makes a difference to objectify any issues to avoid a client perceiving that they are being 'difficult' or that the worker is 'dumping' them.

Dispersal: different experiences in different towns and cities

'Dispersal' refers to the government policy of moving asylum applicants from the South East and London to other areas to 'prevent the stress' placed on areas where asylum seekers were arriving or moving to shortly after arrival. As previously mentioned, NASS applicants will be moved from emergency accommodation to a 'dispersal area' on a 'no-choice basis', where they will be housed by private or social housing providers with a NASS contract until the outcome of their claim. Dispersal areas are located throughout the UK, and vary greatly in their demographics. Some areas will have diverse existing populations, others will not. Dispersal areas include major cities and more isolated boroughs.

The huge difference between the areas used for dispersal means that the experiences of refugees will vary greatly. If a refugee comes from an Eastern European country, and they are located in a wholly British Asian or British African area, they may be as isolated from supportive communities as they would be in a wholly white area. They may experience being supported by a small, close-knit host community, or be ostracised – there is no one prescription that fits all. On receiving a positive decision on an asylum claim, a refugee can be faced with a dilemma: to stay in the area of dispersal, or to leave. The experiences of an area whilst in NASS accommodation may have a part to play in that decision. It is here that the issue of 'local connection' may play a key role; some refugees may feel that they need to move to a place where there are other people who hold similar cultural values, or where they are able to worship in accordance with their own faith, or shop for food that they are used to from their home country. The resettlement worker may find that they are working with someone who wants to move from the area they are in, or who has arrived in their area, seeking support.

Different housing departments and local partnerships will have different levels of strategy to deal with refugee housing, ranging from nothing up to strategic and operational partnerships involving the statutory, private and voluntary sector housing and support providers. There are many information sources available on the provision of local services, and many studies published on the resettlement of refugees (Housing Corporation and Liverpool Strategic Housing Partnership, 2004; Bell, Buchan and Lukes, 1999; HACT, 2002). Some key initiatives have been evaluated and recommendations made for regional and national policy (Chartered Institute of Housing, 2003).

Racism, conflict and labels – the impact on resettlement

Such a limited section in this chapter cannot begin to cover this issue in any great depth, but can give the resettlement worker a flavour of what to consider that may provide useful background.

It cannot escape the notice of anyone living in the UK today that there has been a great deal of negative media coverage relating to refugees and asylum seekers. The term 'asylum seeker' refers to someone in the UK who has made an asylum claim, but is yet to receive a decision. In the UK, the term 'refugee' refers to someone who has received a positive decision, entitling them with some form of 'leave to remain', the length of time will vary, depending on current legislation. Few UK nationals are aware of the difference between the two terms, and therefore negative feeling is often directed indiscriminately. This is not to say that it is any more acceptable for asylum seekers to be targeted than refugees, but it does illustrate the point that racism plays a huge part in the lives of refugees, and will impact on their resettlement. This has been touched upon above, when someone considers areas for rehousing.

'Racism', as it is often directed at asylum seekers, is not necessarily an issue relating to colour, or even assumed country of origin. There have been reports from asylum seekers and refugees that they have been verbally abused and attacked, with shouts of 'Kosovan', when they have been from Afghanistan, for example. Such abuse relates only to their assumed asylum status, with ignorance as to their actual origin. Non-asylum-seeking overseas students have been attacked for being 'asylum seekers'. The writer worked with one Roma man from the Former Republic of Yugoslavia, who would pretend to be Italian to avoid assault or negative treatment when out socially. The stigma was simply that he was an 'asylum seeker'. As a Roma man he had been attacked for 'being Black' in his home country, and would remark that such racism was absent for him here, as long as people thought he was Italian.

It is very much worth looking at some of the basic facts about asylum seekers in the UK, and there are a number of well-researched studies and websites which include figures and information, clear answers to frequently asked questions, and 'myth-busting' leaflets. Good easy-to-access information and links can be found on the Refugee Council website (see end of chapter).

It is not always helpful to assume that communities that are well-established and include high percentages of people from visible minority groups will be accepting of asylum seekers. The political issues here can be highly complex.

As touched upon above, a large percentage of refugees will have fled from countries that have faced war and oppressive governments, and active 'rebel' forces. Some countries have had lengthy histories involving complex struggles between a number of factions, tribes and parties. These issues and conflicts can be apparent, though generally to a far lesser degree amongst people after arrival in the UK. Here it is important not to assume that any client you are working with will immediately identify with a community group or organisation from their country of origin.

Again, it is important when working with a client to listen and ensure that their concerns are taken seriously when planning for and working through a resettlement plan.

It is important to also remember that many refugees are people who have come from positions of empowered community activism, as this is often a key reason for fleeing their home country. As a result, it important for the resettlement worker to avoid labelling their client as a 'victim'. Just as good practice would involve supporting the abilities of a UK-born homeless person, so it does for refugees. Here it can help if the resettlement worker gets some basic country information relative to the background of their client, although this in itself can only enhance actively listening to the client.

Statutory and voluntary sector support systems

Support systems vary hugely from area to area. It is useful for the resettlement worker to be aware of what is available locally. Dispersal and area is a key factor, as discussed above. Broadly speaking, three of 'types' of support available are outlined below:

Statutory bodies

A number of local authorities will have 'asylum teams', which may also deal with support issues for people with 'refugee status' – particularly during the 28 day period of moving from NASS accommodation. Some housing and social services departments have specialist workers or teams for single people or families. Some education departments may also have specialist officers for refugees and asylum seekers. Statutory bodies also include primary care trusts and other health departments, who may have specialist workers for refugees and asylum seekers or people from visible minority groups; this may include maternity staff, mental health teams and health visitors.

Voluntary organisations

Some areas may have strategic partnerships, including voluntary organisations who assist with integration projects; visible minority, Black and Minority Ethnic partnerships that liaise with Local Strategic Partnerships. A good starting point for information on such groups would be local Councils for Voluntary Services (CVSs). Other specific voluntary agencies may exist and be able to offer a range of support or information to refugees and community groups: some of these may be part of national organisations such as the Refugee Council or Refugee Action; others may be local independent groups. Voluntary organisations will vary hugely in size, funding, types of support offered and ethos.

Community groups

Community groups may or may not fall into the category of voluntary agencies, but it is worth giving space to them separately. Community groups may be refugee-led or otherwise. Community groups may be well organised and 'constituted' groups (groups with a defined purpose), or loose support groups, perhaps attached to a community centre, mosque, church or other religious base. A community group may be seen as different to a voluntary agency as it is usually smaller, with less funding and can provide more flexible support. In some dispersal areas, particularly where less structured specific services are available, local communities have grouped together to provide friendship and support and to welcome refugees and asylum-seeking people. Such groups can be invaluable in providing practical and emotional support to refugees outside of structured support.

Information on local provision, including all of the above sections, may be available from the local Council for Voluntary Service, or in some areas there are excellent websites detailing and cataloguing this information. The refugee client may have specific information on services, having researched this or used them during their time in the area. However, for some, there may have been little contact with any agencies.

Empowerment and refugee community organisations

A good resettlement package will aim to empower the service user, and foster a sense of self-belief. As front-line resettlement workers, it is a key goal to ensure that a service user can move on from a support package, equipped with both knowledge and an ability to function within their accommodation better than they could have done before. This is not to suppose that they will never need support again – as individuals, all of us require some level of support, depending on our ever-changing circumstances.

Arguably, those of us in need of resettlement support are, for at least a time, in a situation where we are disadvantaged in some way due our circumstances. This may be due to issues relating to mental health, drug or substance use, illness, lack of experience (e.g. a young person leaving care or home with no parental support) or having lost a previously dependent or co-dependent relationship (e.g. domestic violence, leaving an occupation with tied living arrangements). Some people facing these experiences will not need resettlement support, as they may have support from peers or extended family. Many people who are refugees lack these support systems, or any experience in UK systems. Some refugees receive support from (and give support to) Refugee Community Organisations (RCOs).

Throughout the UK, there are many RCOs operating as other community organisations outlined above. These organisations vary greatly. Some organisations have grown considerably and evolved into voluntary organisations that employ full-time staff and provide a wide range of services, including housing and resettlement support. Other RCOs are very small with limited, if any, grant funding, and only offer advice or mutual support groups. In some areas there are umbrella groups that bring together a number of RCOs to ensure a strategic voice locally, and to share resources to provide more support for their members.

Support available via RCOs can make a key difference to refugees. Some issues are difficult for refugees to discuss with mainstream providers, or even with refugee-specific services. The level of cultural understanding and accessibility can ensure appropriate support is given.

> Hope has lived in the UK for two years with her three children. Prior to leaving her country of origin she was raped, and has experienced ongoing pain and discomfort since then. Her GP was male, and she felt unable to discuss her health and the rape with him. Hope eventually started to attend a community group of women from her country, and over time, after regular meetings, discovered other women had suffered similar trauma. Hope felt able to tell them about her health worries, and was supported in attending a clinic. She received medical treatment and was referred for specialist counselling.

For a refugee who is very isolated from any apparent peers, it can be useful to explore refugee-led provision in the area. This provision may differ considerably to other community-based support and voluntary agencies, as it is led by refugees for refugees, and can enable and encourage empowerment and involvement in community development. To be an asylum seeker, then a refugee, can in itself be experienced as a humiliating and degrading experience, with widely held prejudice apparent throughout the media, and with far fewer rights to experience work or to become self-supporting. Many refugees have previously been involved in community activism (this may well have been a reason for fleeing their home country) and to become involved with other people from the same or similar backgrounds can provide a sense of empowerment that is difficult to get from another source. RCOs can also be valuable in supporting other mainstream voluntary and statutory support organisations through advice, information and training to enable the provision of more user-friendly services to people from asylum-seeking and refugee backgrounds.

It can be difficult to find information on all of the refugee-led provision available in an area, but the local CVS will be a good start. Contacting Refugee Action, the Refugee Council, or local authority may also help.

Many refugees will already have a good working knowledge of available support, and some may choose not to use existing provision, either because the groups they are aware of do not cater for their specific needs, or because they prefer not to access this type of community-based organisation. Some clients may choose to remain apart from close-knit communities: for example, a gay Jamaican man may fear that the local

Jamaican community would be less accepting of his sexuality. An HIV positive African woman may fear stigma if her status is revealed to other members of a community association. This is not to suggest that RCOs are less accepting than other UK based community associations, but stigma and prejudice can exist anywhere – and the fear of it can be very real. The key here again is to listen to the individual, and to be open to possibilities for support and empowerment.

Summary and conclusion

Resettlement issues will be different for all individuals, whether or not they are classed as a refugee. There are some key issues that will impact upon refugees differently to people who are UK, or even, EU nationals.

There are many studies and texts relating to 'resettlement' and refugees in existence, but many of these relate either to resettlement of refugees as an *integration* issue, or to specific projects, or general theories. These are incredibly useful, and can help to drive changes for the overall improvement of services to refugees, they can influence local and national policy, as well as agency development, but they do not necessarily aid the resettlement worker in providing a good one-to-one service for their client. It is recommended that resettlement workers read up and research what is available in their area, but also that they look at their own practice and awareness in order to provide a holistic service for clients.

There are many refugee-specific support agencies and community groups through-out the UK. Some of these have expertise in rehousing, and some also in resettlement, but there is not the level of provision available to satisfy the level of need.

This chapter would propose that it is a productive approach to ensure that 'mainstream' statutory and voluntary homeless agencies enable their workers to become better equipped to support refugees as with other diverse client groups. This will help ensure that resettlement and homelessness issues are more effectively covered for refugees.

As has been developed successfully in the last ten years with an increase in specialist knowledge amongst resettlement workers with young people, drug users, drinkers and people with mental health issues; so resettlement models can be as effective for refugees if front-line workers are given the opportunity of gaining good background information, knowledge and support in the relevant issues.

Chapter 5

Difficult people? – Unresponsive services! Working with homeless people with multiple needs

Pip Bevan

Introduction

This chapter aims to be an introduction to the issue of people who are homeless and have multiple needs. It will give a definition of multiple needs, explore who homeless people with multiple needs are, and outline the prevalence of this group. It will then explore issues of accessing health care for this client group, the challenge of this client group for health services, and the issues facing young adults with complex needs. Three current examples of agencies working with people who are homeless with multiple needs will follow, and I will finish with recommendations for the way forward.

In 2001, at the dawn of a second Labour Party victory, I wrote in Homeless Link's magazine *Connect*:

> We pride ourselves on the fact that we belong to a civilised society where we seek the 'common good'. The 'common good' cannot exist without there being human rights for people in our society, and that we always have options for the most vulnerable. The time has come to stand up for those who are often unseen, passed by, silent or silenced in our society. The combination of being homeless and suffering a number of serious and at times life-threatening needs and illnesses, can be overwhelming.

(*Connect*, July 2001)

It is disappointing, in 2006, to be writing another chapter on the needs of this group of people who, though they are now recognised as the most vulnerable group of people who are homeless, are still awaiting services which treat them in a holistic way.

Often seen as 'difficult people to work with', they in turn see services as unresponsive to them at the point of their need. If they do not conform to the structure of the services in drug and alcohol, mental health and so on, they are seen as the problem. On the contrary, people who are homeless, with multiple needs in particular, need services that are creative, flexible and work in a multi-disciplinary way to enable their interacting needs to be met.

However, as we shall see, there are some promising changes of attitude, and strategic appointments in both the Department of Health and the Office of the Deputy Prime Minister (ODPM) which could enable a fresh approach. Homeless Link has worked with homelessness agencies and homeless people to try to define what is meant by 'a homeless person presenting with multiple needs'.

The definition of multiple needs

A typical homeless or ex-homeless person with complex or multiple needs often presents with two or more of the following, and usually lacks effective contact with services:

- *Mental health problems.*
- *Misuse of various substances.*
- *Personality disorders.*
- *Borderline learning difficulties.*
- *Physical health problems.*
- *Offending behaviour.*
- *Challenging behaviour.*
- *Vulnerability because of age.*

And where one issue is resolved, the others will still give cause for concern.

(Homeless Link, 2002)

This definition was recognised as describing this group of people who are homeless, was accepted by homelessness agencies, and was used by Geoffrey Randall in describing the needs of this group when writing the guidelines for local authorities to consider when bringing together their homelessness strategies (DTLR, 2002).

Who are the people who are homeless with multiple needs?

Often the hard core of people who are homeless with multiple needs will narrowly fail to receive a diagnosis of mental illness, or an assessment as having learning difficulties, or will not have a sufficiently serious dependency problem. However, where two or more of these needs are present within an individual, they interact, and often cause considerable conflict and suffering with negative outcomes for the person concerned. The result is an extremely chaotic and vulnerable person, who becomes part of one of the most excluded and marginalised groups in our society.

The core needs of this client group mainly revolve around a combination of mental health and drug and alcohol needs, referred to as 'Dual Diagnosis'. Dual Diagnosis often forms the core of the needs, and it was out of this concept that the definition of multiple needs developed. Dual Diagnosis was clearly as much about specification of services as about people's needs. Mental health services often would not engage with a person because of their addiction problems, especially if they presented to mental health services while under the influence of various substances. Addiction services would often not work with a client who also clearly had mental health problems, as they had not received training in this field. This meant that clients were 'ping-ponged' between the services for mental health and substance misuse. The clients had to be supported by two different teams who, at that time, did not communicate well, either with each other, or even with the client. Work was done on this issue in the United States, and the consensus of opinion was that these clients needed an 'integrated service', either from dually trained workers in mental health and substance dependency, or with the two teams involved communicating well with each other and, equally importantly, the client.

In people experiencing homelessness, Dual Diagnosis will often be compounded with physical health needs, particularly if the person has been living on the streets for a long time, or if they are 50 years of age and presenting with health problems that the general population will exhibit at 65 or 70 years. The voluntary homelessness sector has been aware of these people for many years, with very little and sometimes no long-term help and support. Even though each local authority has a homelessness strategy, few of these have strong links to the Health Improvement Plans of the Primary Care Trusts. This is essential, so that not just the numbers of homeless people, but, an accurate assessment of their health needs also are taken into account in putting appropriate and sufficient services into place.

The prevalence of people who are homeless with multiple needs

In February 2002 during the week 11–18 February, Homeless Link tried to improve the accuracy and reliability of reported figures of service users with multiple needs. Respondents were asked about people who are homeless with multiple needs, using the definition developed by the Multiple Needs Project at Homeless Link and used by the then DTLR in their *Homelessness Strategies: A Good Practice Handbook* (DTLR, 2002).

The vast majority of respondents (88 per cent) said that they worked with people who were homeless with multiple needs. Agencies reported 47.8 per cent of their service users had multiple needs, and that there was no significant difference for male or female service users. The report said that many respondents had commented on the need to speed up access to specialist services, particularly those concerned with substance misuse, and also to address the barriers to providing statutory services support. Most substance dependency services were rationed by whether the client was motivated to change, and most mental health services needed a diagnosis of 'severe and enduring' before engaging with the client.

Accessing health care for homeless people with multiple needs

A question arises regarding the degree to which this group of people who are homeless are problematical, i.e. they are seen as difficult and complex, but to what degree is this complexity about the co-ordination and demarcation of services as opposed to about the individual? In February 2004, Crisis produced *Lost Voices* (Croft-White and Parry-Cooke, 2004) which sought to: 'explore the characteristics and life experiences of individuals struggling with competing health issues, critical life situations, which are further exacerbated by stigma, poor social and life skills, and limited opportunities' (ibid.: 2).

This important report found that people who are homeless continued to experience considerable difficulty in obtaining information, accessing services and receiving any coordinated response from health providers. Sometimes inflexible structures within the system of provision and the very real needs of the clients meant that the tensions were never resolved. *Lost Voices* cited a range of obstacles that prevented homeless people with multiple health needs from gaining the support they so clearly needed:

- **Availability** of services was problematic for this client group.
- **Flexibility,** or lack of it, presented a further hurdle, revealing the tension between the desire to provide flexible services and the practical realities of delivering services within traditional but sometimes rigid structures.
- **Provision of appropriate care** has continuing gaps, especially in the need for comprehensive check-ups, health screening, and lack of drug and alcohol detox services.
- **Non-prejudicial treatment** is an issue, with some services working in a non-prejudicial way, but others perceived as holding negative attitudes towards homeless people, thereby discouraging their use of services.

What emerged most clearly was the need for dedicated health and homelessness services that have the capacity to go out to people in hostels and other venues. There was concern that individuals often received inappropriate, inadequate, and sometimes no treatment due to prejudicial attitudes and 'buck-passing' between healthcare professionals. Due to the diversity of need and the often transitory and elusive lifestyle of many homeless people with multiple needs, health care services should be creative and opportunistic in their design and delivery.

(Ibid.: 3)

Challenging the structures

People with multiple health needs challenge the very structure of the way in which the Department of Health and the National Health Service operate. They have grown up with clearly defined silos of medical specialisms that are seemingly watertight: mental health, drugs and alcohol (sometimes even these are split), physical health, learning disability, and so on. Each has its own long history and its own philosophy, borne out of years of focusing on a single discipline. This has been necessary in order to have the greatest knowledge about the particular medical condition. But the very thing which has led to excellence will often militate against a holistic approach and the multi-disciplinary way of working which this client group so desperately need. Take, for example, motivation. Whether someone is motivated to change or not is not an issue for mental health services, but it is clearly an issue for drug and alcohol services, and is often used to ration services in some areas.

> *Like the rest of the population, homeless people have a right of access to appropriate health care services . . . this research found that, in reality, it was not always easy for homeless people to use these services even when presenting with a single health issue. Where multiple needs were present, professional boundaries frequently intervened, as a 'dispute' appeared to arise between health care specialists as to which need should be addressed first.*

> (Crisis, 2004)

Single issue services have been reluctant to engage with people with more than one need, often playing one need off against another. This approach is not acceptable if we are to engage effectively with this client group. Each health care service needs to be mindful of the client, and the way in which their service impinges and relies on the other service inputs. No one agency can successfully support people with multiple health needs. It requires a team effort and a new and creative exploration of the methods of multi-disciplinary working. General Practitioners (GPs) are the main gateway into primary care, and the Royal College of General Practitioners consensus statement from their Leeds Conference in 2002 has said:

> *Primary care practitioners should provide a welcoming and sensitive service to homeless people and enable them to access the full range of health and social services required to meet their needs. Homeless people should be registered permanently wherever possible and integrated into all health prevention and promotion activity within the practice.*

> (Royal College of General Practitioners, 2002)

The Multiple Needs Briefing by Homeless Link (Bevan, 2002) felt that GPs and other primary care providers need to be more understanding of homeless people with multiple needs. Consultation slots are usually aimed at a single issue diagnosis, clients with a number of interactive and complex needs take more time to diagnose and treat, but if these clients are to receive an appropriate service adequate time must be found for them.

In 2004, The Institute for Public Policy and Research and Turning Point published the important piece of work, *Meeting Complex Needs: The Future of Social Care*. This report opens by saying:

Too many health and social care services are failing to meet people's complex needs ... we do not believe that complex needs should function as another service label to determine eligibility, but rather as an active and useful description to highlight those people who need a more targeted intervention from service providers. People's complex needs can have breadth (range of need) and/or depth (severity of need). It is valuable shorthand to describe multiple interlocking problems where the total represents more than the sum.

(RCGP, 2002)

The report calls for radical changes and the setting up of 'Connected Care Centres', one-stop-shops bringing together health, education, addiction, employment and other services under one roof. This work looks beyond just the homeless population to a wider problem of people with multiple needs in society, seeing 'hundreds of thousands' of people being failed by a system that is both wasteful and expensive for the taxpayer. Lord Victor Adebowale, Chief Executive of Turning Point, said in the press release to this document:

People do not come clearly labelled with 'alcohol problem' or 'learning disability' yet too often the current system treats them that way, Often those who need help the most are the least likely to receive it and that's not just a problem for the individual – it means that as a society we're getting bad value for money from the service we pay for. We need a new approach that designs and delivers social care around people's complex needs, rather than expecting people to fit neatly into existing services.

(Adebowale, V.)

The report calls for reform of the way health and social care services are designed and commissioned:

- Commissioners need to accentuate the division between commissioning and purchasing. They must be provided with the support and training to enable them to commission strategically to meet the particular complex needs of their local community.
- Effective commissioning should cut across boundaries including, for example, the NHS, social services, housing and employment services.
- Services need to draw on the best mix from the public, private and voluntary sectors to meet complex needs. In particular, government needs to remove current barriers preventing the voluntary sector from competing on an equal footing with the other sectors – short-term contracts, the inaccessibility of capital and the lack of standard contracts between government and the voluntary sector.
- There needs to be a new kind of professional worker who acts as a 'service navigator' for people with complex needs – ensuring that they have a single point of entry into a network of services.

The web address for downloading this report is: http://www.turning-point.co.uk/NR/rdonlyres/4D78A928-982A-4C33-A85F-C7770090BD26/0/ComplexNeedsReport624k.pdf

Signs of the times

There is a new wind blowing through the corridors of the Department of Health and the Office of the Deputy Prime Minister. They have each created a new appointment, that of Health Advisor on Homelessness. We welcome this move, as it is the fulfilment of years of campaigning on the part of Homeless Link, its previous incarnations, and its member agencies.

In my opinion, the issue of homelessness and complex multiple health needs is the nettle to be grasped; it is the most marginalised and challenging section of the homeless population. The National Health Service is one of the largest employers in this country, and to effect change in such a large organisation is a slow business. But there is a movement, from single issue medical silos towards working across medical disciplines, that is beginning to be felt, and this client group presents a stark challenge to the health service to get it right and moving quickly.

Young adults with complex needs

The Social Exclusion Unit, now part of the ODPM, produced a report in November 2005 called *Transitions: Young Adults with Complex Needs* (ODBM, 2005) which will be very important for 16–24 year olds. This age grouping was not best served by the old demarcation line between child and adult at the age of 18.

Some young people suffer disproportionately from different types of the disadvantage listed above, and are often also at risk of becoming involved in anti-social behaviour, drug use and crime.

- *Over 1 million people in Great Britain aged between 16 and 24 are not in education, employment or training.*
- *Young men are the most likely victims of violent crime. They are also the most likely perpetrators of crime.*
- *It is estimated that nearly half of all 16–24 year olds in England and Wales have used illicit drugs. Reported Class A drug use amongst 20–24 year olds is three times higher than that in the general population.*
- *Suicide is the cause of a quarter of the deaths amongst 16–24 year old men.*

Some disadvantaged young people also have complex needs; interlocking problems where the total represents more than the sum of the parts:

- *Over 90 per cent per cent of imprisoned young offenders have at least one, or a combination of, the following: personality disorder, psychosis, neurotic disorder, or substance misuse.*
- *Substance misuse affects around a third to a half of people with severe mental health problems.*

- *Homelessness is frequently associated with substance misuse problems; and being homeless almost trebles a young person's chance of developing a mental health problem.*

(ODPM, 2005)

Age boundaries

A young person in one of the focus groups commented, 'When I was 16, I was classed as a priority, but now that I am only just 19 they don't really give a toss.'

Modern transitions to adulthood can be described as either *fast track*, or *slow track*. Those on the slow track stay longer in education and remain financially dependent on their parents for longer and experience a slower – but usually more successful – transition. However, young people on the fast track to adulthood, such as young parents or early school leavers, can face a more uncertain future. A person with an unsupported or an unfulfilled need can begin to encounter other problems, and thus begins a downward spiral.

The age structuring on which many policies are based is often complex, inconsistent, and works against the principle of resources following need.

Holistic services and the trusted adult

Many young adults with multiple needs are not supported by current provisions. Some may experience duplication or overlap in provision from single-issue services, while others may fall through the gap.

However, holistic services – that is, services that look at the individual and the range of problems that they face – can manage complex problems and encourage engagement with service providers. Young adults may find it difficult to approach services – either because they don't know that they exist, or because they mistrust them after bad experiences, either of their own or of friends and family.

Support, advice and guidance are vital to an effective transition. For such people, the trusted adult – be it mentor, personal adviser or lead professional – will be crucial.

From the evidence gained, the report (ODPM, 2005) urges five key principles of service delivery for young adults. These are:

- Actively managing the transition from youth to adult services.
- Taking thinking and behaviour into account, and building on it.
- Involving young adults (and their families and carers) in designing and delivering services.
- Giving effective information about services, and sharing information between services.
- Offering young people a trusted adult who can both challenge and support them.

Website

http://www.socialexclusion.gov.uk/downloaddoc.asp?id=785

The way forward for the future

Many of the recommendations from the 2002 *Multiple Needs Briefing* by Homeless Link (Bevan, 2002) still stand, and really need to be highlighted again with some additional explanation of what has happened since:

1. A commonly agreed model of holistic assessment should be developed and used by all homelessness agencies across the UK. This model must be closely linked with training and support to ensure that the planning and delivery of care is appropriate to the individual and their needs

One of the purposes of a comprehensive needs assessment process was to enable the assessor to identify where further expert input was required. Sometimes this could successfully be gathered from other agencies through telephone contact or a request for written reports. However, workers identified three problems; firstly in identifying the most appropriate agency; secondly, in persuading professionals to undertake an assessment of a homeless person who clearly manifested more than one health problem (for example the co-existence of drug and mental health issues); and thirdly, in obtaining an assessment within an acceptable timescale.

(Crisis, 2004)

There are few examples of a holistic assessment; much more work needs to be done. Assessments need to be capable of building a picture of the degree of need, and how these needs interplay with each other in a single individual. The strength of the single assessment would be to say, for example, that a person has X per cent mental health needs, X per cent substance dependency needs, and X per cent physical or other needs. It should not, then, be beyond us to draw down a 100 per cent support package for that person. It has to be cheaper to work in a holistic multi-disciplinary way with a person, than to have to deal with them when they are in crisis and emergency services need to be engaged.

2. Worker to client staffing ratios for teams working with homeless people with multiple needs should be further investigated and enhanced to support effective key working

Clients with multiple needs require consistent, intensive staffing, if they are not just to be contained or warehoused. This allows for the enforcement of boundaries, and positive work with residents in danger of breaching the hostel boundaries in order to avoid their eviction.

3. Access to statutory specialist agencies should be radically improved to support people with multiple needs

Where possible, the 'teams' offering these services should be multi-disciplinary and involve workers from different organisations, both specialist and mainstream. In addition to specialists in mental health and substance misuse, the teams should include nurses and other primary healthcare specialists

(ibid.: 35)

4. There needs to be a substantial increase in the availability of alcohol detox and respite beds

The government has recently increased the amount of money for alcohol treatment, and The National Treatment Agency (NTA) has also produced *Models of Care for Alcohol Misusers* (MoCAM). The NTA website says that, 'Since 2002, *Models of Care for the Treatment of Adult Drug Misusers*, has provided a framework for the commissioning and provision of adult drug treatment services in England. The recent *Alcohol Harm Reduction Strategy for England* (Prime Minister's Strategy Unit, 2004) provided a new role for the NTA in relation to alcohol treatment. In the strategy, the NTA have been given two key primary tasks:

1. Developing a *Model of Care* framework for alcohol treatment services. This will draw on the existing *Models of Care for Treatment of Adult Drug Misusers*, and set out integrated care pathways for alcohol treatment.
2. The development of standards, criteria and inspection work with the Healthcare Commission.

The NTA is working with the Healthcare Commission to develop a system of review for the adult substance misuse treatment system. The reviews will be based on the Department of Health's *Standards for Better Health*, which seeks to establish the level of quality all organisations providing healthcare are expected to meet, or aspire to. This initiative will apply to all Drug Action Team (DAT) areas in England. *MoCAM* needs to take account of these standards.

As well as producing *MoCAM*, the NTA will also publish a review of the evidence base on alcohol treatment, and a review of the cost-effectiveness of alcohol treatment (www.nta.nhs.uk).

Both the increase in the amount of money available for alcohol services and this new treatment strategy should move the work in this area on at a good pace. However, this work, if it is to engage people with multiple needs, should be very clearly geared to working with other agencies, especially mental health services, in an integrated and creative way.

5. Access to move-on accommodation with open-ended tenancy sustainment and floating support should be increased

Work in this area has been moved forward, and in some areas there is recognition that, for some people with multiple needs, their need for support will taper off over the years. For this group of people, floating support always needs to be pitched at the level where, although the person is well and not at the moment needing support, the support worker's case load numbers are not set so high that they cannot keep an active watching brief on this client. For some people with multiple needs, floating support will need to move into tenancy sustainment – a week by week supporting of the person in the tenancy – and there needs to be recognition that for many people this support must be in place throughout the life of the tenancy.

6. Training needs to be provided both nationally and locally in a number of areas, including personality disorders, offending behaviour, physical health problems, vulnerability because of age, and borderline learning difficulties. Initial and on-going training needs to be properly costed and funded

The issue of training is often not a high enough priority for homelessness agencies, and yet the issue is of prime importance as the list of areas highlighted in this recommendation shows. Higher amounts of money need to be set aside for regular training, and this needs to be well argued in order to be reflected positively in the bids for funding projects working with this client group. One of the problems with competitive bidding is that when bids come under pressure for the service to cost less, sadly the training element is often the first to either be reduced or taken out.

7. A comprehensive review of skills, professional development and training within the homelessness sector should be undertaken

Each agency working, or wanting to work, with this client group should conduct an annual training audit with each of their staff. Time should always be taken after each training course for the content to be reflected on in supervision, and the staff member should also be supported in practicing what they have learned in their day-to-day working life.

8. Work needs to be undertaken with member agencies to encourage and support them to have both formal links and information exchange protocols, with mental health teams, drug and alcohol teams, Primary Care Trusts, Probation Services, Frail Elderly Teams, and Leaving Care Teams

The Office of the Deputy Prime Minister produced in April 2004 *Achieving Positive Shared Outcomes in Health and Homelessness* (ODPM, 2005), which is a very important document. The ODPM said that this is a guidance note, and does not represent statutory guidance, but still it carries the weight of the department's wishes. The ODPM's guidance seeks to enable:

Five key positive outcomes which health and homelessness partnerships might work towards:

- *Improving health care for homeless families in temporary accommodation.*
- *Improving access to primary health care for homeless people.*
- *Improving substance misuse treatment for homeless people.*
- *Improving mental health treatment for homeless people.*
- *Preventing homelessness through appropriate, targeted, health support.*

(ODPM, 2005)

9. General Practitioners need to be closely linked with homelessness agencies and understand the needs of the client group

The opportunity for those GP practices which are based in areas with larger numbers of people who are homeless to become centres of excellence in working with this client group, brings the possibility of these practices embracing the 'Enhanced GP Contract'. The new contract is designed to bring about a range of improvements in primary care in providing demonstrable benefits to general practitioners, to other healthcare professionals, to the health service in general and most importantly to patients. One of the areas this new contract should enable is improved access to services by local people through Health and Social Services Boards commissioning enhanced services to encourage the development of a wider range of services.

There is also a new training module, in the planning stage at Oxford University, which will seek to give post graduate primary care providers a lot of background regarding the needs of homeless people, and also good practice in working with them (Kellogg College, 2006). It is to be hoped that this will be on line in the autumn of 2006, and will enable primary care providers to work positively and creatively with homeless people, especially those with complex multiple needs.

10. Work needs to be done with member agencies ensuring that their user involvement strategies specifically set out how they are to engage with homeless people with multiple needs

Often, the most vulnerable and chaotic service users are sidelined in consultation and involvement processes. The interacting nature of their needs can often result in them being seen as difficult and obstructive, and multiple needs clients often withdraw from or are pushed away from consultation and involvement methods designed for people with a lower level of need.

In May of 2003, the ODPM's Supporting People team issued guidance on user involvement for organisations providing housing related services. This guidance recognised that developing user involvement is neither simple nor straightforward. The report says that no one model can be offered to guarantee success.

Making involvement meaningful to service users is a process that has to start with an understanding of the needs, capacities, interests and concerns of individual users. Moreover methods and forms of involvement should be continually developing and improving, reflecting:

- *The increased confidence and skills on the part of users.*
- *Changing relationships between users and staff.*
- *More participatory decision making arrangements.*

This is very useful guidance, and can be found on the website of the ODPM at: http://www.spkweb.org.uk/NR/rdonlyres/2CE966F1-64E9-4CB9-96DA-12AD8B03A06A/176 4/250504aguidetouserinvolvementfororganisationsprovi.pdf

Groundswell have also been working at developing and implementing service user involvement for St Mungo's, and suggested these recommendations:

- Peer facilitators.
- Service users facilitating at meetings for service users in other St Mungo's projects.
- A service user group – which has been set up and works well. It is powerful and has direct access to senior managers. A senior manager attends this group at least once a month.

Notes from Homeless Link's Spotlight on Service User's event, website link: http://www.homeless.org.uk/regionalNational/london/Spotlight_information/serviceuserspot/

11. There is still a need to understand the funding mix of the homelessness sector in seeking to work with this client group

There is a key challenge to the Commissioners of local services to be creative and commission properly bearing in mind the need for holistic, multi-disciplinary services.

12. Every homelessness strategy at the local and national level should detail how they will strategically and practically engage with homeless people with multiple needs

Each local authority should have its homelessness strategy in place, but also should have mechanisms for reviewing it. Each homelessness agency should ensure that this client group is specifically mentioned, the numbers, and the range of health needs that they are presenting with. This information should be given to the Primary Care Trusts to ensure that either present primary care services can respond to their needs, or that money needs to be found for this to happen.

Current examples of agencies working with homeless people with multiple needs

The three examples given are of one peripatetic service, and two residential units, which provide support; agencies might consider these when looking at models of working with this client group. The examples are taken either from annual reports or are written by the agencies themselves.

1. Elmore Community Services – a peripatetic service

Elmore is different, I didn't have to go there – I chose to. They worked with me when other people had given up.

(Client of Elmore Community Services)

Elmore is an independent, community service working in Oxford City. The Elmore Team's Annual Review 2004–5, says that the team works with people with multiple needs who do not easily fit into existing provisions and are not seen as the clear responsibility of any one agency. They base their services on a pragmatic, needs-led approach. They offer practical help, emotional support, advocacy, links with relevant services and outreach. Elmore also provide support and information for other agencies, and local and national training.

An in-depth look at the work of the Elmore Team is set out in the good practice briefing *Inhabiting the Margins*, Leslie Dewhurst and Pip Bevan, Elmore and Homeless Link 2001.

2. Multiple Needs Unit, Focus Futures, Birmingham – residential

Four years ago Focus Futures opened the doors of the Multiple Needs Unit. This innovative project now has a significant track-record of service delivery and partnership. The project was developed as an accommodation resource for men who have been serially excluded from direct access accommodation within the City of Birmingham. These are men aged 25 to 45 who are experiencing a multiplicity of need which might include: mental health issues; substance misuse; behavioural problems; self-harm; mild learning disabilities; personality disorder; and alcohol misuse.

Access route

The access route is via referral only and these can come from both statutory and voluntary agencies.

Provision/services

24 hour supported accommodation, comprising of 15 high quality flats, a communal lounge which offers Sky TV, communal laundry, gardens and a training kitchen. Support is via key work sessions provided by a named key worker as well as collectively by the staff team. The support is needs-led and is both responsive and assertive towards the individual's changing needs or wishes. The support is combined with support provided from specialist and statutory agencies to maximise an individual's ability to sustain their accommodation and work towards independent living.

Staffing

The staff team comprises: 1 manager, 1 senior project worker, 2 project workers, 2 project assistants, 4 night workers and 1 receptionist.

Funding streams

The project is funded from housing benefit and Supporting People.

Partnerships

Key partnerships are with Health and Social Services, Probation, Voluntary Agencies and Birmingham City Council. Working with all these agencies enables us to house and support one of the most excluded groups of people within the City of Birmingham. A key element of the project is the Referral Panel – made up of partner agencies sharing control over access to the 15 units of the scheme. These same partners are often those with the responsibility to provide the specialist support to the clients housed in the scheme.

Strategic involvement

The project meets the criteria for the following government strategies: Crime Reduction Strategy, Homelessness Strategy, Drug and Alcohol Strategy, Valuing People Strategy and the Strategy for Mental Health.

In line with these strategies the project has received visits from the National Audit Commission, SITRA, the Homeless Network, Officers of the ODPM, Ian Duncan Smith

MP and representatives from agencies nationwide, with particular interest being shown in issues of best practice in accommodation and support of those with multiple needs. The project has received good reviews in the housing press and is regularly referred to as an example of good practice in this field by the ODPM and *Homeless Link*. We have also been involved in several training events for providing accommodation and support for people with multiple needs, as well as being involved with the training of student social workers both at BA and Masters Degree level, sustaining good links with Birmingham University.

Highlights

This year we have resettled two residents into mainstream accommodation and we have three residents waiting for permanent accommodation, having completed their four-year stay at the project. All five residents were serially excluded from housing prior to moving to Lancaster Street, and in turn from many community services. One of the above residents now attends College regularly, has completed his NVQ 1 in Woodwork Studies and is planning to return to college at the start of the new academic year.

Following funding received via Birmingham City Council last year the residents have completed a garden project at the scheme which has provided everyone with a place to sit and chat to the other residents and staff during the summer months. What was once a bleak car park area is now a green haven.

An unscheduled visit from Ian Duncan Smith MP, turned out to be a real boost for the Project. Mr Smith was visiting other Focus Futures Projects in the area and expressed an interest in what we do. Residents spoke at great length about where they had come from and where they wanted to be in the future. Following Ian Duncan Smith's visit we received a letter from his office stating how impressed Mr Smith was with the work we were doing at the project and asked us to thank the residents for their time.

Case studies

Mr A moved into 90 Lancaster Street, 18 months ago. Previously, Mr A had been evicted from all direct access within the City, was experiencing mental health problems and his crack habit was costing him about £200 per week. 18 months on Mr A has stabilised his mental health problem with weekly depot injections and he now spends between £20 to £30 on crack per week and has managed to save £900 which is in his account to purchase furniture when he moves into the community.

> Mr B has an alcohol problem, mental health issues and periodically uses crack and heroin. He has managed to maintain his accommodation for the past two years with intermittent spells in hospital. Staff support Mr B to engage with both statutory and voluntary agencies in an attempt to meet his long-term needs and goals.

Plans for development

In conjunction with external supporting services the Project hopes to develop an integrated move-on package to meet the needs of the individual once they are ready to move from the project. This is in line with one of the projects long-term goals, to move people through resettlement into suitable accommodation that enhances their ability to live independently in the community whilst acknowledging their abilities and changing needs.

Figures for 2004–2005

Number of units: 15
Number of referrals received: 20
Number of people accommodated over the year: 21
Ethnicity: 3 Afro Caribbean, 1 Indian, 3 Scottish, 2 Irish and 12 British
Age breakdown: 25 to 45
Number of departures: 7

Contact for Focus Multiple Needs Unit: Stephen Philpott: stephen.philpott@focus.co.uk

3. The Street Worker Project at Look Ahead, Aldgate Hostel, London

Look Ahead Housing and Care employs a Multiple Needs Worker (MNW) at their Aldgate Hostel to support vulnerable, street-working women with substance use issues and who are trying to exit prostitution, by providing keywork support to address their complex needs. The London Borough of Tower Hamlets funds the post.

The service provided by the Multiple Needs Worker aims to accommodate and support a minimum of two female sex workers by having a minimum of two formal one-to-one sessions a week and regular informal support. The worker reviews with the client their support plans and risk assessments at intervals of three months or less. There is particular emphasis on supporting women in changing their lives and in identifying relevant external agencies to work with and refer service users to, if they so wish, to meet the individual goals identified in their Support Plan.

The MNW assists the service users in feeling that they have a right of citizenship. Usually the women have had so many problems with the police or authority, and aggressive or abusive customers, that they have lost their feeling of citizenship and of having any rights at all.

The MNW aims to establish and maintain links with external agencies committed to supporting those involved in street working throughout the hostel and promotes and encourages safe sexual practice and healthy lifestyle choices to all service users.

Outcomes

The outcomes are measured quarterly. The aim is to keep abandonments and evictions to a minimum. The other objectives are:

- To reduce sex working.
- To reduce substance and alcohol use.
- To obtain or maintain a script.
- To register with a GP.
- To maintain a Licence Agreement.
- To address outstanding legal issues.
- To work towards living semi-independently.

Since the project started in October 2004 eight female clients have been housed and supported. Of these clients there has only been one eviction and one abandonment. The remaining six clients have worked with the MNW towards achieving goals set out in their Support Plan. Four of these clients have moved into the main body of the hostel where they continue to work with a general hostel support worker, and are awaiting resettlement into independent living accommodation. Two women are currently receiving support in the street worker project. Within the first three months of women living in the project, they will have registered with a GP, they will have started a benefit claim, obtained a script, and registered with our in-house Resource Centre to develop life skills and reduce street working.

Contact for hostel based multiple needs worker

Mark Lewis: marklewis@lookahead.org.uk

Conclusion

People who are homeless and have multiple needs are among the most marginalised and excluded groups in our society. Indeed they are the 'litmus test' of whether there is equality of access to our NHS health services. With the loss of ring-fenced funding for the most vulnerable groups, people who are homeless with multiple needs have to compete in a hierarchy of need at a local level. This client group is not one of the most attractive, and can easily get passed over and lose out.

We began this chapter with taking pride in the fact that we belong to a civilised society which seeks the common good. Will we stand up for these often unseen, most passed by, and often silent members of our society? Will we enable people who are homeless and suffering a number of serious, often life threatening needs and illnesses to have their needs met? Will we call them from the shadows and the margins and support them to find a valued place within our society?

Chapter 6

Contesting and working with challenging behaviour

John Ames

Introduction

A conversation with the Editor of this book Mike Seal led to me being asked to write this chapter. I expressed the opinion that 'challenging behaviour' had become a categorisation of the users we work with, and that a significant contribution to this has been 'constructed' by ourselves as 'professionals', partly through a process of labelling and stereotyping. What started as a progressive term has now become, some argue, derogatory. The term 'challenging behaviour' was originally introduced to make workers think more about the behaviour being a challenge to services rather than a problem (Hewett, 1998) and as a move away from the expression 'problem behaviour' (a term that was widely used when I was working with young 'looked after' teenagers in the 1980s).

The British Institute of Learning Disabilities still emphasises this on its website when answering the question, 'What do we mean by challenging behaviour?' It answers, 'We use the term challenging behaviour to emphasise that the behaviour is a challenge to us.' Thus, the term challenging behaviour has become a label, and professionals like me within the homelessness sector (as do the rest of the social care sector) use this term regularly, and at times are guilty of stereotyping and labelling those we apply it to. Perhaps because we lack other options and because, after time, they too would probably be viewed as derogatory or labelling as well, it seems to be a matter of how we interpret the terms rather than what term we use. The word 'challenge' has a positive connotation for me; it signifies opportunity and the potential for achievement, and it would be great if this aspect of the word could be reclaimed in terms of 'challenging behaviour'.

Less and less do we think about challenging behaviour as a 'challenge' to our services and increasingly we are thinking of it as a 'problem' to our services. One alternative is the idea of challenging behaviour being 'exotic communication' (Ephraim, 1998), based on the idea that behaviour is about communication. Ephraim's preference for understanding the behaviour in terms of the emotions and thoughts that generate it is an emphasis that I subscribe to and support myself. I hope that this chapter will help the thought process for workers in our understanding of this term and how we might interpret this into actions. I also hope that the chapter will stimulate some discussion.

It is often through a lack of knowledge and fear that we stereotype and categorise in this way. We put people into categories to make them, in our own minds, easier to deal with. I personally believe that this happens due to a lack of training and awareness, and I mean training in its widest context of learning, not just a training course. Training can be anything from developmental input from managers to action learning sets, learning that lends itself more readily to reflection. If you were to ask most workers within the sector about stereotyping they would be able to give a fairly good definition of it, and probably also give an articulate summary of some of the negative impacts for the recipient of the stereotyping, but I doubt they would have looked at their own, their teams' or their organisations' stereotyping and labelling of the homeless. I think too much training and developmental input in this area currently concentrates on how to *deal* with challenging behaviour, rather than looking at what *lies behind* the behaviour.

In this chapter I want to consider the issue of stereotyping and its potential impact on those we work with, and consider too other ways in which we might contribute as workers to behaviours. Then a significant section of this chapter will be looking at the practicalities and the principles of working with challenging behaviour and how you can apply these ideas to improve your practice. The intention of this chapter is not to put down the efforts of all those who work in the field of homelessness: I have never ceased to be impressed by the hard work, dedication and commitment to the service users displayed by those I have worked with over the last ten years in the field of homelessness, and the quality of the work produced by those people. What I do hope to do is help develop an increased understanding of challenging behaviour through writing about an area that seems to have had relatively little coverage, other than within the context of education, particularly 'special needs' education.

Stereotyping and labelling of users demonstrating challenging behaviour

As most of us know stereotypes are *generalisations* and *assumptions* that we make about people. They are a way for us to categorise people; users, for example, who demonstrate or who have had a history of demonstrating 'challenging behaviour'. McGarty et al. (2002) identifies three guiding principles to identifying stereotypes:

1. Stereotypes are aids to explanations.
2. Stereotypes are energy-saving devices.
3. Stereotypes are shared group beliefs.

No stereotype will share all the principles to the same degree but will often contain elements of all three. We may well feel that we are highly trained and experienced workers who are well equipped to avoid the pitfalls of making assumptions about the service users we work with, but it happens. Partly this is because there can be real and perceived benefits in the inferences we take from the generalisations borne out of the various categories and stereotypes that we have created. It is recognised that such generalisations about people can be necessary in everyday life.

Stereotypes are aids to explanations, they help us to interact effectively, they give us guidance on what people are likely to be like and what behaviours will and will not be acceptable in various situations. The inferences help us predict how people will behave, depending on whatever category we have placed them in. As workers we acknowledge that everyone is different, but at the same time it is comforting to have that element of 'predictability' with users, who otherwise are often viewed as being unpredictable and therefore difficult to work with.

Over time, the rehashing of these inferences relating to the challenging behaviour and specifically those who demonstrate it, can become more and more inaccurate and distorted. It is then that the guiding generalisations that we use to inform our work can become harmful. Stereotypes are largely negative, but, because we use the same processes of generalisation to function in our everyday life and they can appear to be useful, we are prone to fall back on those processes when a situation seems hard to handle or we are scared. In the animal world, animals make decisions all the time that can be about life or death. We have inherited some of these instincts from our ancestors: people talk about a survival instinct, and it can be useful, but if instincts disproportionately influence our responses they can be damaging for vulnerable people such as some of the service users we work with. Another important danger of stereotyping is that we are more likely to pay greater heed to the acts that confirm the stereotype and pay less attention to information that disproves or goes against the stereotype.

Below is an example from my past working life that demonstrates how not having the same opportunity to make generalisations can make a difference. It's not scientific because we do not know what would have happened with these young people if they had been placed elsewhere, but it is an interesting example to consider in the light of this chapter.

About eighteen years ago I worked in a residential project for 'looked after' young people aged 16–18 years. The project's philosophy was designed to try and break down some of the assumptions we make as workers about the users we work with, and the philosophy was very simply called 'a fresh start'. This involved the project refusing all previous information from the social worker about the young people other than their name. All other information would be provided by the young people themselves, the young people would decide what they wanted to tell us about their lives prior to their time at the project, but only if they chose to do so. This was important because stereotypes can be self-perpetuating; if we believe that someone is **aggressive, unpredictable, deceitful** or threatening then we tend to respond in a mirrored fashion. It may be packaged in a different way, but that is often how our behaviour becomes influenced.

Then in turn the service user will respond in an aggressive, unpredictable, deceitful or threatening manner, therefore confirming and living up to the original stereotype that we had of them. Figure 6.1 below has examples of how we might mirror users' behaviours. Indeed, labelling theories suggest that people who are labelled by others they see as being in authority, will then perform appropriately to the role suggested by the label given them. The behaviour suggested by the role becomes the correct or expected behaviour, and as professionals we do hold authority in the eyes of many of our users, and thus they will behave as we predict they will.

However, not only did the young person's project refuse previous information unless provided by the young person, it also took the 'fresh start' idea a step further, in that once you had finished a shift working with the young people you were not allowed to hand over to the oncoming staff or indeed to even meet them. Instead, you handed over to a manager who then went and met with the next worker coming on and handed over to them, taking out your own emotional baggage. So if you were feeling a bit stressed out by someone's behaviour the behaviour that caused the stress would be handed over, but not your own personal anxieties and stresses about it.

This, in effect, gave the young person a 'fresh start' each shift. Though we did not have referral information about the young people it was impossible to not surmise that many of the young people had suffered very troubled pasts and had been difficult to place. The project in Manchester took referrals from all over the country and was a very expensive resource. The assumption to be taken from this was that most of the young people there were running out of placements, as such expensive 'out-of-Borough placements' which were not easy for the social workers to fund. However, the project enjoyed an incredible amount of success, working towards positive outcomes with the majority of young people. I realise that the fresh start policy would now be viewed as totally unacceptable practice and, indeed, it was controversial at the time, but it served as a good indicator of the potentially damaging effects of stereotyping and categorising of service users, as has how the knowledge about clients and what we do with that knowledge, often unconsciously, can be detrimental to them. And research has shown that the effect of unconscious bias can be strong, as a quote from *Psychology Today* suggests:

Psychologists once believed that only bigoted people used stereotypes. Now the study of unconscious bias is revealing the unsettling truth: we all use stereotypes, all the time, without knowing it. We have met the enemy of equality and the enemy is us.

(Psychology Today, May/June 1998)

This quote related to an article on a test developed at Yale University by Mahazrin Banaji who, when she took her own tests, found that she demonstrated very strong unconscious prejudices which she described as very 'disconcerting' for her; I think it is the disconcerting and uncomfortable nature of facing up to our own biases that makes it difficult.

With regards to the notion of being unpredictable I feel that there is no other categorisation of users that we work with in a more **unpredictable** way than those who demonstrate challenging behaviour, which is most commonly expressed in the form of workers inconsistently dealing with situations. One of the main reasons for this is fear. Because of the threat of violence or verbal abuse workers are more likely to turn a blind eye, or just give in on this 'one occasion'. It happens all the time: I have observed it in my work and workers have spoken about this to me candidly on a course that I run on Working with Difficult and Dangerous Behaviour. No one would dream of criticising anyone for feeling fearful or scared and I myself have experienced those emotions at work, it is human nature and often the survival instinct kicks in. The fact that this inconsistency can perpetuate the behaviour, is widely acknowledged, but is still commonplace.

In terms of **deceit**, we could look at the, until very recently, common practice of writing risk assessments about users and not sharing these with them. To some extent I understand the thinking behind this, but would not support it as accepted practice. The justification for this practice, I have heard, is that 'the means justifies the ends'. But the user can also justify keeping information from us that, for example, might affect their chances of resettlement. As workers we often talk of the dangers of sharing this piece of information or that piece of information with the service user, but we need to think about the dangers if we don't. We also need to make sure that we do not use deceit as a form of intervention. I have heard numerous accounts where this has happened: one example of this being the worker who offered a user a cigarette to calm them down and suggested that they step outside to have it, and the user was then locked out of the hostel. The worker argued, that the means justified the end. They wanted the user to take time out to calm down, which was an appropriate intervention in itself, but the use of the deceit was not acceptable.

I have seen **aggression** expressed in terms of controlling rules, particularly in hostels. We all know that there is a need for rules and structures in communal living situations: even in my time as a student living in shared housing we had rules and structures. However, there is a difference between rules that are there for the good of all, to help the harmonious running of the project, and rules that are based on control. I once sat down with my team in a hostel to look at what rules we could get rid of. This was a hostel with a history of very aggressive and, at times, violent, challenging behaviour. What we got from reducing the rules was: less aggression and violence, more user participation and a greater sense of mutual respect. Obviously this was not all down to creating a less controlling atmosphere, but it certainly contributed to it. In my experience the more someone demonstrates aggression the more we impose rules and conditions upon their behaviour, which can itself be interpreted as an act of aggression and hostility by the user. This can degenerate into a step-by-step mirroring of aggressive behaviour, with ever more stringent rules and conditions. I would suggest that we should think very carefully about how we use rules, particularly within residential settings: of course we need them, but let's not turn them into punitive rules. One of the fundamental principles of the *United Nations Guidelines for the Prevention of Juvenile Delinquency* adopted in 1990 states, 'Young persons should have an active role and partnership within society and should not be considered as mere objects of socialisation or control.'

The context is very different but the sentiment is the same; let's ensure that the homeless people we work with have an active role and partnership within our organisations and let's not slip into making them objects of our control, even if they do demonstrate aggressive and challenging behaviour. We must make sure that what rules we do impose are reasonable.

Figure 6.1   Examples of how we might mirror users' behaviours

With regards to the practice of not accepting information about service users, it is important to note that I do accept the need for risk assessments, carefully planned interventions and the role that information about our users plays in informing this process. But perhaps it is a question of degree; how much information do we need? To what degree are we involving the service users? How relevant is the information we are using? I understand that many will consider my example project to demonstrate unacceptable practice, but I hope that people will at the same time acknowledge that sometimes the more 'creative or eccentric' (some professionals might say naïve) ways of working with people are often successful. How many times do you see a story of some small independent project or team working with a user group in a less traditional or accepted way and having great success? It is from these stories that we can often learn a great deal. We do not have to copy what we might see as unsafe or unprofessional practice, but just maybe there is something for us to learn about human interaction, and why those projects are successful, in our increasingly bureaucratic sector.

I also think that we have gone too far with risk management: we are at a point where it can be difficult to re-house people because some Registered Social Landlords (RSL's) and other housing providers don't want to take the 'risk' with more challenging users. Hostels and supported housing schemes are becoming more 'fussy'. Young (Community Care, 2004) reported in an article called *No Room for Nuisance* that, 'The government's crackdown on antisocial behaviour has left social landlords keen to wash their hands of problem tenants'. I support the concept of risk assessments and good risk management, but we need to be careful that some of the most vulnerable users are not excluded from services.

However, to conclude about the young persons' project that I worked in, this was an incredibly empowering message to give to young people; to say 'we want *you* to give us your past history as we are primarily interested in what *you* want to achieve in the future. That was our referral criteria: the young person had to come with an idea of what they wanted to achieve and an idea of how they felt we could support them in this. As I said at the start, we will never know what would have happened to these young people if the project had not existed, but I am in no doubt about the powerful effect that this had on the young people that I worked with.

What is challenging behaviour?

Within the homelessness sector the term challenging behaviour has been used to describe behaviour which clashes over a period of time with what would be considered the 'norm'. This might manifest itself as breaking rules, ignoring requests, being disruptive or being threatening or aggressive to others, including workers, but can also be more passive behaviour such as lacking self confidence or generally being withdrawn. This section will look at the more aggressive behaviours and how we deal with them.

It is widely accepted that behaviour, including 'challenging behaviour' is a form of communication, and when dealing with a situation it is helpful to think about what the person is trying to communicate. Behaviours are also learnt, and what might seem an effective and acceptable behaviour in one context can be the opposite in another. So, as workers dealing with the issues of homeless people, we also need to give regard to the environment and backgrounds from which our service users have come and the environment and backgrounds within which they may have learnt, or at least developed, some of their behaviours. Within these environments these behaviours would have made more sense to the user and others around them. It is when we start to understand more about what people are trying to communicate through their behaviour that we will truly be able to support them in moving on to develop more effective forms of communicating.

Below is a **very brief and simple** overview of what some other people have said about a very complex subject. We should always seek to work with the individual rather than try and fit them into some psychological box; and trying to achieve a greater understanding of our users is very important. Whenever working with users who present with difficult, challenging or dangerous behaviour, you should be working collaboratively with your manager and your team, and beyond in some circumstances, to come up with planned interventions.

Maslow (1968) categorised aggression into:

- *Natural or positive aggression*, aimed at self defence; combating prejudice or social injustice.
- *Pathological aggression*, resulting from an individual's inner nature being distorted or frustrated.

Aggression, Maslow argued, is primarily a result of frustration caused by unfulfilled basic needs. In other words, aggression is not essentially a part of human nature, but is more likely to be a reaction to circumstances in which essential requirements of our lives are unfulfilled. If you think about Maslow's hierarchy of needs in terms of many of the users we are working with, it is clear that many are without some of the most basic of needs.

Buss (1961) interpreted aggression in terms of the type of goal that the aggressor was seeking: aggression was either *hostile* or *instrumental*. Hostile aggression was when the sole intention was to cause suffering to the victim; and instrumental aggression, when the suffering inflicted on the victim was caused in the attainment of another goal. Someone shouting abuse at you might be considered hostile aggression, while someone attacking you to rob you might be viewed as instrumental. Another example of the categorisation of aggression was Moyer (1968) who came up with seven categories based upon the stimulus that precipitated them; these were:

1. Predatory aggression.
2. Inter-male aggression.
3. Fear induced aggression.

4. Irritable aggression.
5. Territorial aggression.
6. Maternal aggression.
7. Instrumental aggression.

Many of these categories will overlap, but what all of these explanations try to do is explain some of the possible causes of aggression. The *Nursing Standard* said of aggression:

> *It appears to be a mathematical equation; aggression is the answer, the challenge is working out how that answer is arrived at. It is not just about discovering possible impelling factors, it is also about the value, function and meaning of that answer to the aggressor and the victim.*

(Nursing Standard, 25.3.98)

I think this is a very powerful quote because aggression is, for some of our users, the answer; and our job is to work in partnership with these users and support them to come up with different answers in their lives. But also it is very important that we, as the quote suggests, try to understand how this came to be the answer for the user.

Other common explanations for challenging behaviours are:

- **Instinct** – aggression happens because we are all born with an aggressive instinct, it is innate and therefore unavoidable, though not necessarily uncontrollable.
- **Frustration** – the theory is that if we are frustrated in achieving our goals we become aggressive, especially towards those we feel are holding us back or standing in our way.
- **Learned behaviour** – this theory suggests that we react aggressively because that is all we know, it is the way we have learned to deal with life.

In all instances, it is important to focus on the behaviour, not the person, and try to understand the factors influencing the behaviour. Some of the reasons might be:

- The person feels threatened, depressed, powerless; justified in being angry.
- They expect to be treated with hostility.
- They are unable to communicate effectively.
- They feel it is the only way to achieve their goals.
- Aggressive behaviour usually works for them.

There may be other reasons, but, as mentioned at the beginning, it is important that you discuss these issues either with your manager or in team meetings, so that a considered, and if appropriate a team, plan can be put into place to work with this behaviour.

The term 'challenging behaviour' is an umbrella term that encompasses many different behaviours, but which can actually act as a hindrance to finding solutions by misrepresenting a behaviour as more or less serious than it is. Most commonly we associate challenging behaviour with the more aggressive or threatening emotions such as anger, but even anger is a complex emotion, as the four faces of anger matrix (Gorkin 2000) below demonstrates:

Four Faces of Anger Matrix		
	Constructive	Destructive
Purposeful	Assertion	Hostility
Spontaneous	Passion	Rage

It suggests that, quite correctly in my view, anger can be both *constructive* and *destructive*. The skill for workers in the social care sector is to develop an ability to accurately interpret and understand the anger that is demonstrated by the users we work with, rather than interpreting all anger as negative. In these incidences we need to be careful that we don't label users as being enraged or hostile when they are simply being assertive or passionate. Gorkin suggests that the matrix itself can act as a tool for workers and users in understanding and accepting the power of aggression and anger expression.

How do we contribute to situations and behaviour?

Earlier in this chapter I spoke of how I felt that we might unconsciously contribute to the notion of challenging behaviour. I think there are other ways in which we affect challenging behaviour both positively and negatively. As part of the training I offer I get people to think about what they bring to situations of challenging behaviour that they have dealt with and often the group is amazed by the length of the list. Below is a table (Figure 6.2) showing just some of the responses I have received:

While this shows only some of the responses, it is numerically indicative of the split between negative and positive emotions and feelings. No matter how 'professional' we pride ourselves on being we will not always be able to counter the effect of bringing these emotions into situations. If emotions were that easy to switch on and off we probably wouldn't be doing the work we do. However, what we can do is to be aware of this as an issue. By increasing our awareness we are likely to minimise the effects of bringing the more potentially negative emotions and feelings into situations we are dealing with. In its most simplistic terms, it can be the difference between you being effective or not in dealing with any given situation. In the training I deliver, the workers then go on to explore how the various emotions can affect the way we work with people, and are often surprised about the impact they can have. Though it appears obvious, we do not always give ourselves the opportunity to reflect more concretely on such issues.

I am not, in any way, trying to lay the blame for challenging behaviour at the door of workers within the homelessness field, but what I am trying to do is raise awareness

fed up with your job	fearing confrontation	confident in the knowledge you have
angry at having to be at work	feeling confident	feeling at a loss because you have no relationship with the person
under pressure because of workload	having personal worries or anxieties not connected with work	unsupported because there are no staff around or a lack of support structure
feeling anxious or scared because the people you are working with have a history of violence	feeling full of energy	feeling pressure to act consistently, rather than act as you see fair at the time
feeling positive about work	feeling uninformed	feeling tired with little to give
disliking the person you are working with	feeling supported	feeling very stressed

Figure 6.2   Feedback from training to the question 'what do you feel you bring to a situation of challenging behaviour?'

of the various issues that may help us, as a profession, to ultimately improve the service and support to our service users, while helping to keep us, as workers, as safe as possible. Having considered some of the ideas about what challenging behaviour is, it is important to think about how we work with the behaviour.

The foundations for effective management of challenging behaviour

Before we consider the build up to an incident the important things that you should have at your disposal are:

(a)   A policy, procedure or guidelines, produced by the organisation that you work for, which will give you a framework for working with and managing challenging behaviour.

(b)   The knowledge of how to call for help in an emergency if you need to, and the means to do that. This knowledge would include a manager's on-call number, if it is out of hours, and a mobile phone if you are working in the community.

(c) Some information about the user you are working with, most notably a risk assessment, though I realise that this is not always possible, such as when an outreach worker meets a new user on the street for example.
(d) Hopefully some training or developmental input from your managers about dealing with incidents of challenging behaviour. This may be a recent, or if you are a more experienced worker, something you did initially a while ago or have repeated.

These are the foundations that should be provided by your employer, and it is on these that your own skills of communication and working with people will be based to allow you to more successfully manage incidents of challenging behaviour. An important point about these incidents is that you will not always manage them to a successful conclusion, and this will be covered more in the section on debriefing.

The pre-incident period

The nature of incidents involving challenging behaviour is that the build up to them is never going to be the exactly the same; they can build up over hours or even days or they can just suddenly blow up without any apparent warning signs. When I worked as a main grade worker there were many shifts when I took the handover with a sense of doom at the impending crisis that was bound to happen – only to have a lovely quiet evening with all the service users interacting positively. On other occasions the predicted peaceful shift was not to be. This equally applied when I was working in people's homes offering floating support. I remember receiving an irate phone call in the morning from a user I was to visit and prepared myself for some hostile interactions only to find that this issue for the user had passed. The important point here is to always be aware, to *observe* what is going on and not to be too reliant on your *sense* of what is going to happen. Having said that I do think that your 'gut feeling' can be very important when dealing with challenging behaviour and you should never totally disregard this feeling. Avoid relying blindly on your 'feelings' to inform your understanding of any given situation, but use them alongside your knowledge, experience and interpretation of the situation to guide you.

Essentially you need to be communicating and working as a team at this stage (if you work in a residential setting). Is everyone in the team aware that there is potentially an incident developing? If not, then you need to make sure everyone is informed. It is good to have a discussion about what you are going to do now, how you are going to handle the situation if it escalates, what has worked before and what should everyone's role be. All of these issues are much easier to deal with at this point rather than later on.

There are some important issues to consider in the build up to an incident. As stated before, incidents often build up over time, be it a matter of days or hours. For some users we will know about their 'triggers', the things that can potentially make them feel aggressive, agitated or frustrated. To assist with the people that you work with who might demonstrate challenging behaviour be knowledgeable about triggers for such behaviour. This is a team responsibility, as well as an individual one; you need to have discussions in team meetings, in handovers and supervisions, about what you have noticed. The trigger could be mental in nature: a family member's birthday, the words of a song; or they could be physical: noise, the temperature or hunger. It is imperative that the team observes and records what they see to build up a picture of potential triggers, as it is then that you can try to minimise the service user's exposure to those triggers in the short term and work with the service user to deal with the issues relating to the triggers in the longer term. During the build up stage you could even remove a trigger to allay the escalation of an incident, by removing someone to a quiet area, for example, if the trigger is noise; engaging with them in an activity if their trigger is boredom; or giving them some food, if their trigger is hunger.

This links into another tool that can be used in the build up stage: the idea of diverting or distracting the service user. This can be most usefully deployed at this early stage, and it can also be used while dealing with the incident, though the likelihood that the service user will pick up on the fact that you are trying to divert or distract their attention away from the issue that is causing them to become wound up, will have increased at this point. One of the most common ways to distract someone or divert their attention is through getting them involved in an activity, as mentioned above. This obviously can only be used when you have some warning of the impending challenging behaviour either via noting trigger points or through verbal and non-verbal signals being given off by the service user. However, many residential projects will proactively use this tactic to lessen the incidents of challenging behaviour by having a programme of activities, both within the project and in the community. This would not usually be directed at any one individual but would be a more blanket approach to diverting and distracting.

The incident itself and dealing with it

The following guidance for dealing with a serious incident or situation of challenging behaviour is based on the Dealing with Difficult and Dangerous Behaviour training that is offered to the staff at Thames Reach, Bondway, where I currently work as a training officer.

Stay calm

This is not always as easy at it seems. The principle of calmness should be adhered to from the very start of the time you begin to deal with the incident. I have seen staff running to a situation when it is not necessary. Except in extreme cases, walk over to the incident. If you rush, you immediately create a sense of urgency that can take away from your sense of calm. Walking to the incident can also give you the added advantage of having that little bit more time to think about what you are going to do. This is of the utmost importance, and essential in terms of good practice; it is not acceptable for workers to lose control, no matter how frustrated or angry you are feeling. You need to stay in control to enable yourself to make the best decisions on how to deal with the situation. You should understand your own triggers and buttons, and it may be necessary for you to let another member of the team take over at times or you may need to just walk away. Try to find and use techniques that work for you, counting to ten really does work.

Give some clear messages

Some of the messages that you should consider giving include:

- Request the behaviour to stop.
- Acknowledge that you have understood what they are saying.
- Express concern about the situation they have created or found themselves in.
- Remind them of what they potentially have to gain or lose.

You may not choose to use these in every situation, but I think they are very important messages that should come into the vast majority of interactions. The statements may vary in the actual wording, but the message should be the same.

Try to create win-win situations

If you can try to give the service use who is demonstrating the challenging behaviour the opportunity to save face, this will often de-escalate a situation very effectively. Do not go into a situation with the idea that you are going to 'win' at all costs and that you won't back down, you need to be willing to compromise. The most important thing initially is to calm the situation down; analysing the unacceptability of the behaviour in any depth should be saved for another time when they are calmer and you can discuss it with them.

Work as a team

If you have the opportunity to, be prepared to hand over to another worker if it feels that it is getting too much. This can also be a great way of creating a win-win situation. If the issue has become polarised between one particular worker and the service user, the intervention of another worker can successfully defuse the situation. This is not usually about skill levels but just about the situation and often if the roles were reversed the outcome would be the same. A note of caution here: do not just barge in and take control, as this can be very undermining of the worker dealing with the situation. Instead be around, and visible, and observe. If you feel your colleague is struggling, offer a way out for them and a way in for you.

Be aware of the guidance and policies of the organisation

Most organisations will have policies and guidelines for incidents; bear these in mind while you are dealing with the situation – they should help you and give you a framework in which to operate. These should also include knowing how to call for help in an emergency if you need to. If your organisation does not have any such policies or guidelines, then talk to them about introducing them; they are very important and a mark of good practice in this area.

Continuously assess the situation

It sounds obvious but it is a real skill to reassess the situation as it happens, to change tack or direction if necessary. This is sometimes known as 'reflection in practice', when you are reflecting as the incident is happening and thinking about how you can do things differently, what skills and tools do you have at your disposal that might help resolve the situation.

Be aware of environmental factors

The physical environment is important. Much has been written about the use of soft colours to create a warm environment, which will help to create a space that lends itself to a more relaxed and calm atmosphere.

Split up any antagonists

Often where an incident is between two or more people it can be very difficult, if not impossible, to resolve the situation while they are still in close proximity. Where possible it is usually a good idea to try and split up the antagonists.

Use good communication and interaction skills

Some examples of this include the ability to ask open-ended questions, which helps the person to let off steam if they want to. This would mean asking questions like, 'How did you feel about that?' as opposed to closed questions like, 'Did you do that?' This can be very useful in defusing situations, as the person often just wants to have their say and be listened to. By allowing this you will often find that the person's mood will come down. *Empathise* and *sympathise* where appropriate and where you feel able. Empathising means being able to acknowledge that you know how someone is feeling. You won't always be able to feel empathy, but if you do then it can be a powerful tool to use. Sympathising is agreeing with and understanding someone's frustration, acknowledging that they are right to feel angry and helping them find ways to deal with the anger. Another way of communicating effectively can be to *normalise* the person's feelings, let them know that they are 'not alone in feeling like that' and that 'they are not the only one who has gone through this'. As with the ideas of empathising and sympathising you will not always be able to use this. All these *interaction tools* should only be used when you genuinely feel that emotion, whether it be sympathy or empathy. Finally, refer to past achievements and successes, try to create a more positive view for the user of themselves – often challenging behaviour manifests itself when the service user is not feeling very good about themselves.

Be aware of your non-verbal communication

'Sometimes non-verbal messages contradict the verbal; often they express true feelings more accurately than the spoken or written language', noted Murphy and Hildebrandt in their book *Effective Business Communications* (1991). This is a complex area and a very important one. It has been stated that between 60–90 per cent of communication is non-verbal. Non-verbal communication includes everything from voice intonation to your stance, and I have broken them down into the sections you see below.

Voice intonation: This should be calm. Don't raise your voice but try to keep the intonation at an even volume level. You should try and create a reassuring tone, speaking at a moderate pace with pauses. It sounds very contrived but it works and if you have a naturally loud voice, or tend to speak quickly you may need to practice.

Eye contact and facial expression: You should show that you are being attentive in your facial expression; challenging behaviour is usually at least partially about demanding attention and you should show that you understand this. As with the voice the facial expression should be steady and even, and your facial expressions should compliment the use of the voice. You should be very wary about smiling, though using your sense of humour can be a great tool in defusing an incident. Here timing is crucial, it would most commonly be appropriate when the service user had 'come down' in mood and would not usually be appropriate when they are in a heightened state of arousal. Note, though, that a reassuring flashed smile while nodding in agreement over an issue may be appropriate, and is very different from a sustained smile. As for eye contact, you should try and maintain a good level of steady eye contact, without staring and make sure that you pay attention to the user's own eye contact. If they appear uncomfortable you may want to lower your eyes slightly for part of the time so that the eye contact does not seem so intense to them.

Body language: Make sure that your arms are down with the palms showing; don't fold your arms, wave them about or put your hands on your hips. In fact, your whole body should be still, not in the way it might be if you were playing the children's game 'Statues', but more in a way that says you are calm and relaxed. Something else that will give the message that you are calm and relaxed is if you stand with your weight slightly to one side. In terms of your positioning, if you stand square on to someone, face to face it is confrontational and may be perceived as so, try to stand slightly to the side of the user with whom you are dealing.

Spatial awareness: You must be aware of spatial issues and keep a reasonable distance from the service user; this is important in terms of both respecting personal space, which can become even more important when someone is feeling aroused and angry, but also in terms of your potential safety. A minimum of an arms length, but preferably a bit more, is the commonly accepted guidance, but use your own assessment and the verbal and non-verbal signals from the user to also inform your decision. I have known people to touch the aggressor and I would say this is very unadvisable. If you touch them, it is giving them permission to touch you, and it may be returned in a more aggressive or damaging way. In terms of spatial issues, although not really to do with non-verbal communication, is awareness of your environment; try to avoid corners or small enclosed spaces, though this is often dictated by where the incident is taking place.

As I stated earlier this can all seem very contrived when written down in this way, but much of it will come naturally. You should, however, be prepared to work at aspects of non-verbal communication; I have known some otherwise very good workers who have not been particularly skilled in this particular aspect of their work. Finally, I would say that it is very important that you pay close attention to the non-verbal communication of the user; you will find that you get signals and feedback which will help you read the situation more effectively.

Debriefing

It is important to always *debrief* after an incident and not just for those directly involved. Other workers who may have witnessed the incident may also be carrying feelings that need to be dealt with and depending on their threshold for such incidents, or sometimes their experience in dealing with them, they can be more affected than the worker who was directly involved. Equally, if other users are around they can also be deeply affected by this.

Ideally the debriefing should consist of two processes, the first being directly after the incident and the second taking the form of an **incident analysis** with the whole team involved. Directly after the incident it is important that the workers get the chance to discuss what has happened, so they can leave it at work; venting any negative thoughts at this time in this safe environment can play an important role in protecting good practice. The initial debriefing session should ideally be created by finding a safe environment, which should be as disturbance-free as possible, in which the worker and a colleague can focus on the worker's experience of the incident. The worker's feelings should be emphasised, with no judgements made about actions at this stage, and immediate and further support needs should be identified. It is always important to remember that no one will always get it right in dealing with situations of challenging behaviour; with the benefit of hindsight you will usually be able to think about something that you could have done slightly differently, that may have been more effective.

A second form of debriefing, the incident analysis, involves a more detailed look at what led up to the incident and the stages of the incident itself. The incident analysis, in my opinion, is best done in the next team meeting, assuming that regular team meetings are taking place. Ideally it should be done within a week of the incident and preferably not longer than two weeks after, though I think it is always a good exercise to do whatever the time lapse. My preference is to do this in a structured way, picking out a time period before the incident happened (this could be two hours, one day or a week, any time period you choose and consider to be useful) and looking for indicators or actions at critical points and examining how these could have been done differently or what could be learnt from this. When doing such an incident analysis it is important to make sure that the workers involved are not left feeling devalued or inadequate, but supported. This can be easy or difficult dependant on the incident itself and the supportive nature of the team. An often less obvious but nevertheless important element of debriefing is the recording and monitoring of incidents, important for several reasons including: to identify trends and levels of stress with any given team or service; to act as a benchmarking process that can promote good practice; and to let the workers know that these incidents are being noted.

Conclusion

The nature of a chapter such as this is that you can never be totally happy with it, because the notion of challenging behaviour is such a complex one. As I have previously stated it is not positive to always get it right, but what we can do is increase our awareness of many of the issues surrounding this area of our work. Whether it be on an individual level or as a team or organisation, we need to question the way we work with users who demonstrate challenging behaviour. Think about whether you have ever been guilty of stereotyping some of the users that you have worked with and who have been labelled as falling into the category of challenging behaviour? Whilst it is important to re-iterate that ultimately the responsibility for the behaviour remains firmly with the user, nevertheless I hope that we all wish to improve our practice and to gain a more sophisticated understanding of those we work with. This level of sophistication will not be gained from this chapter or this book alone, and hopefully this chapter will also raise as many, if not more, questions than it answers. In light of this I would like to offer the following recommendations for improvements that we could all be making when working with users demonstrating challenging behaviour.

Recommendations

For organisations to look at the way they relate to their users in terms of unconscious bias and stereotyping.

This could be done through a programme of raising awareness amongst their employees, through training, team discussions, whatever seems most suitable and appropriate to the organisation. Within the organisation where I currently work, we recently introduced a traineeship for service users and former service users to enable them to become employees, as frontline workers. Speaking to people as it developed from the planning stages to the inception of the scheme, I sensed both an excitement that many felt, but also a tangible fear amongst some of the workers. I feel that this was based on some of the unconscious prejudices of workers for the user group with which they worked. However, now speaking to those same workers the fear has dissipated and been replaced with unbridled enthusiasm. That's not to say there won't be any of those prejudices and biases there, but this scheme has unintentionally helped some workers to face up to some of their own prejudices. The point is that if we accept that these prejudices are there, should we not put far more effort into raising awareness of them?

For all organisations to ensure that they have a policy for working with challenging behaviour (including information about debriefing) and offer training or access to training at different levels, i.e. introduction, intermediate and advanced courses.

It is important that the training does not just relate to how to deal with challenging behaviour as covered in the second half of this chapter, but also looks at potential sources of the behaviour, and some of the theories of aggressive, challenging behaviour. I would also suggest that looking at our conscious and unconscious stereotyping of users' challenging behaviour and the implications of this for our practice, would be a positive step to understanding this issue.

To review internal selection criteria that is making it increasingly difficult to place people, and to work with external agencies including Registered Social Landlords' to make sure that a vulnerable group does not become increasingly excluded from services.

To work with users, to look at the labels they carry with them and so support them in replacing the negative labels with positive ones.

Positive labels can help the user to increase their self-esteem and their feelings of self worth, whilst negative labels can contribute to the self-fulfilling prophecy effect and can leave the user with feelings of resentment and anger.

Section Three:

Identities and cultures in the homeless sector and societal and personal reactions to homelessness

Chapter 7

Homelessness and its impact on our personal and societal identities

Mike Seal

Homelessness is becoming the destiny of the world.

(Heidegger, 1977)

When the third world is no longer maintained at a distance out there but begins to appear in here . . . (when it) emerges at the centre of our daily lives, in the cities and cultures of the so called advanced or First World, then we can perhaps begin to talk of a significant interruption in the preceding sense of our own lives, culture, languages and futures.

(Pratt, 1992)

The ice that still supports people today has become very thin; the wind that brings the thaw is blowing; we ourselves who are homeless constitute a force that breaks open ice and other all too thin realities.

(Nietzsche, 1884)

Introduction

Lifton (1992) suggests that we 'engage in destructive patterns of symbolising homelessness'. It is that phenomenon that is the subject of this chapter. In my previous book I traced how society has constructed homelessness in terms of policy. I contended that homelessness had been constructed along conflicting ideological lines. It was seen historically as either an individual failure, the homeless person being 'bad, sad or mad' or as a structural failure, the by-product of failed housing policy (Balchin, 1998). What I did not attempt to address were the reasons why we would construct homelessness in such a way. This is the subject that I would like to explore in this chapter.

I want to argue here that the way we construct homelessness goes beyond the need to 'deal with it' as a social problem. Our reactions to it are a result of a deeper crisis. I will argue that encounters with homelessness evoke in us a deep-seated unease, both societally and personally. By **personal encounters** I mean the way that we experience homeless people, as individuals, through encounters with them on the street and in our reactions to representations of them in the media. By **societal encounters** I mean how we subsequently respond to it, as a society, through policy and service provision.

The three quotes above make points that weave through the argument I wish to present here. Firstly, I will argue that we feel threatened by homelessness, because it is a reminder both that our society fails certain people, and because it is a mirror to our own vulnerabilities, again personally and as a society. Secondly, I will argue that we respond to it in contradictory ways. On the one hand we deny it, displace it and demonise those who are homeless. On the other hand we pity them and recognise it as an indictment of society. We may even romanticise it (which the Nietzsche quote hints at). Finally, I wish to propose that we mythologise homelessness, and use it as a lens to focus on how we would like our society to be. I also believe that the myths underpinning these constructions are bound up with notions of 'Britishness' and that these inform how we construct policy on homelessness. I will also contend that many homeless people buy into these myths, and are damaged by them.

Personal constructions of homelessness

Homelessness is a flashpoint for people, exemplified in Tony Blair saying that 'homelessness should not be tolerated'. This statement cuts two ways (Jordan, 2001): we should not tolerate the conditions that precipitate it; but also we should not have to experience seeing it. Here, then, I want to concentrate on people's thoughts on encountering homelessness, normally in the shape of a beggar or person on the streets.

> *Homelessness can be seen as both causing, and being reflective, of a broader legitimation crisis in modern society. They are reflective of a social breakdown.*
>
> (Daly, 1996)

As I said earlier, the homelessness encounter invokes a cultural crisis that works on two levels. Firstly, as Daly expresses, we are being faced with the obvious failings of society and the failure of structuralist solutions to a variety of social ills, including homelessness. It is a point of crisis for the homeless person and for ourselves, for we are complicit in their situation as more 'fortunate' members of society.

However, this does not account for the extremity of some of our reactions. In my experience people who would not try and locate other social issues, such as racism, violence or sexual attacks, as originating in the behaviour of the victim, would still contend that many homeless people 'choose' to be in their predicament. As a physical consequence homeless people are 13 times more likely to be the victim of an assault than the general public (Grenier, 1996) meaning at least that many people have an antipathy towards homeless people. We need to ask ourselves why this might be.

> *Being outcast or homeless among the insiders (i.e. members of the public) must be rationalised by the insiders. The insiders see themselves as rational and caring*

individuals who, through willing participation, maintain a system that is also believed to be rational and caring. So, when confronted with such a wretched situation, the insiders must attribute the situation to the behaviour and attitudes of the victim and not themselves to the system, which affords them their insider identity.

(Kramer and Lee, 1999)

We have acknowledged the embarrassment of the homelessness encounter, where we are confronted with the structural failure that homelessness can be. Kramer and Lee (1999) note above how it is quite human, upon any difficult encounter, to try and rationalise our experiences, and distance them. I would contend that this process is more difficult with homelessness than other issues. While racism has a structural dimension, as pointed out by the McPherson Report (1999), it is easier (at least for those who do not experience racism directly), upon encountering it, to construct it as an individual's problem, and not ours. It is possible to construct it this way for when a racial attack or harassment is witnessed, it is normally possible to identify a perpetrator or 'cause' of the violence, that is outside of us. Witnessing a homeless person on the street is more difficult, as the cause of this situation is not visible or easily identifiable. The lack of a perpetrator prompts an uneasy sense of guilt and complicity in the observer and the easiest way to deal with it is to blame the homeless person themselves.

Homeless people draw us into their plight, because they're here, and many people say in different ways that we cannot avoid them . . . They thrust their homelessness right before us and they ask us for money or for some attention.

(Lifton, 1992)

To compound this feeling of unease, homelessness is both a physical encounter and a common one. As Lifton says above, an exacerbating factor with homelessness, at least in the case of rough sleeping, is that it is a public event. It is played out in front of us, encroaches on our space and invades us in a way that racism and unemployment etc. rarely do, unless we ourselves fall victim to them. This 'invasion' is not always a deliberate strategy by homeless people (although it can be, as Butchinsky has explored in this book). Homeless people breach boundaries by bringing private functions into public space. They often eat, sleep, drink, defecate and socialise in the street. Given these factors, we then need to consider how we react to homelessness, both as individuals and as a society, in how we construct it and legislate for it.

On another level, both Pratt and Heidiger point towards another, deeper, crisis with which homelessness confronts us. Many authors (Giddens, 1996; McGuigan, 1999) document as a feature of late modernity (or post-modernity, not a debate I wish to enter into here) that our identities are becoming increasingly fractured. The reference points and certainties that have traditionally given us a sense of self are increasingly being contested (Giddens, 1996; McGuigan, 1999). It is homeless people's invasion of our sense of our own lives that makes us uncomfortable as it reminds us of our identity crises, both as individuals and as a society. It reminds us of the degree to which we are all homeless, lost, insecure and fragile.

A common way I have heard homelessness rationalised, or humanised, is that we are all only a few mortgage payments away from it (Seal, 2004). As a practitioner I joked with colleagues that we were only a drink away from the clients. While these constructions can be a genuine attempt to challenge our distancing of homeless people (and I will explore that reaction more later), they are rarely materially true. Such constructions are also in danger of denying the nature of poverty and class as they affect housing (Balchin, 1999). To become homeless, as well as falling behind on a mortgage say through redundancy, I would have to have no possibility of gaining new employment, be unable to downsize, have had the mortgage company give up on me, have lost my accommodation, and have alienated all friends and family I could stay with etc.

I think that many people, particularly practitioners, are aware of the falseness of the construction that we are all materially close to homelessness, or could easily see this with a little thought. Yet these images still have resonance and poignancy. I think their power is at the psychological level, rather than the material level. While we may not be in danger of imminent homelessness, we fear that it would not take much for our lives to start unravelling. Our sense of self is fragile and to be confronted with people who are nakedly fractured can mirror our own insecurities. It is easier for us to cope with our unease by reducing it to a practical level, even when that does not bear scrutiny.

Explanations as to the troublesome nature of the begging encounter cannot be found on purely financial or economic grounds. How much upset would be caused to most of us when discovering that we have lost 10p?

(Macintosh and Erskine, 2000)

We have discussed the unease of the homelessness encounter and touched on one aspect of how we try, but fail, to deal with the unease we feel in the encounter through rationalisation, often through blaming the individual. Returning to the Kramer and Lee (1999) quote, we can see why various authors (Dean, 1999; Lifton, 1992) have detailed how we deal with homeless people by disassociation, displacing feelings of resentment, fear, pity, contempt, guilt, shame and a sense of conflict, although these feelings are often sublimated. Daly (1996) observes that those who are homeless are often referred to as 'the homeless' as opposed to 'homeless people'; the guilt and contempt we feel when confronted with homeless people making us de-personalise them.

Rather than take collective responsibility, an attitude of disengagement and disaffection sets in. Hewitt (1995) describes observing a man giving to a homeless person in Kings Cross. He notes the emphasis with which it was said that it was 'for food' to the point of it being an accusation. The homeless person himself was a party to this interaction, having a sign saying 'hungry and homeless' next to him. The man probably knew, or suspected, that the money would not be spent on food. Nevertheless the homeless person felt obliged, again quite accurately, to appeal for money in this way: this is the nature of the discourse.

Public and media constructions of homelessness

It is also important to look further than these individual encounters to see what the 'public' perception is of homeless people. It is an important consideration for, as Southard (1997) has noted, both media images and the consequent reactions homeless people receive from the public have 'discernible impacts on the development of self-concepts within the homeless population'. However, as Liddiard cautions, 'public attitudes towards homeless people is a notoriously nebulous area to delimit' (Liddiard, 1999) and we should be wary of generalising. Boydell et al. (2000) contend that the messages we receive about the value of homeless people, both explicitly and implicitly, are important. They detail how images of and attitudes towards homelessness are encountered within the family, educational institutions, the judicial system, and mass media, and are articulated in public opinion. However, how audiences interpret the multitude of images they receive (Liddiard, 1999) is equally contentious and I therefore will go into detail on this subject here. It has been dealt with in depth by other authors (Hartley, 1993; Liddiard, 1999; Maxwell et al., 1972; Mowbray, 1985).

Liddiard notes the media tendency to sensationalise certain newsworthy aspects of stories about homeless people: to personalise, and hence de-politicise, their experiences; to emphasise the 'other-ness' of homeless people, characterising them in terms of 'personal fecklessness and shirked responsibility' (Liddiard, 1999). Widdowfield (2001), in a textual review of five newspapers, characterised portrayals of homelessness as criminals, victims or 'other'. How this translates into public opinion is unclear, although a typical list of homelessness myths, drawn from a number of sources (Centrepoint, 1997; Crane et al.,1999; Gale, 1998) lists such things as: 'they make loads of money from begging'; 'they don't want to work'; 'couldn't they could just go home?'; 'surely social services would look after them?'

Public policy and homelessness

In terms of public policy we deal with homeless people in a manner underpinned by these myths. In a previous work (Seal, 2005) I showed how this is perpetuated in terms of blaming the individual. Here I would liked to expand on the other dimensions of seeing people as 'other' and of criminalising them.

We deny homeless people's humanity by denying them the space they occupy and seeking to reclaim it. Daly (1996) talks about the 'peripheralisation of the centre' whereby cities are spatially stratified with some sites being central (new office towers) while next door others are peripheral (poor council estates). In the case of the extreme, homelessness, the space is actually denied. Daly draws a parallel with ethnographic work he did in Nairobi where he worked with squatter communities. He found over 100 'informal settlements', including one that had a population of over 200,000 and had existed for 30 years, that were registered on the official maps as forest. As such shanty towns were not recognised then, the government was not obliged to provide infrastructure or services and, crucially, could destroy them at any point.

I noted in my previous book (Seal, 2005) the example of the closing of the 'Bull Ring' at Waterloo in London, which was torn down to make the way for a new cinema. While agencies provided services for the displaced (indeed it was a planned eviction, cited as good practice) the idea of the Bull Ring as a homeless people's space was not countenanced. At that time, even squatters, another much maligned group, gained rights to their properties after a number of years.

A similar example occurred in Lincolns Inn Fields. Again, hundreds were evicted for aesthetic reasons: the lawyers were fed up of having them on the doorstep and felt they were putting customers off. This was despite the fact that it had been a recognised cardboard city for over 20 years and at times had a population in the hundreds. I knew some of the residents and ex-residents of both these places, which they definitely viewed as their homes. Once, I was taken on a tour of the Bull Ring, which had a structure like any community. There was a central part where everyone came in to talk and drink, and surrounding this there were pocketed communities. The drinkers had one place, the drug users were elsewhere, and people with mental health issues were in a different part again. On the outskirts there were often couples who had built elaborate 'bashes' with separate living and sleeping areas. These were called 'the suburbs' and my guide had just moved there himself. Nothing now remains.

It is this contesting of space that we find a threat. When I worked in Kings Cross in the late nineties, a policy of zero tolerance was brought in and among the 'crimes' to be dealt with under that zero tolerance was street drinking. Street drinking is often cited as a problem, without qualification, in an area. Sitting on the pavement drinking a can was considered a crime while sitting at a table outside a pub ten yards away drinking from a glass is not. The problem of homeless people's drunken behaviour is then cited as though everyone else goes home from the pub in silence and without incident at closing time. Focault (1986) recognised the importance of space both in experiencing communal life and in the exercise of power. Echoing previous arguments, the issue of homelessness has been blamed on a perceived loss of community, or a symptom of it (Wagner, 1993). Yet a civil society, one based on community, does not like to be reminded publicly about its failings.

Other crimes would include the rise in 'concern' over phenomena like 'aggressive begging' (if a person is fearful of the repercussions from refusing to give money or property to a beggar, this is classed as 'robbery' under the Theft Act 1968). The power to use ASBOs against there begging, rough sleeping or street drinking are just a continuation of the criminalisation of street activity that started with the Vagrancy Act 1836. In my opinion the explicit linking of street work or street rescue teams with the police (with the threat that non-engagement will eventually lead to prosecution) is, in my opinion, another aspect of this criminalisation.

The myth of home and homelessness

While we have explored the myths, and how they manifest in terms of public policy, what remains to be explained is why the media, and by extension the public and society, needs to create such myths. I think the work of Girling (1993) who explored the power and function of myths, is useful in analysing how we deal with our encounters with homeless people in this country by sustaining certain myths about homelessness.

Girling (1993) says that myths are emotionally charged beliefs, expressing the way people experience and make sense of formative periods in their history. They are symbolic representations of reality, which is why they are hard to challenge with facts, but they are also authentic responses. Creating myths is how we respond to social change and other phenomena which make us feel powerless (something that we have already explored as being pertinent to homelessness). Girling holds that stable and routine eras of history are conducive to the use of reason, but during times of stress, and economic, political or cultural crisis, 'latent emotional feelings are revived, finding their expressions in myths'. He holds that myths enable believers to adapt to and to shape the reality of powerful, impersonal forces at work in society. They do this by:

1. Helping people to cope with the existential condition of suffering which becomes patently more acute in times of crisis, and thus by extension to cope with the existence of evil in the world.
2. Allowing people to feel they belong to the community (us against them) in which they can shelter.
3. Inspiring a good community, i.e. appropriate norms of conduct and the motivation for action to achieve them. Myths provide both meaning and identity.

For us myths about homeless people and mythical solutions to the issue solve the unease caused by our encounters with homelessness. It allows us to cope with the crisis of suffering which cannot otherwise be resolved; it allows us to distance ourselves from homelessness, create a 'them and us'; to demonise them, and means we need to differentiate between 'the deserving' and 'the undeserving' homeless people. Myths are thus useful to 'solve' or manage some of the aforementioned existential angst that homelessness evokes in us. While this helps us to understand *why* we create myths about homeless people, it does not explain why we create *these particular* myths.

The nature of these myths

Some authors (Arnold, 2004; Kramer and Lee, 1999) consider that the way in which the media portrays homeless people echoes our societal insecurities, and in turn we construct them through, and in terms of, these insecurities. Kramer and Lee (1999) say that the American media categorises homeless people in terms of three 'characters':

- 'The Nietzschean (anti) hero, the drifter, the wanderer, with no ties that bind, the militant individualist.'
- The 'pathetic refugee', who unlike the hero does not wander from a lust for independence but is forced into homelessness by circumstances.
- The social isolate, hermit or nomad who has rejected the idea of 'normal' social intercourse.

What is of note is that Kramer and Lee recognise that these constructions say as much about American society, as they do about homeless people. They see the American dream as the lens through which these constructions are created. These roles are all variations, distortions or inversions of this cultural myth, a playing out of accepted cultural roles within that 'imagined community' (Anderson, 1983).

Kramer and Lee see the American Dream as the myth through which the USA media constructs homelessness. To explore the implications of this for Great Britain would entail a more detailed examination of how the media portrays homelessness; and an engagement with the concept of a 'British Dream' or 'way of life', both of which are beyond the scope of this book. However, what follows in the next few paragraphs is intended as food for thought and as a pointer for further research work to be conducted.

Galvin traces the experience of America, Germany and Britain and their creation of national myths. While America had the American Dream and Germany had notions of the *Volk*, Britain had the myth of 'progress' and 'property', both intrinsically linked to capitalism and the Protestant Work Ethic. It is these constructions that I will argue are part of the myth of 'Britishness' through which we construct homelessness, along with a notion of 'fairness' and 'decency' which helped us justify colonial expansion (Gilroy, 1993) under a moral cloak. The notion of British 'fairness' has been evoked by many from Patricia Hewitt regarding the NHS (2005), to the Fabian Society (2006) and was one of the main characteristics that the Commission for Racial Equality found that British people liked to attribute to themselves (Ethnos, 2005).

However, we need to find an anchor for such myths. A possible link seems to me, at least for Britain, to be the concept of home, and how 'home' relates to the wider concept of 'Britishness', often conflated with 'Englishness'.

Home brought together the meanings of house and of household, of dwelling and of refuge, of ownership and of affection ... this wonderful word 'home' ... connotes a mythical place but also has a more abstract sense of a state of being.

(Rybczynski, 1986)

The question of home, is intrinsically linked with the way in which processes of inclusion or exclusion operate and are subjectively experienced under given circumstances.

(Brah, 1996)

While home is just an example of how a myth of Britishness is perpetuated, it is nevertheless a powerful one, and the most pertinent for this study. If we mythologise home, we mythologise homelessness; and as soon as this is done, homelessness can be denied or dismissed as unwieldy, abstract or diffuse, even intractable. Therefore, if we understand how we conceptualise home, our own home, we may start to understand how we construct ideas of homelessness and homeless people.

Watson and Austerberry (1986) have traced a myriad of concepts of home: material conditions and standards; safety; security; privacy; space; control; personal warmth; comfort; stability; choice; self-expression; and physical and emotional well-being. In feminist discourses meanings of home are bound up with ideas of compassionate marriage, children and shared activities. Those who deviate from these conceptions are stigmatised. For many the concept of home is directly linked to the idea of a site for the reproduction of the labour force. The emphasis is on private space, which can be a site for family values and for socialisation. Indeed, this is relatively uncontroversial. Winston Churchill famously said that communism would never take root in this country because we are a nation of homeowners.

Authors such as Saunders (1998) have associated home with ideas such as 'ontological security'. The more secure we are in our homes, the more we have security in our sense of self. Gurney (1994, 1999) rightly says that those who have secure homes are more likely to have other factors, linked to ontological security, present. Homeowners are more likely to be middle class; to have security, stability, and status; and therefore to have 'ontological security'. Kemeny (1992) argues that the state and other powerful interest groups justify housing policies through such assumptions, that falsify and mystify the way housing tenures operate. He argues strongly against the mythological reverence for home (Kemeny, 1992) in English-speaking countries and demystifies a number of widely held preconceptions about the 'natural' desire to own our homes, have security of tenure and view capital accumulation as a sign of security and achievement. He cites the dreams of home ownership of yeoman farmers and pioneers in contemporary America and Australia as evidence for ideologies of home ownership, sustained by moral tales of a promised land (Kemeny, 1992).

Anderson (1983) says that the need to claim a place of origin, of authentic place, of history can be linked to imagining a national identity. He also explores how these imagined communities reached an apex at the end of the nineteenth century, although claims were made that their roots went back much further. He shows how claims that are made for 'national communities' and 'ways of life', are in fact as much an issue of the present as one of the past. Such myths help us deal with our identities being threatened in the three ways Girling mentions. We perpetuate a myth, a myth of the age of progress that we are trying to return to, where a home is a cornerstone, we are settled, we are responsible and we work. All other lifestyles are denied and derided. In this myth people who are homeless cannot have skills and have no validity.

In recent manifestations we have seen Thatcherite calls for a return to 'Victorian Values' and Major invoking such myths as an 'Olde England' of cut grass, the crack of leather against willow in a village game of cricket, and warm beer. New Labour talks of developing communities and sustainability, returning to an imagined time of community co-operation and mutuality. However, such images are easily contestable. Brah (1996) points out that for every cold Victorian night spent in front of a roaring fire in a mansion, there were people standing around a makeshift fire on the streets. She also talks about how we forget the stratified nature of this huddled group, with its probably mixed ethnicity of Irish, Jew, Indian and African. For her, our ways of imagining 'Britishness', and in particular 'Englishness', eradicates such multi-cultural-isms, such social exclusions. Kemeny sees the ideology of home as a part of this wider ideology of Britishness.

Curiously, if we return to the aforementioned public myths about homelessness we see variations, distortions or inversions of the cultural myth of Britishness as I have explored it. The statements, 'they make loads of money from begging', 'they don't want to work', 'they could just go home', 'social services would look after them', have resonance with the importance of capitalism, property, the Protestant Work Ethic and the supposed 'fairness' of the British way. In particular, the statement 'they make loads of money from begging' evokes both the importance of capitalism and is an inversion of the work ethic. The phrase 'they don't want to work' is a classic condemnation of someone failing to adhere to the Protestant Work Ethic; 'couldn't they could just go home?' invokes the infallibility of the family and the supposed British characteristic of 'fairness' that the family would display. 'Social services would look after them' dismisses them because the British sense of fairness would not allow this to happen and therefore they must have chosen this lifestyle themselves.

These myths are again sustained within the solutions and services provided to homeless people. There is a perpetuation of the ideal of the home, the Englishman's castle, as being the solutions to all their ills. I traced in my previous book how many homelessness agencies are very practical in orientation, seeing the new accommoda-tion as the key, if not the complete solution, to homeless people's issues. Linguistically these myths are expressed through certain constructions of autonomy and individual-ism. We talk about individuals not community, choice and customers, independence not inter-dependence; even empowerment is redefined in New Right terms as self-help and not mutuality. For those resettled the majority of provision is single flats, which is then perpetuated as being a 'holy grail'. I also catalogued in my previous book how workers often distance themselves from their clients, something we will see again in the next chapter. As a part of this distancing, what Gurney sees as the second role of a myth, there is a perpetuation of 'them and us' attitudes towards homeless people.

Conclusion: homeless people making sense of these myths

Looking back to the opening words of the Introduction to this book, I want to return to the contention that homeless identities are also continually created and contested by homeless people: that this narrative is negotiated in the encounters and dialogues we as professionals and as members of the public have with homeless people. The question then arises of how homeless people respond to these myths and create a sense of themselves from them.

As to capitalism (or money making) and the work ethic, I have found many homeless people to possess, and actively see themselves, as entrepreneurial. Some years ago I ran a participatory workshop with homeless people on the topic of begging. They saw begging as an economic arrangement, echoing Dean's (1999) findings in *Begging Questions*. They also felt that to be successful (economically) you trod a fine balance between playing on people's guilt and annoying them (and therefore being at risk). One participant talked about how he begged in Oxford Street, but not in the City: 'You never get anything off the rich. They hate the poor, let alone us. It's the normal people who give money; they feel guilty.' There was however a line not to cross: 'Don't do it at night, then they're pissed and will have a go, don't do it in no poor areas either.' There was a deliberate policy of playing to stereotypes: 'Got to look like you need it, have a card, look scruffy, look poor, give 'em what they want.' One telling attitude that was discussed was their general disdain for those who gave. Exploring this, their reasoning was 'well, they always want a piece of you, make you feel small'. Macintosh and Ervine (1999) say that one of the public discomforts with homeless people is that there is no transaction taking place. However, taking note of the previous participant's comments, I feel that there may be a transaction or an unwritten contract. As givers we buy part of the beggar's dignity, and on one level I would prefer to know that the money will buy beer not food, to justify my own preconceptions. It is easier to accept Murray's (1990) idea that the homeless are an 'underclass of poor who live off mainstream society without participating in it' than as Macintosh and Ervine (1999) conclude, that 'choosers cannot be beggars'. Interestingly, the group very much described these economic activities as 'working' or 'grafting'.

Sometimes, however, people would actively invert these myths. Something I observed in my practice was the pride in getting loans or grants from the DSS on false pretences. It was not for monetary reasons, as the money was often as not shared out. There was a definite idea of 'getting one over on the system', a system with which homelessness workers are very much identified.

As to notions of British 'fairness', I have discerned not only profound rejections of this idea amongst homeless people, but also entrenched internalisation of the fact that this all must be their fault. The other chapters in the book have explored how service users often resist agencies. Snow and Anderson (1987) examined homeless people's construction of their identities and found a strong factor was 'institutional distancing', i.e. rejecting the services that are offered. They put this distancing down to individuals trying to deal with the inconsistencies of their self-conceptions and their reality. A different interpretation might be that they are resisting the micro-power at the point where they can. Service users 'getting one over on workers' is part of this culture as Butchinsky explores in Chapter 1. I have found homeless people to be often acutely aware of the inconsistencies in the way they are treated and the differing philosophies of the agencies they engage with. As a worker I would see the same person, who a few hours before was rationally explaining to me why he viewed his family background as a root cause of his homelessness, saying to a nun at a night shelter that he would repent his sins as this is what had caused his homelessness.

On the other hand many homeless people I have known have, to various degrees, blamed themselves for their predicaments. This can take the form of depression and low self-esteem (Bao et al., 2000); a rejecting of 'normal' morality, revelling in a renegade image (Taveccihio et al., 1999). Or, as Flynn describes, there can be a re-creation of the moral codes and roles (often in an exaggerated form) within the homeless community, of the society denied to them. It is this last aspect that I found more telling, especially in the myths people created about homes they had lost or fantasies about 'homes' that had been denied to them.

Gilroy (1993) sees the concept of a denied home as a site of trauma, separation and dislocation, but also as the potential site of new hopes and beginnings. Either way it is a myth that sustains us, rather than a truth we will realise. One of the commonest phrases I have heard from homeless people is the cry of 'if I just got a flat it would be all sorted'; echoing the 'magical' solution of the home, forgetting to ask what would be sorted, and why a flat would be the solution. Some older people, with whom I have worked, had a longing for, and perpetuated a romantic notion of, their previous life, prior to being homeless, even when they were largely constructing a myth. They looked back to a time of full employment, when they did casual work, as the time they were alive. Younger homeless people talk about wanting 'a job, a house and a family, just the same as everyone else', not knowing that this is itself a construction. These views are negative because, while they express the traumas and feelings of displacement, they do not replace the lost home with a new identity of new hopes and beginnings, but with a lie that maintains an unfilled longing.

This can be especially poignant when some homeless people move into their new accommodation. At this point they are confronted with the myth, which they bought into, that we as practitioners bought into, that this would magically transform their lives and solve the problems we had labelled as 'homelessness'. For many the reality does not match their expectations, either physically or psychologically. The accommodation may be in an area where they have no links or support, they may be lacking basic furniture and the accommodation may be in poor repair. Even if some of these physical things are in place, the new accommodation often falls far short of the remembered or idealised 'home'. Unable to establish themselves in their new community, and perhaps with other ongoing issues, people bring their old street community with them, which is likely to cause friction with new neighbours. Unable to cope with the resulting problems, such as threatened eviction or Anti-Social Behaviour Orders, people may leave their accommodation.

When the first batch of rough sleepers resettled under RSI were surveyed, 40 per cent had returned to the streets (Randall: 1994). I saw this many times in my practice, where people have been unable to maintain their new accommodation. There are three main reactions I have observed in those who have left their new homes: they blamed themselves; or possibly someone else; or it was incorporated into their fantasy identity. Only some started to question their received notions of home. Some rejected the idea of home altogether and started to 'accept their fate', what Snow and Anderson called 'embracing' of their homeless identity. This could either be in the form of valuing what a transient lifestyle can give, or more negatively, just 'giving up'. Others recognised 'accommodation' for what it actually is. Four walls, often in a run-down area, which may well be a start but it's certainly not the end of their journey towards 'home'.

It seems we have a task ahead of us, as workers, members of the public and as a society. My first call is for more research, both into media portrayal of homeless people and the myths that we have about them as a society. Part of this research is to investigate where these myths come from and how they are sustained. My idea that these myths and constructions are tied up with notions of Britishness may or may not be a good starting point for further research: at least I hope they will inform the debate. We will then need to challenge ourselves as to why and how we construct homelessness. Agencies, which I think have lost their campaigning and consciousness-raising emphasis of late, need to rethink the importance of these areas of work. While it is understandable that they have been concentrating on dealing with the front line practical needs of homeless people, they need to remember also that how homeless people see themselves portrayed in the media, and how they are treated in their encounters with the general public will have a direct influence on their needs and sense of themselves. Furthermore policy makers in forming policy, and agencies in reacting to those policies, should give attention not only to the New Labour mantra of 'what works', but also what ideas are informing perceptions of 'what works'. I would challenge the New Labour notion that we should just 'be practical', and 'not be bound by ideology'. The obvious practical solution does not always work, and for me ideology is always there: the point is to uncover it and see if we agree with what it is saying.

I certainly think this is something that homeless people are aware of and are engaged in challenging. I recently read *The Big Issue Book of Home* (2000), which has printed a series of homeless people's poems and short stories on the subject of home. I was both heartened and saddened by it. Many of the poems were rejecting received notions of home, while some were romanticising it and expressing the unfulfilled longing I mentioned, although often being unconscious of doing it. I just want to leave you with two of those poems that epitomised to me these different positions.

A House

You can't sell me
what I already have

Take your rose covered cottage
Your lace curtains
Embroidered Wisdoms

And plastic dreams

A foot print
Is deep enough to have walls:
This is where I put my name
This is where I sign.

(Christina Park: 2000)

Be a Home

Be a home
where love is
Be a home
that houses all that is beautiful and real
Be a home
where everything in it is loved and cared
for
Be a home
where the only disharmony is the soft
aching to want to house everyone who
doesn't yet feel where home is
Be a home
Where love is
at home
(Len Ball, 2000)

Chapter 8

Homeless sector culture

Andrew Van Doorn and Mick Kain

Introduction

Over the past five or ten years there has been an increasing focus on the policy and strategic approaches needed to tackle homelessness and social exclusion. This has resulted in a report (SEU, 1998) and targeted strategy (DTLR, 1999) to reduce rough sleeping, with new duties for local authorities to produce homelessness strategies, a new strategic funding framework for housing related support – Supporting People – and multi-million pound investment programmes in all aspects of homelessness provision, prevention and housing.

Alongside this has been a drive to pull together the available knowledge and evidence base about homelessness in the UK (Fitzpatrick et al., 2000), the scope of key aspects of the sector (Harrison et al., 1991; Harrison, 1996; Van Doorn and Williamson, 2001; Johnsen et al., 2004), its services and practice (Bevan, 1998; Van Doorn and Williamson, 2001; Bevan and Van Doorn, 2003; Homeless Link, 2004; Crane and Warnes, 2000; Pannell, 2002; Crane et al., 2005), its implementation of government policy (Randall and Brown, 1993, 1996, 1999) and the numbers and lives of people who experience this who are homeless (Croft-White and Perry-Crooke, 2004; Willcock, 2004; Homeless Link, 2002; Pannell and Palmer, 2004; Kenway and Palmer, 2003; Crane and Warnes, 2001). Significant focus is often placed by researchers on the complex lives and experiences of homeless people, some researchers working with them over time to obtain a greater understanding of their lives and the impact of service intervention (Crane and Warnes, 2002).

The exploration of culture within the available literature has predominantly focused on people who are homeless, or more specifically 'street culture' (Randall and Brown, 1999) concentrating mostly on rough sleeping, street drinking and begging. *Coming in from the Cold* (DTLR, 1999) the Labour Government's strategy for rough sleepers, challenged the ways in which the sector delivered street services, such as soup runs and outreach teams, and how they contributed to 'street culture'. This aspect of culture has warranted investigation and has been joined by a policy focus in terms of interventions and strategies for these groups.

Unfortunately, very little research and investigation focuses on the culture of organisations offering those services. Although subject to significant investment and change, homelessness organisations have not been subject to the same exploration of culture that the individuals they support have. With the intensity of change in how the sector is configured and the needs of those who are homeless, and the increased scrutiny of organisations that support them, there is and should be an increasing interest in all aspects that influence service delivery and outcomes for individuals. Therefore the culture of organisations and the sector warrants greater investigation in order to establish a better understanding of what drives the thinking behind, and the experience of, the models of service and support for people who are homeless.

Over the past few years, there has been some discussion about looking closely and critically at the culture of the sector (Van Doorn and Kain, 2003; Cloke, Johnsen and May, 2005). Some government officials talk about the need for a 'cultural revolution' (Housing Today, 27.01.06) as do some organisations and individuals working in or with the sector. No one, however, has attempted to define the culture or open up the debate for further examination. This chapter attempts to do just that and encourages the reader to reflect on how the culture can both help and hinder the sector's responses to the changing needs of people who are homeless and the wider policy and funding environment.

A time of change

In 2003, on the threshold of major changes in the sector introduced through Supporting People, we charted the changes and began to think about their potential impact and the 'readiness' of homelessness organisations and the sector to meet them. In our paper *To Boldly Go . . . Where the Homelessness Sector has Never Gone Before* (Van Doorn and Kain, 2003), we showed that the homelessness sector has undergone and continues to experience considerable change. This is as a result of a number of factors, but primarily driven by the introduction of new programmes such as Supporting People, and the changing needs and complexity of people who are homeless. We conceptualised six main areas of change, framed by the extension of quasi-markets of welfare to the homelessness sector through Supporting People, already begun in other areas of public service delivery in the 1980s and 1990s, such as in Health, Education and Social Care (Knapp et al., 1994; Wistow et al., 1994; Challis et al., 1994). These changes were:

- A shift from a provider-led to a purchaser-led sector.
- The introduction of local strategies defining service provision, away from the dominance of national policies.
- The move towards a stronger evidence base to define service intervention, previously driven by common sense.
- The introduction of quality, review and outcome measures where very few previously existed.

- The integration, at all levels of service design and delivery, of service user involvement, which at best was patchy.
- A shift away from crisis responses to homelessness, to one of prevention (Van Doorn and Kain, 2003).

To help us understand the solutions offered by and the potential impact of these changes on homelessness organisations and the homelessness sector we turned to Levy and Merry (1996). Their book combined a number of different authors' understanding of organisational change, concluding that there were two levels of change – *first* and *second order*. *First order* change is a change in one or two aspects, in content that doesn't change the world view or paradigm. *Second order* change, however, is multi-aspectual, a change in context that results in a new paradigm. They warn that to successfully deliver change the strategies used must match its 'order'. If organisations try to meet *second order* change with *first order* solutions they simply make plans at the structural level so as not to question paradigms. If paradigms change then staff in organisations need to change their conceptualisation of problems, their attitudes, and their understanding of their roles (Van Doorn and Kain, 2003).

We believe that the change required in the homelessness sector is of such a magnitude (*second order*) that it is at the level of organisational culture where it is most required; and the need within the sector to shift paradigms that define problem identification and service design and delivery are paramount.

The nature of the organisations in the homelessness sector

Although important, we do not want to spend time debating here what defines the homelessness sector or organisations, nor what is meant by homelessness. We do, however, want to give the reader some sense of the organisations we are talking about. The majority of organisations within the homelessness sector are voluntary and community organisations, some with a faith-base, some not, including housing associations, large and small, operating at the local, regional and national (and UK) levels. The majority of homelessness organisations would define themselves as such and say that they work predominantly with homeless people, the majority of whom are single or couples without resident children (often referred to as the 'non-statutory' homeless) (Van Doorn and Williamson, 2002). Alongside direct service delivery organisations, there are other bodies who support, campaign and provide infrastructure, local, regional and national ones who, although not working directly with individuals, embody much of the same culture as those who do.

Here, we are writing about our own and others' perceptions of culture which we consider to be pervasive, not only *through* individual organisations, but *across* all organisations working in the sector. We are observing organisational cultures that, to a greater or lesser extent, become repeated across the homelessness sector.

What is organisational culture?

Organisational culture is a set of pervasive principles that can be observed through what happens in practice in an organisation. Each culture has a range of different principles that do not necessarily fit together logically, and are often outside the conscious awareness of those involved in it. This means that actions based on cultural principles are almost automatic, and often hard to question.

Argyris (1976) identified two levels of communication existent in organisations:

- **Espoused theories:** what is said; for example, mission statements, policies and procedures.
- **Theories in use:** based on the behaviours of others, particularly managers.

Where these two are not congruent, the 'theories in use' are believed. Employees, service users, and volunteers are not fooled by the façade of espoused theories, though an environment may make it difficult for a person to say what the unwritten rules are. The theories in use, the unwritten rules, are the level of organisational culture. Working to change this level of organisational functioning is more difficult than changing policies, but in the end produces much greater results in performance, and offers greater scope for an organisation to change. As culture is the most powerful driver of practice, it is a useful tool for managing an organisation.

Within the culture, different principles have different weight. Some principles can be changed and adapted to needs. At the other end of the scale there are some principles which are deeply ingrained. These principles are the deeper assumptions which organisations rest on. While they may not be linked directly to the espoused value-base or mission of the organisation, questioning these principles can feel like challenging the very basis of an organisation's sense of meaning. We are calling these principles 'cultural anchor points'. They are the deeply rooted principles which, when all else is under challenge, will drive the behaviour of an organisation. Particularly when an organisation is overstretched or under stress, it will turn to its anchor points to recognise what is a problem and what is most likely to solve it. A boat at anchor will move around on the surface of water moved by tides and currents, but always moves in relation to where the anchor is dug down into the sea bed. Similarly with a cultural anchor point, an organisation may make changes and adaptations of the surface level, but in its thinking, planning, and problem-solving behaviour it will only be changing in relation to its cultural anchor point.

Organisational culture is always present, and needs to be consciously and strategically managed to support the organisation and its task. In times of organisational change, conscious management of the organisational culture, and particularly its anchor points, is essential for enabling adaptation. A danger in trying to manage organisational change is that structures, policies, and mission statements may be changed, but the culture is not, resulting in little change in behaviour. Some cultural anchor points are so deeply embedded that there is no thought of questioning them and, at times of change, they are rarely revisited and thought through. This often results in changes being 'bolted on' to frameworks that are trying to resist being different.

One of the main difficulties for an organisation in identifying its own culture is that it is so much part of the thinking of the organisation. It requires people within the organisation to think about how they are thinking. Culture is also pervasive throughout the organisation, particularly in those with long histories. It is not therefore possible to stand in one part of the organisation and be objective about another. Some of the same culture, and particularly the anchor points, are informing the observations of that observer.

When new people join organisations they may be in a good position to notice what the cultural anchor points and assumptions are. However, they also wish to be accepted within their new organisation and rapidly adapt to the environment around them (Chen et al., 1997). This makes a healthy culture a strong training tool as it absorbs new staff into it. On the other hand, an unhealthy culture is a destructive force because it will still absorb staff into it, even though new staff may want to challenge it. We also learn our individual norms from organisational cultures we have been part of, for example school, clubs, and previous work settings (Nwachukwu and Vitell, 1997; Weber, 1996). So people who work in many different organisations in the sector will take the culture with them and reinforce it in other organisations.

The way to discover the culture of organisations is to notice patterns of behaviour, listen to the stories and anecdotes that staff tell each other, observe the symbols that exist, and ask visitors to comment on the reality that they see – to search for the 'theories in use'. To do this requires an open and non-defensive attitude, and a willingness to explore the very human level of an organisation.

The culture of a sector

The culture of a sector will be made up of pervasive principles and anchor points which can be observed across organisational boundaries. Different organisations will each have their own individual cultures, some of which will coincide with the sector culture, and some of which will be different and independent. It is important that different organisations maintain their individuality: this enables them to respond to particular requirements of their area of work, geographical area, and to provide choice for the users. It is also important for the sector as a whole to have a healthy culture to provide consistently high standards of front-line work, to enable the sector to adapt to changing circumstances, and to be able to act as an effective advocate for its client group in wider local and national planning about how best to meet the needs of people experiencing homelessness.

This chapter wishes to suggest what the key pervasive anchor points of culture are across the homelessness sector, and to think about the implications of those for service delivery and working with change in the sector. We particularly focus on the role of strategic managers. Chen, Sawyers and Williams (1997) identified that the organisational norms that people adjust to come primarily from the roles of power, such as the top management of the organisation, and the Team Leader for individual teams. They can be said to be the 'custodians' of the organisational culture and as such have a key role in reinforcing or changing norms and culture.

The rest of this chapter therefore describes the cultural anchor points of the homelessness sector and explores how these have developed and some of their implications for current practice.

Cultural anchor points of the homelessness sector

Organisations in the homelessness sector have a long history of responding to the needs of a group of people who are different from the rest of society and who feel ostracised by it. Over many decades, voluntary and charitable organisations have provided warmth, shelter, clothing, food and companionship to those who find themselves homeless. Like many voluntary and community organisations working with other client groups, their very existence has been due to failure of government policy and legislation, where statutory services are unable to meet all the needs of vulnerable people, and the State is seen as failing those people they work with, voluntary and community organisations arise to plug the gap. The focus of provision was on meeting practical needs and developing the structures to do this: providing a space to sleep, organising food and collecting and distributing clothing. This is a direct response to the most basic of presenting needs.

The anchor points of the sector can be seen in this initial humane response. Practical needs are met by organising structures that provide practical responses: the problem is defined in terms of a suffering of people, i.e. they do not have the practical things that are necessary for sustaining life. The need for action in providing for these basic needs results in the establishment of structures to gather, manage and deploy the necessary resources: the raising of money to meet the needs; teams of people who will do the tasks, such as collecting and organising clothing, or cooking and serving wholesome food; and the provision of clean and decent sleeping space.

As small organisations with local responses became bigger, their problems become to create structures to regularise the wider organisation and division of labour on a larger scale. The people required to do this work were mostly volunteers and did not need specialist skills outside of those they may already have in their own daily lives, such as cooking and cleaning. What was important in the people providing the service was that they were humane, had a respect for and wanted to engage with service users, and had a strong value base that was shared with the organisation and their co-workers. In the early days as the organisations were mainly from a Christian background this value base may also have been described as love (*agape*) or charity (*Caritas*) (Cloke et al., 2005). The respect ingrained in this value-base often meant that service users were not quizzed or interrogated about themselves. People providing the service, usually untrained volunteers, were dissuaded from asking about what led someone to become homeless and exploring that.

The **cultural anchor points** that have therefore developed in homelessness organisations are:

- Seeing the client group in terms of primarily a housing need.
- Meeting perceived needs by action, and practical tasks.
- Seeing organisational challenges in terms of structures to provide practical responses.
- Believing that the State's welfare structures and 'Professionals' have failed the client group.
- Needing 'helpers' with the right values rather than with specialist expertise.

These cultural anchor points have in some respects served the sector well. Its strong action-and-value-base has maintained its engagement with some very chaotic people, so it is constantly striving to create more provision to meet increasing need. However, as the sector and understanding of the client group have both changed, these anchor points have inhibited the sector's development to meet new challenges.

The homelessness sector has changed

Once predominantly a loose network of concerned individuals and organisations providing basic shelter, food and companionship, the homelessness sector has over the past 20–30 years transformed itself into a multi-million pound industry. In the 1980s and 1990s the sector experienced considerable expansion, responding to a growing problem of homelessness and changes in government legislation. In the major cities, the larger dormitory style hostels, such as the DHSS Resettlement Units, were replaced by smaller hostels. At the same time provision of small, more permanent, night shelters and hostels began to emerge in larger towns and in some rural areas, and the numbers of day centres grew from just seven in the 1970s to over two hundred in the 1990s (Crane et al., 2005).

During the past twenty years the nature, experience and understanding of homelessness has evolved. The changing needs of people who are homeless has been well documented, with agencies increasingly working with people with multiple needs, mental health difficulties, personality disorder and misusing alcohol and drugs (Van Doorn and Kain, 2003; Bevan and Van Doorn; Randall and Brown, 2002; Fleman, 1999). As the client group has become more complex, so there have been greater increases in understanding multiple needs and the social problems they face: consequently the sector has tried to broaden its own response.

A school of thought and provision has emerged that sees homelessness as not exclusively a housing issue. The growth of accommodation with staff support, access into professional services and the emergence of resettlement characterised the sector in the 1990s (Ham, 1996; Bevan, 1998). At the local and national level work has been undertaken on how to respond to homelessness and create effective ways of enabling people to be housed. This has led to organisations being asked, and required, to provide a more intrusive and organised response that focuses on the individual moving into and sustaining their own housing.

The homelessness sector has grown and adapted, but also struggled with how to meet the changing needs of individuals in a changing environment. It would seem that the needs both of the client group and the external environment have predominantly been met with changes of the *first order* i.e. with minor adaptations that do not change the paradigms, the cultural anchor points, of the organisation. Our observation is that the changes have been of *second order*, requiring the paradigms of the sector, its cultural anchor points, to change.

We can see how the cultural anchor points, having remained unchallenged and unchanged, still drive the operation, planning and development of the sector, at times *inhibiting* its response to change rather than helping.

Seeing the client group in terms of a housing need

This is one of the most entrenched anchor points whose acceptance dominates the shape of the homelessness sector. When you talk with people within the sector they are very clear that the reason the client group come to them is because of a range of serious life difficulties, such as exclusion from the family, drug and alcohol difficulties, mental health difficulties, coming out of institutions such as local authority care, prison and the armed forces, and histories of sexual and physical abuse. That they have also become homeless is the most recent crisis in a life of great trauma and deprivation.

Describing these very complex and painful experiences simply as 'homelessness' results in the primary response being one of housing, with other aspects seen as outside the remit of the organisation, or the remit of other specialist agencies. If the sector more accurately described its client group they would be seen in terms of their trauma, rather than in terms of their housing situation: thus the trauma would be the primary concern of the organisation that they have made contact with. Continuing to view people in terms of their homelessness rather than their trauma means that organisations and their funding streams, such as Supporting People, have been formed to deal with the secondary need rather than the core of most of their clients' difficulties. We therefore suggest that using a housing perspective to meet the needs of complex trauma is leaving unresolved difficulties for the sector.

Meeting perceived needs by action, and practical tasks

People who work in the sector tend to be very busy. This is partly because there is a lot to do, but also because people tend to do rather than reflect. People often say that they would like time to think about things but there is no time to stop and reflect. This means that things are often done automatically and because that's how they have always been done; the sector invests strongly in the cultural assumptions that have gone before. This is also mirrored by the client group, who will often act without thinking through the implications of what they are doing, and react to their immediate situation rather than understanding their trauma. A bias to action is certainly part of the sector's determination to keep providing a service. The focus on action, however, tends to push out the space for thinking and reflection; a space where cultural assumptions can be questioned and new expertise developed.

Seeing organisational challenges in terms of structures to provide practical responses

This anchor point can primarily be seen in the development of service provision and is very strong in managerial responses to organisational challenges. The preoccupation of managers remains the provision of structures by which primarily untrained workers will respond to the needs of service users. This has led to some excellent and innovative structures such as street outreach teams, provision of specialist accommodation for those who have been serially excluded, and small cluster housing. However, responses to service users' trauma have also been met with structural solutions such as time boundaried and formatted Keyworking. Management of structures has driven the organisational development rather than management of expertise in working with people who have experienced trauma. Therefore the role of strategic managers continues to be seen as to plan structures by which front line workers meet the needs of clients – which results in the structures created for recording and measuring activity and quality becoming used as tools for working with trauma.

Believing that the state's welfare structures and 'professionals' have failed the client group

Homelessness agencies have been able to take the side of their clients in seeing statutory agencies and the state as ineffective in responding to their needs. As the needs of service users in the sector have become more complex, and funding streams have dictated more planned work across different sectors and agencies, the homelessness sector has found itself needing to have an increasing amount of contact with statutory agencies. The effectiveness of this contact has been patchy. While there are examples of innovative working, much of the contact remains at the level of difficulties with structures and effectiveness of referral. The sector has looked to creating structures that will access particular services for clients rather than negotiate and establish good working relationships with other agencies based on co-working and multi-disciplinary attitudes. Many organisations within the sector remain frustrated, or hostile, to statutory agencies.

Needing 'helpers' with the right values rather than with specialist expertise

Although the sector has changed a great deal over many years, strong values remain at the heart of individuals and organisations (Van Doorn and Williamson, 2001; Cloke et al., 2005). Often, using staff and volunteers with the right values is seen as more important than the right expertise. It is very easy to have a discussion with workers at all levels in organisations about the social and political implications of homelessness, and an individual's rights to live their own life. This enables organisations to be places where people who experience exclusion are more willing to go. It is also part of why the sector continues to provide services in the face of challenging behaviour and limited resources (Johnsen et al., 2005).

However, as recognising problems, and solving them, is seen in terms of structure, and the values of the workforce is viewed more highly, the role of the worker is seen to be in running that structure rather than in having the expertise to do the necessary work. Although aware that people who experience homelessness have multiple needs, the sector has not invested in the expertise of its workers to understand and work with these needs (Bevan and Van Doorn, 2002).

The sector may recognise many of the changes it is experiencing, and those that are needed, but this cultural anchor point is slow to shift. This means that the provision of a very small amount of training, such as two or three days in a year, is considered as a very large investment and training budgets reflect this. There is a belief that learning from experience and learning on the job will build the necessary skills. This has some merit and is where many workers build up their intuitive skills. The difficulty is, what is learned is how to survive in the face of a challenging situation, rather than what best helps the client. That challenging situation is then also seen in terms of structure, so structures are devised to minimise difficulty rather than workers being trained in the skills to resolve trauma.

This attitude to building expertise for front line workers is also reflected in lack of training for managers and supervisors, because the focus is on devising structures and managing tasks more than on organisational development and skilled reflection.

Impact of the current cultural anchor points on the homelessness sector

The impact that these cultural anchor points have on the sector is significant. Some aspects of this culture have enabled the sector to meet new challenges head on, such as the introduction of Supporting People. However, the limiting nature of the anchors, particularly in terms of working effectively with the complexity of the trauma experienced by service users, results in significant difficulties for workers and organisations.

The development of structures

The dominance of structure has served the sector well in meeting the new contractual requirements of Supporting People, such as the need for written policies, quality assessment tools and performance monitoring. This drive is seen as bringing professionalism into the sector. It means that organisations have tighter financial systems and controls and are more equipped to deal with contracting and increased levels of scrutiny. They are better at having policies across all areas of operation, enabling the building of consistency and baseline standards for procedures and work. It also results in a stronger awareness of the need to assess quality and have procedures for recording work, achievements and outcomes.

However, Supporting People has been a challenge to many small organisations, and organisations across the homelessness sector have found that they have had to formalise their organisational structures and systems (Lowe, 2005). The structures that have been adopted tend towards the obvious pyramidal structures with managers identifying, clarifying and assessing the tasks of their subordinates.

At times of stress this focus on creating structures can dominate. Problems, challenges, and chaos can be seen as failings in, or a lack of, structure. This means that perceived problems can be met with creating new structures for tightening up existing structures. These tighter structures can appear, especially to strategic managers, as clear and providing solutions, but may be inappropriate ways of responding to the chaos of the client group, or providing creative and professional flexibility.

At an extreme level this can produce an organisation which has become very good at writing funding bids, can demonstrate all its policies and procedures, but where frontline staff are more clear about how to fill in forms than they are about how to work with the complex challenges of service users. Investing in structures without investing in expertise can result in service delivery failure (Park, 2002)

Action and structure over thinking

The frame for organisations in the homelessness sector remains the practical and structural. In the face of a demanding work place, the cultural anchor points push people towards action, with reflection and learning being seen as secondary. This means that spaces for reflection, study and learning, however relevant to the work, are not invested in and do not have strong cultural support. More time is put into action than basing intervention on reflection using coherent models. What can therefore be seen in the sector are changes in the way the client group is responded to by means of a number of innovative models of structure. There is not a strong development of models of working with trauma, change and human development. Time to reflect, such as in supervision, is too often taken up with task management – the delivery of structures.

An example of action and structure being dominant over thinking can be seen in how Keyworking has developed in the sector. Within the approach used, there is an expectation that service users will benefit from a formal Keyworking session every 2–4 weeks. Given the severe difficulties some service users experience it is unlikely that they will benefit from intervention with such long gaps, and it is even more unlikely that they will be able to manage fixed length meetings at pre-arranged times. Attendance at Keyworking sessions is consequently often poor.

Similarly, the process of Keyworking that has developed in the sector is planned around a structure – the Keyworking form. The basis of human change is in skilled guidance and reflection, not in following a set structure of questions. A form with headings used for Keyworking is useful for categorising and recording outcomes. It is very poor and ineffective in promoting change in the individual. Because workers are told by their organisations that this is what is offered to service users, they become frustrated that the clients are not engaging with the help offered. Initially, service users are much more likely to engage in support which is less formal, more flexible, has less boundaries, offers more regularity of contact and is more skilled in the nature of the trauma of the client group. If strategic managers understood this, they would plan the work based on the expertise to meet the needs of service users, leaving workers less frustrated and more able to help their clients.

By increasing the structures and requirements for service users, there may also be a danger that homelessness agencies become as inaccessible as the statutory agencies from which they wish to remain different.

Lack of constructive relationships with other agencies

Organisations within the sector continue to have difficult relationships with other agencies, particularly statutory ones. As a result research suggests that staff in specialist agencies are isolated from other organisations, with professional cultures constituting barriers to cooperation both within and between organisations and professions (Pannell and Parry, 1999). A number of the anchor points come together to inhibit change in this area. The continued feeling is that statutory agencies are failing the client group and the implicit blame in this remains dominant. This is influenced by an ambivalence about expertise, seeing the role of 'expert' as something belonging to those other organisations which they do not want to be like.

The reliance on structures results in time being invested in creating fixed and clear referral procedures, where an individual's specific need is identified and then formally referred to a specialist or statutory agency. The recurring pattern is for a referral to be made to statutory agencies without first having made a working relationship with that agency. Then when service users fail to get help, this re-confirms the belief that the statutory agencies have failed the client group.

Structural responses will never be very effective. Client needs will best be met with a multi-agency, multi-disciplinary response based on expertise in multiple needs and complex trauma. This is achieved by negotiating, building and maintaining ongoing working relationships at all levels, and for each service user.

Resolution of the situation would be for homelessness sector services to acknowledge that other services and sectors also have inadequate resources, experience restrictions and are coping with pressures within the current framework. Successful inter-agency work means replacing 'statutory services are bad and they have nothing in common with us' with 'we are all struggling: how can we work together?' The anchor point needs to change to one of co-working, and learning multi-disciplinary skills from others' including the statutory sector.

Repercussions of not investing in expertise

The failure to value expertise and the resulting lack of investment into building expertise at all levels of organisations is perhaps the most damaging of all the cultural anchors within the sector. As we have already discussed, this can be seen in the scant investment in training and development of all staff, and the paucity of skilled reflective practice. There are some significant repercussions of the underinvestment in expertise to be seen in the sector: under-skilled managers; workers confused about their role and seeing expertise as something someone else has; discounting the impact that working with clients' trauma has on staff and the organisation; and viewing, and often labelling, service users as 'difficult'.

Suspicion about expertise is seen throughout organisations. Strategic management is under-trained in the key aspects of the challenges affecting the sector – organisational change, organisational development, demonstrating quality, provision of service for multiple needs, and inter-agency or multi-disciplinary working. Management continues to be seen in terms of the development of structures to meet essentially housing needs rather than the management of expertise to respond to people's trauma. The action-based culture means that managers do not spend the time investing in the questioning of the assumptions they base their planning on – the use of reflection for strategic management, and cultural anchor points are being reinforced in apparently new developments. This sets the culture (including mission, policies, use of budgets etc.) for middle managers and front line staff, perpetuating the barriers to more responsive development.

Workers seeing that they need to address client trauma are also caught by the message that this is going into territory that is not their remit. Workers can find themselves trapped between responding to the needs of service users without the full approval and back-up of the organisation, and without adequate training; or restricting themselves to housing-related advice and guidance which will not in reality meet the needs of the service user. You hear this voiced as 'we are not counsellors'. Here the 'counsellor' is the name given to expertise.

Service users may be ambivalent about receiving help, and by turns, suspicious, aggressive and needy. This means that workers are regularly facing challenging and upsetting experiences. Even highly trained and experienced workers can feel overwhelmed by it. Because cultures are pervasive throughout organisations it is most likely that managers do not debrief from the stresses of their responsibilities, nor from the impact of difficult relationships in the organisation.

Lack of coherent models of working with client trauma, and lack of time to reflect, leads to little conscious management of the impact of the work on the worker. Talking about the impact with workers tends to focus on describing the problem; for the front line worker, the client, for the manager, the funding or contracting. What is often not worked with is debriefing from their experiences and letting go of the anxiety it causes them.

There is a great danger that managers do not recognise either how the impact from the client group creeps up through the organisation, nor how the anxiety about funding issues seeps down through it and impacts on frontline staff. When anxieties and stresses are not dealt with they do not go away but begin to drive the nature of problem solving and planning (Goleman, 1998). As the anxieties are increasingly denied it becomes ever more difficult to be aware of how they are influencing the thinking: but the solutions become less and less effective in resolving the problem, which in turn increases the anxiety.

This has severe implications for organisations:

- Workers and managers become hardened and cynical.
- Workers and managers begin to behave inappropriately and become 'difficult' workers.
- Increased sickness and disciplinary issues.
- Macho or aggressive and authoritarian behaviour.
- Increase in personal problems such as relationship tensions or drink problems.
- Blaming others, particularly managers, Supporting People teams, or other agencies.
- Blaming the clients for being 'difficult'.

Service users' 'difficult' behaviour is also seen in terms of their actions. The cultural anchor points create a response based on seeing the person in terms of housing need, focussing on action, and avoiding reflection and expertise. Where the trauma is not recognised the service user becomes labelled as 'difficult', or worse, they are related to in terms of their actions, and their needs are not responded to.

Workers' 'difficult' behaviour is similarly seen in terms of their actions and responded to with actions to deal with the behaviour. What is often not recognised is that most 'difficult' worker behaviour is from the impact of the 'difficult' work they do. Where workers have expertise in the client group and are skilfully de-briefed, they are less likely to begin to act in inappropriate ways.

There is a mirroring of how 'difficult' workers and 'difficult' service users are viewed and treated. The lack of reflection and expertise means the trauma is not addressed, so the behaviour of the individual becomes difficult. In these circumstances managers are most likely to label staff as being 'difficult' in the same way that staff may label clients as being 'difficult'. Where people are labelled 'difficult', they are most likely to continue to live up to that expectation. Understanding the anxiety and trauma is more likely to resolve the difficulty.

'Difficult behaviour' increases the sense of dissatisfaction throughout the organisation, and the organisation can expect an increase in the level of sicknesses and absenteeism, a lowering of the worker's motivation, and probably an increase in disciplinary procedures. It is the job of strategic managers to work with not only the tasks and policies of the organisation but also to manage these emotive impacts on the human beings who are the workers that do the work of the organisation.

Conclusion

Homelessness organisations and the sector have come to a critical point. Over the last three decades the sector has developed from a network of small local agencies, offering basic shelter, food and companionship to a complex multi-million pound industry offering a range of accommodation, support and specialist services to meet the complex needs of people who experience homelessness. Its anchor points, which developed out of the very practical nature of services thirty years ago, have enabled the sector to grow and maintain engagement with a group of people that are often excluded by other services. However, these paradigms that have served the sector well are now its major barrier to meeting the current needs of its client group and also that of government and local commissioners.

Throughout this chapter we have taken a close and critical look at the sector's cultural anchor points, highlighting how they came about and what impact they are currently having on service design and delivery. We have shown how culture is an important driver in organisations and can both inhibit and promote the very best of practice and outcomes for service users.

We believe that homelessness organisations find themselves caught between feeling driven to provide a service by their can-do attitude, often without the resources and relationships they would like, and hindered by misdefining the client group as simply homeless, and seeing the issues in terms of structure. The failure to invest in reflection and expertise means they are not finding a means of questioning themselves about these assumptions or basing their work on skilled responses to the actual needs of the client group. Only by reflecting on and challenging the deepest paradigms, the cultural anchor points of the sector, can the sector begin to create the solutions to the challenges it currently faces.

The sector requires mature managers who can think beyond their experience and training. This requires self-critical reflection. Managers need to learn how to test the cultural assumptions against the world around them and the needs of the client group, and enable whole organisations to adapt and change their culture in relation to meeting the client groups' needs in the current funding and political environment.

But more than this, the sector needs to explore, discuss and identify, through honest appraisal and reflection, its culture and how it both supports and frustrates its work and its ability to meet the changes it faces. We hope that this chapter will contribute to opening out this debate, encouraging others to reflect on the observations we make and the challenges they present.

Chapter 9

Workers in the homelessness industry: towards an identity

Mike Seal

The problem of homelessness is intrinsically bound up with the self conceptions and interests of those who define and respond to it. Workers depend on the homeless for their sense of identity and or livelihood.

(Brandon et al., 1980)

Youth work is a profession 'in itself' (it meets all the objective criteria) but not yet a profession 'for itself' (self-conscious and aware of its identity and its obligations).

(Sercombe, 2000)

Introduction

Perhaps unsurprisingly, the question of whether workers in the field of homelessness have a discernible 'identity' has not been the subject of much concern in the literature. Even anecdotal evidence on the make up of the workforce, such as in the discussions I have had with agencies or as expressed in their annual reports, have tended to emphasise its heterogeneous nature, with a pride in this supposed diversity. However, as Brandon (1980) indicates, the question of who works with homeless people is not neutral. It is not enough to say we are a broad church or that we have a diverse workforce. Taking Sercombe's framework (2000), albeit about another related field in another country (youth work in Australia), I contend that we are indeed a profession 'in itself', having many of the characteristics of a profession, but we have yet to develop effective self-awareness. While law and statutes concerning homelessness and homeless provision have made us aware of our obligations, who we are, the 'cultures' we work within (see Chapter 8), what the attitudes we bring to and develop through the industry are, remain more of a mystery.

This chapter is therefore an attempt to take us closer towards becoming a profession 'for itself'. It will attempt to do two things. Firstly to explore what the characteristics of those who work with the homeless are, whether these characteristics coalesce into a worker 'identity', or identities, and what factors influence the formation of such identities. It will secondly examine how we learn to be a worker in the homeless field, and, perhaps most importantly, how we can therefore impact upon these cultures and identities.

As well as existing literature, I will be drawing on an ongoing survey I am conducting with workers, which explores demographic makeup, working conditions and the attitudes they bring to the work. As a rough approximation of the limitations of the survey, I would say that it surveys paid workers for whom working with homeless people is their occupation. It has a bias towards the south of England, towards people who access skills-based training and for workers in hostels. In terms of numbers 102 (at time of writing) is not a huge sample, but neither is it insignificant. As such I do not claim that these figures are definitive: rather they are indicative, and I intend them to inform the debate. To complement and hopefully enrich the raw survey data, I will draw on my experiences of training workers on these issues (over 2500 practitioners in the last 14 years) where the debates about what it means to be a worker in this field are often played out.

Exploring worker identities: the literature

Eraut (1994) feels we should not underestimate the socialisation process of becoming a professional, with its learned set of solutions and understandings. In particular we should not underestimate the psychological barriers to breaking away from this homogeneity. To illustrate, I remember talking on a Groundswell promotional video (an organisation working to increase user involvement in homeless services) about how, having worked in the industry for years, I felt challenged by the organisation's ideas. This was despite their views encapsulating my position on entering the service. I had become encultured into a way of viewing things, and clients, that had become my 'common sense'. Bandura (1977) starts to examine this homogeneity, saying that to understand our professional identities we need to look at how we learn to be professionals.

Lave and Wenger (1991) defined the ways we learn how to be a professional as *situated learning*. Learning is less about the acquisition of certain forms of knowledge but resides in social relationships of the workplace, and how we learn to 'be' a worker (Smith, 2002). As William F. Hanks puts it in his introduction to their book: 'Rather than asking what kind of cognitive processes and conceptual structures are involved, they ask what kinds of social engagements provide the proper context for learning to take place' (1991). It not so much that professionals acquire structures or models to understand the world, but they participate in frameworks that have that structure. In this there is a concern with identity, with learning to speak, act and think in ways that make sense in the community. To these ends this helps me define what I mean by the term 'characteristics' of workers. As well as looking at some of our demographic characteristics I want to explore how we speak, act and think in our roles.

However, I also want to reiterate the importance of my second aim for the chapter, an examination of how we learn to become a worker in this field. To these ends Tucker set criteria that any explanation of professional identities would need to meet to be effective. He considers that such frameworks should:

1. *Explore the impact of ideological effects on the socio-political terrain and the condition of existence for those working with homeless people.*
2. *Assist analysis of those forms of discourse that are used to define particular forms of work.*
3. *Show how ideas are struggled over and contested at various levels of experience.*
4. *Demonstrate how such matters directly impact upon the professional identities which individuals and groups adopt in their everyday work.*

(Tucker, 2004)

These criteria will therefore form the framework for my conclusion, and to a degree will shape my analysis. In examining workers' professional identities I will seek to explore how those are constructed and contested and the impact of this on the work that they do. I will seek to explore also the constructions of homeless people that underpin the content of these identities, how they are re-enforced by the structures of services performed in the name of homeless people and the ideological positions that lie behind them.

Existing characterisations of homeless workers

Interestingly, Smith and Wright (1992), in one of the earliest explorations of user perceptions of the old resettlement units, also surveyed workers' views on clients and the service. They found that there were two dominant perspectives, which is as close as we get to identities so far.

The traditionalist view

- The client group is seen as inadequate, almost culpable, and beyond help.
- The client group, and the hostel regime, represented a problem to be contained hidden and policed.
- The hostel regime should be highly controlled and strictly enforced.
- The underlying attitude towards residents was oppositional, even hostile.
- There was a resentment of the independence and 'comfort' of undeserving poor and complaints of leniency and softness towards them.
- Reforms were disapproved of, seen as inappropriate and resisted passively or actively.

The reformist view

- The client group are unfortunate fellow humans.
- They need patient support rather than control.

- The hostel regime should be essentially one of 'treat as would be treated'.
- The rules should be kept to a minimum – and be implemented flexibly and liberally.
- The emphasis should be on help in solving the underlying problem behind residents' current positions.
- The emphasis should increasingly be on resettlement.
- The traditionalist regime is needlessly repressive and not a long term solution.

This typology is useful both as a starting point and as a reference point for our current exploration. While I would not seek to produce such a binary account, I would like to establish if there are tendencies in workers' views and construction and importantly, if any of these groupings are likely to conflict.

Factors in being a good worker

I set out in table form below workers' ratings of what they thought were the most important qualities in a worker:

Worker qualities	Most important (%)	2nd Most important (%)	3rd Most important (%)	Totals (%)
Been homeless	4	13	12	29
Caring	16	20	21	57
Experience	16	13	18	47
Knowledge	10	24	37	71
Listening	45	30	10	85
Qualified	7	2	3	12

People seemed to have an obvious model of what makes for a good worker. Interestingly, these results were fairly uniform across different types of workers, i.e. hostel based, floating support etc. Being able to listen to clients was the most popular reason by a significant degree; a fairly close second quality being the level of knowledge a worker has, followed by caring, and then experience. An interesting message here is the weight given to listening skills and knowledge. People seem to be operating very much on a model of people skills and specific knowledge being primarily important.

As a model of working this is an interesting combination. I talked in a previous work about there being several models of resettlement (Seal, 2005) with Australian models tending to emphasise the importance of the worker and client relationships and (Winteringham, 2000) a more British model that emphasises practical knowledge. Workers seemed to be seeing the value of both.

However far less value was placed upon having personal experiences of homelessness, general work experience, or being qualified. Perhaps value being placed on experience of homelessness is due to the low levels of ex-users becoming workers, with the survey finding 16 per cent of workers having previously been users of care services. Unfortunately there is little comparative data on the extent of ex-service users becoming workers in other fields. However, there is a policy that may give us an indication on rules about service users coming back as workers, or volunteers.

> *Current and former drug and alcohol misusers should not be considered or overlooked with regard to employment by reason of their substance misuse alone. People with experience of drug misuse and drug treatment can be effective employees in drug services, particularly if they receive the support required for all new employees, including induction and appropriate training.*
>
> (NTA, 2004)

The above quote is taken from *Guidelines on Employment in Drug Treatment Services*. The guidelines were a reaction to the common practice of bans for periods of years before an ex-user could become a worker again. Groundswell (2006) recently found that many agencies reflected this attitude and are still running arbitrary rules about when a user can come back, normally one or two years. It is interesting that in the parallel field of drug use, where it could be argued that there is a more genuine fear of people relapsing, government guidelines advise against such arbitrary rulings. Most agencies to whom I mentioned the 16 per cent figure for service users were surprised by how high this was. This seems to indicate that admitting that you are an ex-user is still taboo for worker', and also how under researched this area is. Regarding workers' attitudes towards qualifications and experience, Brandon is illuminating on the subject:

> *Workers were recruited for a sense of mission and political or religious commitment. Idealism was preferable to pragmatism. There was a suspicion of the more structured and less impassioned approach of the professional.*
>
> (Brandon, 1980)

Brandon's quote seems only half-true here. Caring was only third in the list of values, knowledge and skills being rated above this. However, the suspicion about qualifications is borne out and reflects my experience in training. There seem to be two factors at play here, a justification of people's positions and a cultural attitude. The self-justification may stem from the fact that only 21 per cent of respondees had a professional qualification, and only 14 per cent a professional qualification from the care sector. This figure is indeed low compared to other care fields. In nursing the figure is 74 per cent qualified (NHS, 2002) and in youth work, 57 per cent (JNC, 2004), though this latter figure is even deceptive as, within the remaining 43 per cent, a large number are locally qualified. Even in social care, where the government has set a target of 50 per cent of the workforce being qualified as a minimum standard and recognises that there is a serious issue with unqualified staff (Skills for Care, 2005) the figures are 39 per cent for children's homes, 34 per cent in adult learning and even 28 per cent for domiciliary care workers.

There is a common thread of sentiment across a wide range of (homeless) organisations that represents an ambivalence about learning, training and qualifications. What matters is what people can do, not the qualifications they have.

(Matthews, 2005)

As Matthews above indicates, people not being qualified seems to have fostered a culture where qualifications are not valued. I have noted elsewhere this anti-intellectual and anti-professional trend (Seal, 2005) amongst workers and organisations, as have Cain and Van Doorn in Chapter 8 of this book. However if we examine people's levels of education we find respondees tended to be well educated with 44 per cent being educated to degree level and 11 per cent to post-graduate level. Twenty per cent were educated to 'A' level standard (NVQ level 3) and 20 per cent to GCSE (NVQ level 2). Only 5 per cent of people had no qualifications at all. There seems to be a big split between those who are university educated and those who are not. Whether these differences are divisions is unclear, but they would seem to have at least the potential to be so, particularly when there is an anti-intellectual culture to clash against. Otherwise graduates would seem to need to buy wholesale into the idea that they have not got anything to add to the sector by their qualifications.

That people did not necessarily value experience in the field was interesting and seemed in contrast to what I pick up in training, experience being seen there as the alternative benchmark to qualification. Of interest here is what we mean by experience, as at worst it can simply be time served. Sercombe (2000) notes that in professions that resist professionalisation and accreditation, there often exist 'grandfather clauses' that give people credit simply for having worked in the sector a long time. By this measure our result can be seen positively, in that people are valuing skills over the length of time people have been practising. However underneath these figures there was a more basic explanation of self-justification: 33 per cent of workers had been in the field for one year or less, with 50 per cent having been in the field for two years or less.

There may be several reasons for this; there has undoubtedly been an expansion in services since the development of Supporting People and a consequent influx of new workers to the sector. There was also a direct correlation between people's length of service and the value they had put on experience, the longer they had worked in the field the more they valued it. Length of experience seemed to have more potential to be a more general source of division. The average time served in the field was five years, which, given the above, indicates a distinct division between workers who had been in the field for some time and those who were relatively new. Indeed, for those 50 per cent who had worked in the field for over two years the average length of service was seven and a half years. The important question would seem to be whether these potential divisions are played out elsewhere in people's view of their work. Unfortunately we will see later that they are.

Motivations for working with homeless people

When asked for their motivations for doing this kind of work, the responses were:

Motivation	Primary motivation (%)	2nd most important motivation (%)	3rd most important motivation (%)	Totals (%)
To help people	17	38	32	87
To help people to help themselves	67	24	4	95
Because there were jobs in the sector	3	10	6	19
Because I did not want to have an office job	7	6	6	19
To help people get their rights	6	24	50	80

Perhaps unsurprisingly, people said helping people to help themselves was their primary motivation, both overall and as a first choice. This is notable as being more popular than to help people, which as an answer is similar but has a different implication for our role and for where we locate the possible solutions, i.e. in ourselves or in the client. In terms of bias this may well be the answer that people felt they ought to put as opposed to their genuine motivations (a common response in surveys such as this – Miles and Huberman, 1994). Even in this case, the result is useful in illuminating the common culture that people feel they should have. It seems in direct contrast with the traditionalist view, noted by Smith and Wright (1992) and the missionary zeal sought by agencies that Brandon talks about.

The desire to make 'important contributions to individuals and society' showed a significant negative effect upon people's interest in working with the poor and homeless ... these findings raise questions regarding the extent to which altruism is useful in shaping people's desire to work with the poor or homeless.

(Perry, 2003)

The above quote by Perry is interesting in that he found those with altruistic motivations were likely to become disillusioned quite quickly and leave the service. This calls into question the usefulness of the motivations in the table. Perry found that an alternate perspective, such as the worker feeling they had a professional skill and were taking that skill to a particular context was more sustainable. Linked to this is the fact that a sizeable minority of people listed other motivations, such as not wanting to work in an office or simply that there were jobs in the sector, as one of their top three motivations. I found this interesting, not least that people would admit this as it may again be marking a moving away from people having to see this work as a vocation, or a calling. Whether people would admit this in a 'public' arena is another thing. Sometimes one forgets how powerful, and hidden, cultural assumptions can be. For example, I remember my first training session in which somebody admitted such a motivation. I had asked people to give their names and how they got into the job. Most people had given motivations such as expressed above, they were drawn to the work, they had wanted to give etc. Then one man said that he had been a miner, and when he was made unemployed he realised he needed to retrain. He noticed that there were a lot of jobs in the Guardian on a Wednesday (where jobs in social care are advertised), found out that the way to get into the field was to volunteer, which he could do for a while on his redundancy money. Now he worked in the field and enjoyed it. It was strange to hear this tale, for while no one denied his skills, his colleagues could vouch for that, and no one could say that his motivations were not reasonable, it jarred somewhat: such is the nature of culture.

Attitudes towards work

Respondees were given a series of attitudinal statements about their work and asked whether they strongly agreed, agreed, disagreed or strongly disagreed with the statement. The idea of this was again to establish whether there is a common culture amongst workers with regards to their approaches and beliefs about the work. Of these statements there were nine where people had a strong feeling one way or another (defined as 85 per cent or above taking one view), seven where there was a clear majority on the issue but also a sizeable minority of opinion (defined as 65–85 per cent), and eight statements where opinion was divided (defined as where opinions were between 45–55 per cent either way). There were no opinions where people were between the 55–65 per cent either way, which says something in itself.

Issues where there is a consensus

People strongly agreed with the following statements:

1. Most clients need a 'reality check' about the housing they are going to get.
2. Most clients need help to make sense of their lives.
3. Clients may need to be educated to believe in themselves, as they have often been 'educated' not to.
4. The power to change, within limits, lies with the client themselves.
5. We should admit our mistakes to clients.
6. If we think a client is doing something that is not in their interests we have a duty to tell them.
7. It is the duty of workers to bring to the attention to those in power the activities of agencies or colleagues that contribute to hardship and suffering of clients.

8. It is the duty of workers to train, become qualified and keep up to date with developments in practice.
9. We should make more use of the informal support clients give each other.

The first five statements are largely about the nature of the relationships we should have with clients and where the dynamic of change, where it is needed, lies. Statements one and two say something about the state clients are when they come to us. They call into question a simplistic advice model of homelessness as being about 'sign-posting', which is the mainstay and backbone of many homeless strategies (ODPM, 2002). Given my experiences of training I was not surprised to find workers thought most clients were unrealistic about their housing options; it is a common complaint. However, such things have implications for services, at least in the relative emphasis in workers' jobs. In a previous work (Seal, 2006) I noted how many agencies, with regards to housing, portrayed the worker role as something like 'to help clients access appropriate housing for their needs'. In fact a closer approximation of the role would seem to be 'to help clients come to terms with the accommodation that they will eventually get, and see how it could help their situation'. While one could argue that the latter role is implicit in the former, I think it goes deeper than this.

When I have used this as a training exercise, workers have tended to see the agency version as the aforementioned sign-posting role, rather than a more developmental process. The emphasis was on 'accessing' and 'housing', rather than 'helping' and 'appropriate'. Similarly the fact that workers felt most clients needed help with making sense of their lives, reinforces the importance of our cognitive work with clients (Seal, 2005). Again, looking at my previous work, the common role given to workers of 'working with people towards gaining and sustaining appropriate accommodation' should be more appropriately expressed as 'helping someone to understand the situation they are in, and the part accommodation plays in them changing it'. This emphasis also has implications for what people think is the client's role in assessment, an issue that workers were divided upon and one I will come back to later.

Statement three is about self-belief, as are two and three, but also takes a more political stance. It is reminiscent of Friere's notion of 'conscientisation' (Friere, 1972) whereby people need to be educated to develop consciousness of their situation, to understand what has happened to them and why. This is not necessarily because people do not have the innate capabilities or the intelligence to do so, but that the processes they have been through, personally and particularly structurally, have discouraged them from doing so. I traced in my resettlement book (Seal, 2005) how the homelessness sector itself can take an active part in this process of deskilling. Workers at least seemed to recognise the first element of this, that homeless people are skilled, but that they may need to be helped to see this. This means that workers acknowledge that part of their role should be educative, not in the information giving sense but as a dialectical process with the client. However, this attitude was not consistent, as we shall see when it comes to looking at attitudes towards assessment.

Statement four, about the power to change lying with the client, develops on from the third statement, but from a slightly different angle. It has several implications. Firstly that many of the changes to be made are internal to the person, rather than being about external changes. Secondly, by implication, that the person themselves needs to want to change, or at least has ambiguities that can be worked upon. I think that combined this gives out an important message about the limitations of the power of the worker. Many practitioners have complained on courses about being expected to work with people who do not want to, or show any potential of being able to, engage with them. Examples are: when agencies are expected to 'rescue' failing tenancies, often through local authority arranged contracts, regardless of whether the person wants an intervention; or where the tenancy is unlikely to succeed, even if they do engage, the issues the person is facing make sustainment unrealistic.

Statements five and six again relate to our relationship with clients but are more about workers' responsibilities in the relationship. While number five, admitting our mistakes, seems to be obvious, many practitioners on my courses admit to worrying that to do so may make the client lose confidence in them; or even tell the manager who will hold this against them. This is all the more complicated by the tendency of many workers (Seal, 2005) to promise, often unconsciously, more than they can deliver, especially when the client is pushing for us to be able to achieve or provide miracles. Number six, telling clients they are acting against their own interests, seems important, as it makes a statement that a worker has a duty and a right to intervene in such situations. This is important because it is counter to many formulations of being 'non-directive' or 'person centred' (Grant, 1999). Workers seem more drawn to other interpretations of person centredness that can embrace more direct interventions (Bozarth and Evans, 2000). This would seem to be compatible with the adoption by many agencies of such tools as 'motivational interviewing' and 'solution-focused therapy' as frameworks for intervention (Seal, 2005). However, workers' access to such courses are by no means universal, nor are they always valued by the workers themselves, as we shall see later.

Statements seven and eight are about the more general responsibilities of workers, I would say as professionals, to keep up to date with current developments and to report any bad or damaging practice we encounter. These kind of statements are common in Statements of Principles of other care sectors (Banks: 1995) and as such can be viewed as statements about our professionality, although unlike most other professions, the sector still does not have a consistent statement of values. The debate as to whether we should professionalise as a service has, to a degree, been had (Seal, 1999), at least at a strategic level. Interestingly this consensus has not been borne out in the survey. When asked whether the service is becoming too professional or not, while 71 per cent of workers agreed with this, 29 per cent did not. The interpretation of what we mean by 'professional' is a debate in itself and certainly workers' responses probably came from a multitude of perspectives and interpretations: there is also a sizeable minority that has a negative reaction to the term. Positively, even for those that do not embrace the term, these two statements seem to be important to people. A question it seems to throw up for the sector is how they are to put them into practice.

A part of this is training, something to be explored in greater detail in the final chapter of this book, Conclusion. Attitudes of workers towards training were generally positive, although it is important to say that there is a bias here as respondees were accessed through training. Positively, 75 per cent of respondees regarded it as essential and 71 per cent saw it as valuable time to reflect on their work. In spite of the biased sample, people were still sceptical about training. Fifteen per cent saw it as taking away from face-to-face work, 10 per cent were there under protest, having come only because their manager had sent them on it and 3 per cent thought that training can be an excuse for not changing things. This echoes earlier reflections that sometimes more structural issues in organisations can be dressed up as issues for the worker, rather than recognising that they are more fundamental.

In terms of what training people can access, it seems that people are still given limited options. Positively, 24 per cent felt that they could access any relevant training, presumably after they had made the case to their organisation. The most popular type of course people felt they had access to was one or two day courses (53 per cent), such as the ones people were on, and 51 per cent had access to in-house training. Fewer people felt they could access vocational qualifications such as NVQs (19 per cent), and only 11 per cent felt they could undertake courses that involved day release (11 per cent). Perhaps reflecting the aforementioned anti-intellectual tendency, only 4 per cent of people felt they could have access to academic qualifications. Even if this figure includes people who may have access, but are not interested in such courses, it is still a reflection of an anti-intellectual tendency in the sector, or at least an explanation of people's cynicism – you cannot value what you do not get. These last few figures on qualifications seem to give out a clear message that people want them, but are not necessarily getting access to them.

Issues with a clear majority view but also a sizeable minority opinion

While having a relatively clear majority may seem like a positive, to have a sizeable minority is potentially divisive in that the minority may become marginalised and a defensive clique. People mainly agree that:

1. Many projects end up making clients dependent on them.
2. Clients should be responsible for assessing their situation and what to do about it.
3. The needs of individual clients should be balanced with the needs of other clients in the service.
4. We do not involve clients as much as we should in our services.

People mainly disagreed that:

5. On balance, homeless agencies do more harm than good.

6. The service is becoming too professionalised.
7. The power we have over clients gets in the way.

The first statement seems to me to be a powerful one. For as long as I have worked in the field, there has been a debate about the extent to which we make clients dependent on our services. It seems this debate is still a real concern. What we mean by making dependent, which services we are talking about and how they do this remain issues to be explored. The most extreme expression of feeling seems to be elicited through statement five, about doing more harm than good. While a majority of people disagreed (84 per cent), 16 per cent of people thought this was a true statement, 6 per cent strongly agreeing. The figures may well have been higher if it had been phrased as 'occasionally', or 'in some respects'. As it is, people are asked to make an overall judgement, and 16 per cent do this quite harshly, and this is people who work in the field. Whether this is a 'considered' judgement or one given out of frustration we do not know. Even if it is borne out of cynicism, we need to ask ourselves as a sector how a worker could get to the point of making such a statement about something they are involved in.

Taking these issues on a more personal level, most workers (71 per cent) did not feel that the power they had over clients got in the way. I examined people's work context to see if this was a significant factor in the research, because it could be argued that this view may be more predominant in accommodation-based projects where workers have a housing management as well as a support role. However this did not seem to be a factor. As always there is a question of interpretation, but is seems that for 29 per cent of people power was an issue. I have observed a similar divide in training when issues of power come up. The contention in training is whether we are considering direct power, such as the ability to kick people out, or implicit power such as assumed knowledge in the worker or fear of the worker's power, even when they do not have any. For this reason I suspect it is an issue for more people than this. Nevertheless, it seems that it is an issue that a sizeable minority are struggling with.

While one might expect that workers would feel that clients are responsible for assessing their own situation (statement two), it was this statement where people were most divided in this category, with 66 per cent agreeing and 36 per cent disagreeing. Interpretation is again an issue: in training people tend to find contentious the word responsibility (the worker often having an ultimate legal or organisational responsibility), and embark upon semantic debates around the word assessing (whether this is something which a person can do about a third party) and the limitations to both in terms of an individual's cognitive functioning. However these points normally arise from the 'yes, but' camp rather than the 'no' camp. The dominant 'no' view tends to take a stronger line that reflects the quote below.

The emphasis in the eighties on pathos and pathology on the streets has obscured the strengths of the homeless and the very poor and has tended to portray them as judgemental dupes who lack political and social awareness of themselves and of their conditions.

(Warner, 1993)

For some workers, clients are not capable or knowledgeable enough to make assessments. One view of professionalism is that the professional is the person who takes responsibility and has capability, and that the nature of a client is that they do not. However, as Hoch and Slayton (1994) note above, professionals often assume that homelessness can only be helped with the aid and through the guidance of professionals. The ensuing debate is, as one might imagine, often about workers' fundamental attitudes towards their clients and echoes Smith and Wright's (1992) traditional and reformist views.

The fourth statement, that we do not involve clients enough in services, seems to stem from this debate, albeit often at a more organisational level. While there was slightly less of a divide, with 72 per cent agreeing with the statement and 28 per cent not, this still seems nonetheless significant. The wider factor here is that user involvement in services has become more of a policy and practice debate in recent times, with it being a core feature of the *Quality Assessment Framework* (QAF) for supporting people (ODPM, 2004). It seems, again, that while a sizeable majority are accepting its prominence, a significant minority are rejecting it. In training, a common reaction to the idea of user involvement is a cynicism about the organisation's motives. However, this does not seem to be the sentiment expressed here. One could argue that perhaps this is because user involvement is fully developed in those organisations. I would contend that this is unlikely as many authors (Valasco, 2001; Wyner, 1998) note how user involvement and participation is particularly underdeveloped in homeless services. Why this may be will be the subject of a forthcoming book. All I will say here is that there are barriers to be overcome with workers, and probably managers, and a barrier that is attitudinal. Wilcox (1995) gives us a starting point for this when he discussed how fears about user involvement normally stem from a fear of letting go of control and a lack of trust throughout the system, from managers down to the clients.

Finally, people seemed overall to have a utilitarian view of balancing a user's needs with the needs of others using the service. However, the divide was again 68 per cent for and 32 per cent against. In training, the divide has largely been along ideological lines between those who are utilitarian, often seeing themselves as involved in managing a community, and those who come from an individual rights perspective, and see themselves as advocates for their clients. Indeed the split is 50/50 on this statement for those who see fighting for the rights of clients as one of their primary motivations. Interestingly, my experience of organisational responses to this dilemma is that they are contradictory, and determined by practical needs rather than principles. Again in training, when participants have explored their agency's policy statements and assessment guidelines, they tended to talk about examining and meeting the needs of individuals. However, cultures of practice very much seemed to be about creating 'balanced communities' or even just avoiding what are seen as volatile mixes of clients, particularly in residential settings. These considerations seem to disappear if there were voids, financial imperatives dominating. Given this lack of consistency, one could see potential for the existing divides to be exacerbated.

Disagreement

While the previous group of statements had the potential to isolate a sizeable minority there were a number of statements where people were evenly divided. Though it could be argued that they may not be significant and are just differences of opinion, I would argue, at least in some cases, that they are evidence of underlying tensions and cultural clashes. This is particularly so where the organisational stances on those issues exacerbate the situation, often through conflicting messages. Statements where people were divided in this way were:

1. Working with homeless people is largely common sense.
2. The practical support we give to people is the most important thing.
3. Supporting People has meant that we spend less time with the clients.
4. It is more important to spend time talking to clients than writing up our interventions with them.
5. Most clients do not like things to be written down about them.
6. We should share our opinions of other services with clients.
7. The care system does not work.

The first statement seems to be a classic debate in this field, and having trained many workers I was not surprised at this result. I discussed the notion of common sense amongst workers in my previous book (Seal, 2005): suffice it to say that this view tends to go along with an anti-intellectual and anti-analytical stance on homelessness and working with homeless people. Positively, this stance did not correlate much with the statement that we have a duty to train and keep abreast of current developments, but it does betray what kind of training and developments people may value. Regarding the second statement, I also traced in my previous book how organisations have tended to over-emphasise the practical aspects of the work, reinforced by some narrow interpretations of Supporting People's definitions of housing related support. In training, it is a noticeable divide amongst workers. My training does tend to emphasise the non-practical aspects of the work, both as a counter and also because this is the aspect I think we often do well. Reactions to this emphasis reflect this divide, some welcoming the different tack and others feeling it to be not as relevant. More recent developments have tended to emphasise other aspects of the work, such as the importance of social networks and attending to the emotional side of homelessness (Lemos and Crane, 1998; Lemos, 2006). The relative importance of practical aspects of the work seems then to be a division reflected both in organisations and in policy, reinforcing worker divisions.

The next three statements relate to the collation of information. Again, I have previously traced how, historically, workers did not have to write down much, largely because of the funding regimes they were subject to, but that, with the advent of Supporting People, they have a larger administrative load (Seal, 2005). Statement three seems to reflect this change, with the perceived expense being the amount of face-to-face work which is done with clients. At the same time, taking our lead from Brandon, workers were recruited for their face-to-face skills, rather than their administrative ability. I would contend that these combine to develop a culture that is antagonistic to recording and to the written aspect of the job.

Statements four and five, on writing, seem to be reflective of this culture, rather than justifications of it. Organisations have had to change, given the administrative burden of Supporting People, but I am sure this has not been an easy transition and may well be seen as a necessity rather than a positive development by said organisations. Interestingly, this was a divide along time-served lines: the longer someone had worked in the field, the more antagonistic they were towards administration and Supporting People in particular. Again, it seems that we are experiencing a shift that is reflected in worker attitudes. This has been noticeable in training; I have felt that I have to spend less time winning over hearts and minds to the importance of administration, but the division between new and old workers to the sector is marked.

The division on whether we should share our opinions of other agencies with clients (statement six) was an interesting one. The majority were in favour of not doing so (60 per cent), but it was also the topic with the most extremes, with 11 per cent strongly disagreeing and 8 per cent strongly agreeing. In training there have normally been two debates around the topic. The first debate concerned whether we have a right to give our opinion as it may be biased; the counter being that we will act upon our biases anyway and we may as well make these explicit. The second debate is whether it is 'professional' to talk about other agencies in such a way; the counter being that some interpretations of professionalism (Brandon, 1996) specifically say we have a duty to do so. Organisationally, and in the wider context of policy, there again seems to be duplicity. Government programmes from the Rough Sleepers Initiative onwards have given out a dual message, encouraging organisations to work together, while at the same time making them compete in a competitive funding environment. New Labour, as expressed through Supporting People have accelerated this. On the one hand they encourage 'joined-up thinking' through demanding borough-wide homelessness strategies and specific standards relating to inter-agency working in the QAF. On the other hand agencies remain in a competitive framework for funding and an environment of cut backs which further encourages organisational defensiveness.

A final division was whether people thought the care sector works or not. This may seem a slightly glib comment, but it can also be fundamental as it can shape our interventions. In training I ask people which of the following statements best reflects their roles: 'To refer clients onto the appropriate services and agencies that will meet their needs' or 'to help clients understand what agencies are out there, which of the needs they will and will not be able to help with, and how they should go about getting that service'. The answers people give tend to reflect which side of that division they are on. It may also affect how we view finishing the work with a client. Is it when their needs have been met, or is it that we actually leave when we think they are OK enough? In addition the client's judgment about this may not be the same as ours, and this is part of what we need to prepare for.

On a wider level this divide mirrors whether workers or agencies take the aforementioned 'structural' or 'individual' view of homelessness, although the latter is in a form far more benign than in the literature. Agency positions can often be expressed in mission statements such as 'ending street homelessness'. Is this, as Hoch and Slayton's (1989) view, a reflection of the fact that 'workers and agencies are unlikely to say homelessness is intractable and will tend not towards radical solutions but reformist ones because they serve their interests', or is such an aspirational statement aiming high and not being defeatist?

Conclusion

As I said at the beginning of the last section, I would view these divisions and minority positions as more than just interesting. Returning to Tucker's (2004) framework on understanding professional identities, I have hopefully explored aspects of the last three criteria. The divisions and minority positions of workers are largely mirrored by divisions internal to and between agencies, and in the duplicity of governmental policy towards homelessness. As such they will be played out between workers in how we work with and treat clients, what aspects of the work we emphasise, and how we write them up. Organisationally it affects things like policies, like personal boundaries, our strategic priorities, in such things as the extent to which we involve users. The divisions will mean that our policies may continue to be inconsistent, either in how they are expressed or how they are implemented.

If we examine the first criteria, *to explore the impact of ideological effects on the socio-political terrain and the condition of existence for those working with homeless people*, we find a real hotchpotch of ideas. We are anti-intellectual and skeptical about the idea of qualifications, despite half of us being graduates and most of us being denied any more than basic training anyway. For a worker to have been homeless themselves is not valued despite 16 per cent having this background. We value caring and knowledge, but see experience as less important than we used to, partly because our own levels of experience are going down. We want to help others to help themselves and see the work as a vocation, rather than a job, although this can lead us to become disillusioned. We know the job is more complicated than the signposting we are told to do but are confused about the role of a client in this. We try not to be directive but will intervene if necessary. We know that clients are often educated not to believe in themselves but a sizeable minority of us would still not trust them to take a lead in the solutions to their issues. We think that some agencies make people dependent, but few write off the whole industry, although a vocal minority do. A sizeable minority feel workers are getting too professional, yet the vast majority believe in professional structures.

The ideological constructs behind these views are variable. If we look at the traditional structural or individual divide between explanations of homeless people and the role of workers (Balchin, 1998; Hutson, 1994; Cranes et al., 2000), that as we discussed goes some way to explain Smith and Wright's typology, we find that the structural explanations permeate, with a few vestiges of individual attitudes. However, there are also more post-modern influences at play here, which Neal (1996) sees as the third turn in homeless paradigms, emphasising things like the importance of looking at the play of power, how we relate to each other, the importance of relationships etc. This is probably best brought out in the differences between workers. While I would not want to replicate Smith and Wright's typology, there were trends in workers' thinking that did go together.

Individualist or structuralist trends

- The work is largely common sense and should be practically focused.
- Power is not an issue between clients, and user involvement can be a distraction.
- The administration of the job is not as relevant as face-to-face work and can put clients off.
- Supporting People has made the work more difficult and less relevant to our clients needs.
- It is unprofessional to share our opinion of other services with clients.

Post-modern or post-structuralist trends

- We should focus on issues of power as it is one of the keys for establishing relationships with people.
- User involvement is similar; it is a means to getting people to believe in themselves.
- Administration is about consistency and accountability to the client.
- Supporting People has brought standards to the sector.
- We should break barriers down between clients and workers where we can.

However, and following the post-modern turn, these divisions were not simple and were contested at different levels. People often had mixed views and the differences between ideologies were slippery. To finish I would like to invoke another of Tucker's ideas on the forces that influence the formation of professional identities.

Forces affecting the development of professional identities

I like this model because it gives us an indication of what we can do about all this, how we can impact upon our cultures, becoming a *profession 'for itself', self-conscious and aware of its identity and its obligations* (Sercombe, 2000). It also gives us recommendations for direct stakeholders:

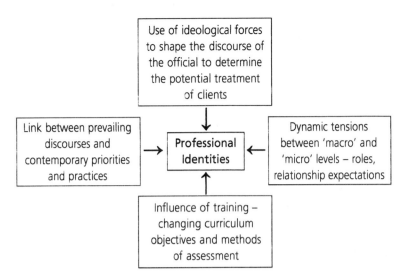

- Researchers in the field need to examine the ideological constructions of homelessness and critique the contradictory messages that can underpin local and governmental policies.
- Trainers, training organisations and commissioners need to have a more comprehensive strategy about training, including critiquing practices as well as the more traditional practical focus.
- Workers need to examine their own views and attitudes, their origins, their underlying assumptions and the way they are played out in the work place and in their relationships with clients.
- Agencies need to examine the underpinning philosophies of their organisations, how they receive policy initiatives and are influenced by them, and how these dynamics are played out in the policies and relations between the staff team.

Chapter 10

Conclusion: lessons to be learnt and actions to be taken

Mike Seal

Introduction

It is always interesting to see how a book develops, as ideas flow and its focus clarifies. The original motivation for this book, as I say in the Introduction, was to develop an understanding of the nature of various homelessness 'identities', how they are formed and their implications. I also note that my interest in the issue of identity arose through having seen particular groups or types of people who are homeless go through the homeless 'system', or rather different 'systems', many times. What I did not say earlier was that I had an accompanying, uneasy, feeling of guilt that I, or the services I was involved with, were somehow failing them.

We need to help people to pay attention to what they are seeking and what they find important rather than reinforcing their problems. People carried strong negative identities, but they also had positive aspects in their lives – which did not necessarily figure in what agencies thought of as examples of positive experience.

(Lemos, 2005)

What Lemos's quote means to me is that I should have been more alert to these feelings when I was a worker, and their importance has been strengthened in the process of writing and editing the book. We, and I would include all in the homelessness sector, policy makers, the media and the general population here, need to pay attention to how homeless people make sense of their lives and the part *we* play within the dynamic of them doing this, including the way we try to 'construct' them. For we are not neutral, and we need to understand this. It is for this reason that the title of this book has changed to recognise this interaction. It was originally to be called '*Constructing and Contesting Homeless Identities*', instead of its present title '*Understanding and Responding to Homeless Experiences, Identities and Cultures*'. The terms 'responding to' and 'understanding' are deliberate and aimed at the sector, for we are the ones who will need to lead the way and push the debates on, in conjunction with those clients who are already active and encouraging others to get involved. The term 'cultures' is there because the book takes a stab at unpacking our non-neutrality, and addresses the assumptions, cultures and constructions we have about homeless people; as workers, agencies, a sector and in society. We, the workers, are also closest to the homeless people. One theme coming out of these chapters is that an important, often determining, aspect of homeless people's experiences (and indeed identities where that is what they have become) is their interactions with services.

Common themes and implications for services

My challenge for the Conclusion was to identify common themes running throughout the chapters. I think there are some to be found.

1. The importance of identity, autonomy and dignity

The general focus of research on homelessness has ignored the inner lives of homeless persons and how they experience their world . . . many social scientists have long assumed that the issues of meaning and self-worth are irrelevant, or at least of secondary importance, in the face of pressing physiological survival needs . . . (however) Maintaining a sense of worth seems to be important and necessary to surviving homelessness.

(Snow and Anderson, 1993)

The results suggest that dignity is an important variable to consider in understanding the experience of homelessness. Policies and programs that support validating the dignity of homeless persons are encouraged. Three outcomes followed the undermining of dignity, including anger, depression, and feelings of worthlessness.

(Keys and Miller, 2001)

Both these quotes back up the general thrust of the chapters, and indeed the book, that identity, autonomy and dignity are important. Butchinsky feels that it is the key to changing services. We need to acknowledge the resourcefulness rough sleepers show in the face of difficult choices. Their autonomy needs to be explored and incorporated into practices, in particular in the relations between workers and rough sleepers. Yet hostels do not place any emphasis on this. The reason Dodson considers being in a couple can be a route out of homelessness is because it brings back self worth and a sense of responsibility, something Keys and Miller see, along with acknowledgement, as prerequisites for a sense of dignity. Yet, as I explore in Chapter 9 on workers, we still feel mixed about the subject: we see that clients are often educated to have no belief in themselves and a sizeable minority of us would still not trust them to take a lead in the solutions to their issues. We are suspicious about user involvement because we are suspicious about things that are not 'practical', as Van Doorn and Kain bring to the fore. It seems that we need to move away from seeing these seemingly 'softer' areas as not *additional* but *fundamental*. User involvement is not a distraction from our job; it actually does our job for us. It is in giving people some dignity, self-esteem and autonomy that they are more likely to be able to resettle.

2. We create negative labels, attaching them to those with problems who do not fit our systems

The cultural anchor points create a response based on seeing the person in terms of housing need, focussing on action, and avoiding reflection and expertise. Where the trauma is not recognised the person becomes labelled as 'difficult', or, worse, they are related to in terms of their actions, and their needs are not responded to.

(Van Doorn and Kain, Chapter 8)

In reality, this group (Dual Diagnosis) has a number of simple needs – a home, friends, income, meaningful daily activities, health needs and so on, which necessitate co-ordinated responses from several agencies. It is in realising this co-ordination that the complexity lies.

(Rorstad et al., 1996)

This was one of the main themes of Ames', Dodson's and Bevan's chapters on challenging behaviour, couples and multiple needs respectively. Bevan is quite clear on the themes, saying that if people with multiple needs do not conform to the structure of the services in drug and alcohol, mental health and so on, they are seen as the problem. He felt quite disappointed to have to be writing another chapter on the subject, reflecting how little has developed. I like the Rorstad quote above because it accurately locates the complexity; it is within us (i.e. services) not clients. Dodson's chapter is perhaps an extreme case of this, there is nothing more 'natural' than people forming relationships, yet for all kind of reasons it is seen as a 'problem' for homeless people. Ames's chapter is also interesting in tracing how attempts to change these constructions can all too easily collapse back in on themselves. The term 'challenging behaviour' was introduced to make workers think more about the behaviour being a 'challenge' to services rather than a problem. Yet it has now become a derogatory term, another 'problem' category of clients to 'deal' with.

3. Homeless people's presentation of themselves to services with particular identities

The central characters – the homeless and the agency workers – respectively play out the role of victims, outsiders or sinners, champions, befrienders or saviours.

(Brandon, 1980)

Research has tended to be through services which in turn tend to serve those in crisis, hence they are found to be vulnerable and in crisis.

(Wagner, 1993)

Brandon sees the interactions between workers and clients as a kind of game or dance, with people playing certain roles. Butchinsky quite clearly shows how people present themselves to us in a certain, deliberate way, hiding the parts they thought we did not want to see and emphasising the aspects of their lives they thought were more acceptable to us. Marshall brings out a similar perspective in the interactions between drug users and the services that are meant to serve them. Understanding the anxiety and trauma is more likely to resolve the difficulty.

On a slightly different tack, Ames talks about how people who have been labelled as displaying challenging behaviour will tend to live up to people's expectations. Van Doorn and Kain see this as applying to both workers and clients. On a service level this has serious implications for our interventions with clients, particularly given that for many clients they have, to a degree, become encultured to our practices. It means that the interventions may well be dances, with both parties fulfilling certain roles without having any real impact. We need firstly to acknowledge that people may be doing this; and to respect when this is part of the reality Butchinsky mentions as being necessary for people to create to make sense of their lives. However, we also need to find ways to break this pattern, and enabling the client to feel safe enough to do this. As Van Doorn and Kain say, 'Where people are labelled "difficult", they are most likely to continue to live up to that expectation. Understanding the anxiety and trauma is more likely to resolve the difficulty.' Ames is quite clear, in talking about challenging behaviour, that it is the client who is ultimately responsible for their own behaviour. However, another way of seeing this is that we cannot change another's behaviour: the only thing we have control over is how we respond to it – we need to learn a different dance.

4. The need to recognise the importance of relationships and social networks

Staff can support people in mapping and understanding their current relationships with family and friends and help service users to identify those they want to strengthen ... staff (also) need openly to discuss lasting and loving one-to-one relationships. Staff should not discourage either the starting of relationships or talking about them.

(Lemos, 2006)

The study found that resettlement was associated with increasing contact with friends and relatives. At the time of resettlement, just 5 per cent socialised at least twice a week with relatives or friends. This increased to 23 per cent after six months; and to 45 per cent after 24 months. These social contacts were associated with a reduction in feelings of depression, worry, pessimism, being unsettled and being dissatisfied with the accommodation.

(Crane and Warnes, 2002)

Most of the chapters brought out the importance of others in the lives of homeless people and being resettled. This is backed up by much research, such as Crane and Warnes, quoted above, and as such is not new. What is new in our chapters is certain emphases within this and messages for services. Butchinsky shows how, for many homeless people, the street is where people develop a sense of community, and that hostels represent respite or time out; which I doubt is what we see the role of hostels as being. She concludes by saying that it is unreasonable to expect rough sleepers to give up their ties to the streets, as these are where people's significant relationships often are. Dodson's chapter is an examination of the implications of this for personal relationships; and, to a degree, the street. It highlights some of the fears of workers and services about relationships and goes some way to explore the reasons we avoid the subject. Geddes's chapter is interesting in that other sectors, at least to some extent, recognise the importance of community, support networks and integration and see them as the starting point for resettlement. Van Doorn and Kain's and my own chapters help explain why we avoid the subject, it being against our practical, action-orientated nature, and against the culture of the services. As to a way forward, I agree with Lemos's statements about how we should orientate ourselves towards this work, but worry about how we will start to overcome the cultural barriers to this. Some of these changes will need to be a part of the second order changes which Van Doorn and Kain talk about, but it will also need individual changes in attitudes. I was heartened recently when talking to John Ames, author of the chapter on challenging behaviour. He has set up a one day course specifically for workers to explore their fears and embarrassment, about bringing up the subject of relationships and how to overcome them. This was a part of a process of mainstreaming the subject, rather than giving people a reason to see it as an add-on or luxury.

5. In-depth knowledge is needed of the nature of particular experiences of homeless people

As Van Doorn and Kain expand upon, the homelessness sector is frequently driven by a common sense view of what needs to be done. As workers, this is often expressed as 'I treat everyone the same' or 'I treat everyone as an individual'. What some of these chapters have shown is that this is not always enough; often to serve someone effectively we need to have an understanding of their experiences and be sensitive to them. Flynn shows how we have to understand the dynamics of sexuality in the homelessness experience. Otherwise, we may not see that by the time the client gets to us they have already had two cycles of rejection, by telling them to hide or subjugate their sexuality we are quite likely to become the third. More to the point, to stop becoming the third cycle will take an act of will on our part; it is not enough to blithely say that we treat everyone equally. Dodson calls for us to understand the dynamics of homeless couples and how their relationships develop, as at present our lack of understanding gives us an excuse to dismiss them. Geddes gives a very detailed account of the nature of the pre-flight experience of many refugees that we ignore at our peril.

A large part of Geddes' account seems to necessitate us having an understanding of trauma, and its psychological effects. While this may make some workers start crying boundaries, as Geddes says, while it is not for the worker to act as a counsellor, it does help if they are able to comprehend that these issues may have an impact on the resettlement process. Perhaps more to the point, to ignore these issues would not support the resettlement process. Interestingly, some work has been done on the importance of trauma work. Firstly Waller highlighted trauma as one of the key unmet needs in 2000 in the report *Closing the Gap*. Glasgow Homeless Network now has a specific trauma team and hightlighted the issue in their report *Disempowerment and Disconnection: Trauma and Homelessness*, (Collins and Phillips) seeing homelessness as a source of trauma in itself. The new Homeless Link manifesto also links homelessness to trauma. Hopefully it is starting to become an anchor point, but it will necessitate a move away from common sense is enough, and practical responses being our lens.

6. Understanding the impact of homelessness services on homeless people

The success of the advocates' campaigns for the homeless is often lost on the homeless themselves, who see the huge shelters built to house them as vehicles to strip them of their individuality and dignity.

(Wagner, 1993)

In my previous work (Seal, 2005), I noted how many workers thought about hostel provision as some kind of neutral holding ground and that many policies reflected this, seemingly to manage the 'containment ' of people rather than seeing it as a person's home and community. The quote above questions this notion, as do I. I remember being at Homeless Link's research conference in 2005, listening to Joan Smith talking about her longitudinal research with Foyers, and her findings that people's mental health issues and drug use both increased during their stay. I also remember being slightly perturbed at the question session that I seemed to be the only one who wanted to talk about that aspect of her presentation.

Another memory I have is of running a workshop on people's fear concerning user involvement. As an introduction, my co-presenter, who was a hostel resident, talked about some of his own fears. He said that his greatest fear was unpredictability. He had grown up in an unpredictable home situation, largely linked to his father's mood swings and behaviour. What he subsequently found hardest of all about hostels was that they reminded him of this: he found life in hostels, and the reactions from staff, were not predictable and this fed his fear.

Many of the chapters of my previous book (Seal, 2005) go on to detail some of these unpredictabilities, and people's general experiences of, and reactions to, our services. Ames develops a whole framework for how we mirror our client's unpredictability, deceit and aggression. Butchinsky describes how rough sleepers resist the lack of autonomy they are afforded by pushing the rules. Dodson details how staff and residents can combine to make life in hostels intolerable for couples, such that they vote with their feet. Geddes and Flynn respectively cover how racism and homophobia can be overt, covert and institutionalised in our provision, but are nonetheless picked up on by the client group.

7. Practitioners and organisations need to value the process of reflection

We must become able not only to transform our institutions in response to changing situations and requirements; we must invent and develop institutions which are 'learning systems', that is to say, systems capable of bringing about their own continuing transformation.

(Schon, 1987)

We have to take certain things as read. We have to fall back on routines in which previous thought and sentiment has been sedimented. As we think and act, questions arise that cannot be answered in the present. The space afforded by recording, supervision and conversation with our peers allows us to approach these. Reflection requires space in the present and the promise of space in the future.

(Smith, 1994)

These two quotes again emphasise the importance of reflection; for workers' development, for organisations and, as Van Doorn and Kain submit, for the sector. While the notion of reflective practice is not uncontested (Eraut,1994), it is accepted as essential by most of the other caring professions. These professions also, as Smith notes above, recognise that we have to build in structures to facilitate it. Within youth work, entitlement to reflective non-line managerial supervision is part of JNC conditions for full time workers.

As I noted recently (Seal, 2006), in this field, most homelessness workers (69 per cent) only receive support in the form of line managerial supervision. Previously (Seal, 2005) I identified three common roles for a supervisor: that of making sure workers are delivering what is expected of them (managerial); to guide and develop the worker, sign-posting them to training etc. (developmental); and to be a facilitator in a worker's reflective practice. When asked what kind of supervision people received, 44 per cent received a managerial model only, 26 per cent a developmental model, 18 per cent a reflexive model and 13 per cent a mix of these.

While there is management training, it (the sector) lacks any widespread belief that improved management of organisations and first line management of front line staff offers the kinds of benefits realised in other sectors. The potential of coaching, mentoring, professional supervision is not apparent.

(Mathews, 2005)

As Mathews and Van Doorn and Kain emphasise, the lack of reflective supervision is probably due to lack of skills in managers who have probably themselves not been trained in doing it. Van Doorn and Kain see that this need for learning has to run through from workers, to managers, to organisation and the whole sector. I will reiterate their concluding words:

> *The sector requires mature managers who can think beyond their experience and training. This requires self-critical reflection. Managers need to learn how to test the cultural assumptions against the world around them and the needs of the client group, and enable whole organisations to adapt and change their culture in relation to meeting the client groups' needs in the current funding and political environment.*
>
> (Van Doorn and Kain, Ch. 8)

For them the 'disinvestment in reflection and expertise' means we do not have a means of questioning ourselves about our assumptions nor a base from which to develop skilled responses to the actual needs of the client group.

8. The need to examine our anchor points and cultures

> *The struggle by different vested interests to impose a particular definition of homelessness on the policy agenda is critical to the way in which homelessness is treated as a social problem.*
>
> (Jacobs, Kemeny and Manzi, 1999)
>
> *Professional identities are created and developed within particular institutional settings; via the 'ideological effects' of social policy; through discursive interactions; and at the level of macro and micro social and political relations.*
>
> (Tucker, 2004)

Van Doorn and Kain outline what they define as cultural anchor points for the homelessness sector. They see these as having arisen over the last three decades, as Tucker indicates, as a reaction to a particular environment. Crucially, they also feel that these anchor points do not serve us, or our clients, as well as they did in what is now a very different environment. They therefore make a call for both reflection and change, as they say:

> *Only by reflecting on and challenging the deepest paradigms, the cultural anchor points of the sector, can the sector begin to create the solutions to the challenges it currently faces ... The sector needs to explore, discuss and identify, through honest appraisal and reflection, its culture and how it both supports and frustrates its work and its ability to meet the changes it faces.*
>
> (Van Doorn and Kain, Ch. 8)

They offer the chapter, and their perceived anchor points, as a contribution to this debate, and hope that it gives others something to reflect on. It is a sentiment I share about my own chapter. I also tried to link into the underlying paradigms within the sector that underpin how we construct ourselves, and the clients we serve. Which homelessness paradigms underpin our attitudes, and indeed our anchor points, is a debate to be had. Sometimes we construct things as the individual's fault, sometimes as the fault of the structures around us. Hopefully we are also beginning to see the importance of more post-modern ideas like identity, self-esteem and the exercise of power. They are certainly things that have come to the fore in this book.

Action points

I said in my Introduction that I would end with an agenda for action. I also said that for any such agenda to work, all stakeholders, and in particular clients, should be involved in moving any actions forward. As an overall statement I would therefore say: all stakeholders, agencies, academics, workers and funders, should view understanding particular homelessness experiences and identities as an ongoing training and research need. Furthermore, policies and working practices should be reviewed in the light of any implications of these new understandings. I have also outlined some specific measures that stem from the eight themes above.

1. Agencies and funders should view working with clients, on how they make sense of their experiences, as a legitimate area of work and seek to develop appropriate intervention strategies.
2. Agencies and workers should acknowledge that they are a part of the homelessness experience and the process of identity formation, rather than being neutral, and should seek to make our influence positive rather than discriminatory.
3. Agencies should examine their policies and working procedures to see how they are structurally discriminating against couples, LGBT clients (in particular transgendered clients), clients with multiple needs and those labelled as 'challenging'. In addition, specific training should be provided on those areas where it is not.
4. Agencies and workers should acknowledge and respect that clients will present to them in particular ways, based on their experiences of services, and that this should be a process of negotiation between workers and agencies.
5. As part of these negotiations, workers, clients and agencies should review working practices with a mind to: challenging unhelpful or 'meaningless' 'patterns' of exchange; in particular, challenging methods of assessing needs that are deficit models, and risk assessments that label people.
6. Developing autonomy, self-esteem and dignity should be seen as an essential aspect of worker interventions, and strategies should be developed for them. User involvement and peer-led work should be valued as fostering these areas of development and be prioritised, rather than being an add-on.
7. Similarly, giving attention to homeless people's relationships, both personal and social, should be seen as a key to successful resettlement. Agencies should develop specific training for workers on interventions in these areas and incorporate them into their assessments.

8. That the homeless community is viewed by workers and agencies as a potential source of support and belonging, as well as a site of distress, and that interventions should build on people's positive experiences of them.
9. That other aspects of people's experiences of homelessness, both in terms of causes of homelessness and in being homeless, can cause trauma. Working through this trauma should be seen as both an appropriate area for intervention and a lobbying point for the whole sector on what is considered priority need.
10. Agencies should challenge their bias towards practical responses to homelessness. This challenge should embrace the idea of reflective practice and develop appropriate support mechanisms and training to help embed a culture of reflection amongst workers and managers.
11. The sector as a whole should explore and critically appraise its cultures and anchor points. It should also seek to establish an ethical standpoint on how it views homelessness and the development of the sector.
12. Mechanisms should be developed to enable workers to explore and challenge their own views and standpoints with the aim of developing consistency rather than conflict in their responses to homeless people and each other.
13. Research is needed into both media portrayals of homeless people and the myths created about them in society. This research should also investigate where these myths come from and how they are sustained.
14. All stakeholders should develop and engage in public awareness campaigns to counteract the negative sides of these constructions. Researchers, academics and practitioners should critique the underlying ideologies of homelessness policy.

Given my initial call for debate in the Introduction, the term 'Action Points' may feel like a slight misnomer, and I will therefore give some qualification for my use for it. If I am uneasy with the term myself, it is not because I do not think the actions I have outlined should happen, for I do. It is because I also accept that in the debate that I hope follows on from this book's publication, they should, and will, change. I would, however, like to keep the term 'action' within the debate, for it should not be a sterile or academic one. The debate should be about what we *should* be doing, and preferably whether what we *are* doing is in the right direction.

References

Anderson, B. (1983) *Imagined Communities: Reflections on the Origin and Spread of Nationalism.* London: Verso.

Appleby, G. and Anastas, J. (1998) *Not Just a Passing Phase: Social Work with Gay, Lesbian and Bisexual People.* New York: Columbia University Press.

Argyris, C. (1976) *Increasing Leadership Effectiveness.* Wiley: London.

Arnold, K. (2004) *Homelessness, Citizenship and Identity: The Uncanniness of Late Modernity.* New York: State University Press of New York.

Baker, O. (2001) *A Dog's Life: Homeless People and their Pets.* London: Blue Cross.

Balchin, A. (1998) *Housing: The Essential Foundations.* London: Routledge.

Bandura, A. (1977) *Social Learning Theory.* Englewood Cliffs, NJ: Prentice Hall.

Banks, S. (1995) *Ethics and Values in Social Work.* Basingstoke: Macmillan.

Bao, W., Witbeck, L. and Hoyt, D. (2000) Abuse, Support and Depression Among Homeless and Runaway Adolescents. *Journal of Health and Social Behaviour.*

Bee, H. (2000) *The Developing Child.* 9th edn. London: Allyn & Bacon.

Bell, M., Buchan, S. and Lukes, S. (1999) *The Needs of Refugees and Asylum Seekers in the London Borough of Hillingdon.* Refugee Action.

Bevan, P. (1998) *The Resettlement Handbook.* NHA: London.

Bevan, P. (2002) *Multiple Needs: Good Practice Briefing.* Homeless Link.

Bevan, P. (2002) Case Study: Specialist Provision for People with Multiple Needs. In *Homeless Link Multiple Needs Good Practice Briefing.* Homeless Link: London.

Bevan, P. and Dewhurst, L. (2001) *Inhabiting the Margins.* Elmore and Homeless Link.

Bevan, P. and Van Doorn, A. (2002) *Fact or Fiction, An Exploratory Study. Multiple Needs Briefing.* Homeless Link. August.

Bevan, P. and Van Doorn, A. (2002) Fact or Fiction? Supporting People with Multiple Needs. In *Homeless Link Multiple Needs Good Practice Briefing.* Homeless Link: London.

Big Issue (2000) *The Big Issue Big Book of Home.* London: Verso.

Boydell, K., Goering, P. and Morrell-Bellai, T. (2000) Narratives of Identity: Re-presentation of Self in People who are Homeless. *Qualitative Health Research.* 10: 1, 26–38.

Bozarth, J. and Evans, S. (2000). *Person-Centered Casework.* Paper presentation at the Eastern Psychological Association, Baltimore, MD.

Brah, A. (1996) *Cartographies of Diaspora, Contesting Identities.* London: Routledge.

Brandon, D. (1998) *Care Planning.* In Bevan, P. *The Resettlement Handbook.* London: National Homeless Alliance.

Brandon, D. et al. (1980) *The Survivors: A Study of Homeless Young Newcomers to London and the Responses Made to Them*. London: Routledge and Kegan Paul.

Brandon, D. and Atherton, K. (1996) *Handbook of Care Planning*. London: Routledge.

Brennan, W. (1998) Aggression and Violence: Examining the Theories. *Nursing Standard*, 12: 27, 36–8.

Brown, M. and Rounsley, C. (1996) *Trueselves: Understanding Transsexualism*. United States: Jossey Bass.

Buss, A.H. (1961) *The Psychology of Aggression*. New York: Wiley.

Butchinsky, C. (2004) *An Anthropological Study of Repeated Homelessness in Oxford*. (Unpublished PhD Thesis). School of Social Sciences and Law, Oxford Brookes University.

Camden Homeless Forum (1998) *The Battle For Street Homelessness*. CHAIN. 3: 34–36.

Carey-Wood, J. (1997) *Meeting Refugees' Needs in Britain: The Role of Refugee-specific Initiatives*. Home Office Publications Unit.

Centrepoint (1997) 'Give Five' production with Demon http://www.uncommon.demon.co.uk/demon/give5/homeless.html

Challis, L. et al. (1994) Managing Quasi-Markets: Institutions of Regulation. In Bartlet et al. (Eds.) *Quasi-Markets in the Welfare State*. Bristol: SAUS.

Chambers (1998) *The Chambers Dictionary*. London: Chambers Harrap.

Chartered Institute of Housing (2003) *Providing a Safe Haven: Housing Asylum Seekers and Refugees*.

Chen, A.Y., Sawyers, R.B. and Williams, P.F. (1997) Reinforcing Ethical Decision Making Through Corporate Culture. *Journal of Business Ethics*. 16, 855–65.

Cloke, P., Johnsen, S. and May, J. (2005) Exploring Ethos? Discourses of 'Charity' in the Provision of Emergency Services for Homeless People. *Environment and Planning*. 37, 385–402.

Cogran, B. et al. (2002) Challenges Faced by Homeless Sexual Minorities: Comparison of GLBT Homeless Adolescents with their Heterosexual Counterparts. *American Journal of Public Health*: 92, 5.

Complete Works of Sigmund Freud. Volume 6. London: Hogarth Press.

Connect (2001) National Homeless Alliance. *Connect*. July, 22.

Crane, M. and Warnes, A. (1997) *Homeless Truths: Challenging the Myths about Older Homeless People*. London: Crisis and Help the Aged.

Crane, M. and Warnes, A. (2000) *Lessons from Lancefield Street: Tackling the Needs of Older Homeless People*. London: NHA.

Crane, M. and Warnes, A. (2001) *Single Homeless People in London: Profiles of Service Users and Perceptions of Needs*. Sheffield Institute for Studies on Ageing, University of Sheffield.

Crane, M. and Warnes, A. (2002) *Resettling Older Homeless People: A Longitudinal Study of Outcomes*. Sheffield Institute for Studies on Ageing, University of Sheffield.

Crane, M., Fu, R., Warnes, A. and Whitehead, N. (2003) *Homeless Fact File*. London: Crisis.

Crane, M. et al. (2005) *The Role of Homeless Sector Day Centres in Supporting Housed Vulnerable People*. Sheffield Institute for Studies on Ageing, University of Sheffield.

Crisis (2004) *Hidden Homeless: Lost Voices*. Crisis.

Croft-White, C. and Parry-Crooke, G. (2004) *Lost Voices: The Invisibility of Homeless People with Multiple Needs*. London: Crisis.

Croft-White, C. and Parry-Cooke, G. (2004) *Hidden Homelessness: Lost Voices, The Invisibility of Homeless People with Multiple Needs*. London.

Cross, E. (2001) B-GLAD 'T-Time' http://dolphin.upenn.edu/~qsa/bglad20001/t-time.html

Daly, G. (1996) *Homeless: Policies, Strategies and Lives on the Street*. London: Routledge.

Dean, H. (1999) *Begging Questions: Street-level Economic Activity and Social Policy Failure*. London: Policy Press.

DeCrescenzo, T. (1994) *Helping Gay and Lesbian Youth*. New York: The Hamworth Press.

Department of Health (2004) *Standards for Better Health*. DoH.

DTLR (1999) *Coming in from the Cold: The Government's Strategy on Rough Sleeping*. London: DTLR.

DTLR (2002) *Homelessness Strategies: A Good Practice Handbook*. London: DTLR.

Eighner, L. (1993) *Travels with Lizbeth: Travels on the Road and on the Streets*. New York: St. Martin's Press.

Ephraim, G. (1998) *Exotic Communication, Conversations and Scripts*. In Hewett, D. (Ed) *Challenging Behaviour – Principles and Practices*. London: David Fulton Publishers.

Eraut, M. (1994) *Developing Professional Knowledge*. London: The Falmer Press.

Erikson, E.H. (1963) *Childhood and Society*. 2nd edn. New York: Norton.

Erskine, A. and Mackintosh, I. (1999) *Why Begging Offends: Historical Perspectives and Continuities*. In Dean (1999) *Begging Questions: Street-level Economic Activity and Social Policy Failure*. London: Policy Press.

Ethnos (2005) *Citizenship and Belonging: What is Britishness?* London: Commission for Racial Equality.

Fabian Society (2006) *The Future of Britishness*. http://www.fabian-society.org.uk/press_office/display.asp?cat=43andid=520

Fals-Stewart, W. et al. (2000) Behavioural Couples Therapy Versus Individual Based Treatment for Male Substance Abusing Patients. *Journal of Substance Abuse Treatment*, 18:3 249–54.

Fitzpatrick, S., Kemp, P. and Klinker, S. (2000) *Single Homelessness, An Overview of Research in Britain*, Bristol: The Policy Press.

Flemen, K. (1999) *Room for Drugs*. London: Release.

Foucault, M. (1986) *Power/Knowledge: Selected Interviews and Other Writings, 1972–77*. London: Colin Gordon Longman.

Freud, S. (1901) *The Psychopathology of Everyday Life*. In Strachey, J. (Ed.) *The Standard Edition of the Complete Psychological Works of Sigmund Freud*. London: Hogarth Press.

Freud, S. (1923) *The Ego and the Id*. Pelican Freud Library (11). Harmondsworth: Penquin.

Friere, P. (1972) *Pedagogy of the Oppressed*. London: Penguin Books.

Gale, K. (1998) *Information and Youth Homelessness: An Assessment of the Information Requirements of Young People in Housing Need and the Role of Information in Preventing Homelessness*. (MA Thesis: Sheffield University)

Giddens, A. (1996) *Modernity and Self-Identity: Self and Society in the Late Modern Age*. Stanford: Stanford University Press.

Giddens, A. (2001) *Sociology*. 4th edn. England: Polity Press.

Gilroy, P. (1993) *The Black Atlantic: Double Consciousness and Modernity*. Cambridge: Harvard University Press.

Girling, J. (1993) *Myths and Politics in Western Society*. London: Transaction Press.

Glasgow Homeless Network (2002) *Disempowerment and Disconnection: Trauma and Homelessness*

Glasser, I. and Bridgman, R. (1999) *Braving the Street: The Anthropology of Homelessness*. New York: Berghahn Press.

Golden, S. (1992) *The Women Outside: Meaning and Myths of Homelessness*. Berkley: University of California Press.

Goleman, D. (1998) *Working with Emotional Intelligence*. London: Bloomsbury.

Gorkin, M. (2000) *Four Faces of Anger*. Selfhelpmagazine.com

Grant, B. (1999) *Principled and Instrumental Nondirectiveness in Person-Centered and Client-Centered Therapy*. Presented at the Third Annual Meeting of the Association for the Development of the Person-Centered Approach in Atlanta.

Grenier, P. (1996) *Still Dying for a Home*. London: Crisis.

Gross, R. et al. (2000) *Psychology: A New Introduction*. 2nd edn. England: Hodder & Stoughton.

Groundswell (2006) *Being Supported: People's Views on Supporting People*. London: Groundswell.

Gurney, C. (1994) *Home and Home Ownership: The History and Ideology of a Concept*. Dissertation, University of Bristol.

Gurney, C. (1999) Glass Houses? Metaphor, Myth and Morality in the Social Construction of Home Ownership. *Housing Studies*. 17: 3, 135–67.

Ham, J. (1996) *Steps from the Street. A Report on Direct Access Hostel Provision*. London: CHAR.

Haralambos, M. and Holborn, M. (2000) *Sociology: Themes and Perspectives*. 5th edn. London: Harper Collins.

Harrison, M., Chandler, R, and Green, G. (1991) *Hostels in London: A Statistical Overview*. London: RIS.

Harrison, M. (1996) *Emergency Hostels: Direct Access Accommodation in London 1996*. London: RIS.

Hartley, J. (1993) *The Politics of Pictures: The Creation of the Public in the Age of Popular Media.* London: Routledge.

Havel, J. (1992) *Summer Meditations.* Toronto: Alfred A. Knopf.

Heidegger, M. (1977) *Letters on Humanism.* New York: Routledge.

Herek, G. and Berrill, K. (1992) *Hate Crimes: Confronting Violence against Lesbian and Gay Men.* Newbury Park CA: Sage Publications.

Hewett, D. (Ed) (1998) *Challenging Behaviour – Principles and Practices.* London: David Fulton Publishers.

Hewitt, P. (2005) society.guardian.co.uk/nhsreforms/comment/0,1520909,00.html

Hewitt, R. (1995) *The Beggar's Blanket: Public Scepticism and the Representation of Poverty.* London: Routledge.

Hoch, C. and Slayton, R. (1989) *New Homeless and Old.* Philadelphia: Temple University Press.

Homeless Link (2002) *Multiple Needs Good Practice Briefing.* London: Homeless Link.

Homeless Link (2004) *Day Centres Handbook: A Good Practice Guide.* London: Homeless Link.

Hopkins, R. (2000) *The Rubicon Society.* Introduction Pack. London: Unpublished.

Housing Association Charitable Trusts (2002) *The Role of Refugee Community Organisations (RCOs) and Refugee Community Housing Associations (RCHAs) in Providing Housing for Refugees and Asylum Seekers in London.* HACT.

Housing Associations Charitable Trust (2003) *Between NASS and a Hard Place.* HACT.

Housing Today (2006) *Supporting Chance.* Housing Today. 27 Jan.

Humphreys, R. (1999) *No Fixed Abode: A History of Responses to the Roofless and the Rootless in Britain.* Basingstoke: Macmillan.

Hutson, S. (1999) *The Experiences of Homeless Accommodation and Support.* In Hutson, S. and Clapham, D. (Eds.) *Homelessness: Public Policies and Private Troubles,* 208–25. London: Continuum.

Hutson, S. and Liddiard, M. (1994) *Youth Homelessness: The Construction of a Social Issue.* London: Macmillan.

Inglehart, M. (1991) *Reactions to Critical Life Events: A Social Psychological Analysis.* New York: Praeger.

Inman, K. and Benjamin, A. (2003) Homeless Couples are More Likely to Have Drug Problems and Spend Longer on the Streets Than Their Single Counterparts. *The Guardian;* 15 October 2003.

Jacobs, K., Kemeny, J. and Manzi, T. (2003) Power, Discursive Space and Institutional Practices in the Construction of Housing Problems. *Housing Studies.* 2: 3, 344–56.

Jary, D. and Jary, J. (1991) *Collins Dictionary of Sociology.* London: Harper Collins.

JNC (2005) *Report of the Joint Negotiating Council for Youth and Community Workers.* Leicester: JNC.

Johnsen S., Cloke P. and May J. (2002). *Homeless Places Project: Day Centre and Drop-in Centre Survey.* Geography Dept., Queen Mary College, University of London.

Johnsen S., Cloke P. and May J. (2005) Day Centres for Homeless People: Spaces of Care or Fear? *Social and Cultural Geography*. 6: 6, 787–810.

Jordan, B. (2001) Tough Love: Social Work, Social Exclusion and the Third Way. *British Journal of Social Work*. 4: 56–67.

Kelley, M.L. and Fals-Stewart, W. (2002) Couples Versus Individual-based Therapy for Alcohol and Drug Abuse: Effects on Children's Psychosocial Functioning. *Journal of Consulting Clinical Psychologists*. 70: 417–27.

Kellogg College (2006) *Health Care for the Homeless*. E-Learning Module. Oxford: Kellogg College.

Kemeny, J. (1992a) *Housing and Social Theory*. London: Routledge.

Kemeny, J. (1992b) *Housing and Social Structure: Towards a Sociology of Residence*. SAUS Working Paper 102. Bristol: School for Advanced Urban Studies.

Kenway, P. and Palmer, G. (2003) *How Many, How Much? Single Homelessness and the Question of Numbers and Cost*. London: Crisis.

Keys, C. and Miller, B. (2001) Understanding Dignity in the Lives of Homeless Persons. *American Journal of Community Psychology*, 29.

Knapp, M. et al. (1994) *Markets for Social Care: Opportunities, Barriers and Implications*. In Bartlet et al. (Eds.) *Quasi-Markets in the Welfare State*. Bristol: SAUS.

Kohlberg, L. (1984) *Essays on Moral Development: The Psychology of Moral Development*. Volume 2. New York: Harper & Row.

Kramer, E. and Lee, S. (1999) *Homeless: The Other as Object*. In Min, E. (Ed.) *Reading the Homeless: The Media's Image of Homeless Culture*. London: Paeger.

Lave, J. and Wenger, E. (1991) *Situated Learning. Legitimate Peripheral Participation*. Cambridge: University of Cambridge Press.

Lemos, G. (2005) *Broadening Out Research into Homelessness*. Presented at Making the Link: Opening up Research into Homelessness. Homeless Link, 4 Oct.

Lemos, G. (2006) *Steadying the Ladder: Social and Emotional Aspirations of Homeless People*. London: LemosCrane.

Lemos, G. and Durkacz, S. (2002) *Dreams Deferred: The Families and Friends of Homeless and Vulnerable People*. London: Lemos and Crane.

Lethbridge, D. (1986). A Marxist Theory of Self-Actualization. *Journal of Humanistic Psychology*. 26: 2, 84–103.

Levy, A. and Merry, U. (1986) *Organisational Transformation, Approaches, Strategies, Theories*. New York: Preager.

Liddiard, M. (1999) *Homelessness: The Media, Public Attitudes and Policy Making*. In Hutson, S. and Clapham, D. (Eds.) *Homelessness: Public Policies and Private Troubles*. London: Cassell.

Lifton, R.J. (1992) *Victims and Survivors*. In Giamo, B. and Gruneburg. J. *Beyond Homelessness: Frames of Reference*. Iowa City: University of Iowa Press.

Lovell A.M. (1992) *Seizing the Moment: Power, Contingency, and Temporality in Street Life*. In Rutz, H. (Ed.) *The Politics of Time*. Monograph Series 4. Washington DC: American Anthropological Association.

Lowe, J. (2005) *Value Added. Small Providers and Supporting People.* London: HACT.

Maslow, A. (1962) *Towards a Psychology of Being.* New York: Van Nostrand.

Mathews, D. (2005) *Report to Homeless Link on Developing an Accredited Qualifications Route-Map for the Homelessness Sector in England and Wales.*

McCombs, M. and Shaw, D. (1972) The Agenda-Setting Function of Mass Media. *Public Opinion Quarterly.* 36: 2, 176–87.

McGarty, C., Yzerbyt, V. and Spears, R. (Eds) (2002) *Stereotypes as Explanations.* Cambridge: Cambridge University Press.

McGuigan, J. (1999) *Modernity and Postmodern Culture.* Buckingham: Open University Press.

McIntosh, I. and Erskine, A. (2000) *'Money for Nothing'?: Understanding Giving to Beggars. Sociological Research Online,* 5: 1 http://www.socresonline.org.uk/5/1/mcintosh.html

MacKnee, C. and Mervyn, J. (2002) Critical Incidents that Facilitate Homeless People's Transition off the Streets. *Journal of Social Distress and the Homeless.* October.

McPherson, W. (1999) *The Stephen Lawrence Inquiry: Report of an Inquiry.* London: Stationery Office.

Miles, M. and Huberman, M.A. (1994) *Qualitative Data Analysis.* Beverly Hills: Sage.

Min, E. (Ed.) *Reading the Homeless: The Media's Image of Homeless Culture.* London: Paeger.

Mowbray, M. (1985). Social Unrest Sparks the Welfare Response. *The Australian Quarterly.* Autumn/Winter, 85–94.

Moyer, K. (1968) *Kinds of Aggression and their Physiological Basis.* In Burglass, R. and Bowden, P. (Eds.) *Principles and Practice of Forensic Psychiatry.* Edinburgh: Churchill Livingstone.

Murphy, H.A., and Hildebrandt, W. (1991) *Effective Business Communication.* 6th Edition. McGraw-Hill.

Murray, C.A. (1990) *The Emerging Bristol Underclass.* London: IEA Health and Welfare Unit.

National Treatment Agency (2002) *Models of Care for Alcohol Misusers,* NTA.

National Housing Federation (2004) *Housing and Support Options for Refugees and Asylum Seekers.* National Housing Federation.

Neale, J. (1997) Homelessness and Theory Reconsidered. *Housing Studies.* 12: 3.

Newburn, T. and Rock, P. (2004) *Living in Fear: Violence and Victimisation in the Lives of Single Homeless People.* London: Crisis.

NHS (2002) *Workforce Census: Section Three: Nursing, Midwifery and Health Visitors.* London: NHS.

Nietzsche (1884/ 1977) *The Gay Science.* Random House.

NTA (2004) *Guidelines on Employment in Drug Treatment Services.* London: HMSO.

Nwachukwu, S.L. and Vitell, S.J. (1997) The Influence of Corporate Culture on Managerial Ethical Judgements. *Journal of Business Ethics.* 16, 757–76.

ODPM (2002) *More Than a Number:* Report on the analysis of ODPM homelessness statistics 2001/2002. London: ODPM.

ODPM (2002) *Homelessness Strategies: A Good Practice Handbook.* HMSO.

ODPM (2004) *Quality Assessment Framework.* London: HMSO.

ODPM (2004) *Achieving Positive Shared Outcomes in Health and Homelessness.* London: ODPM.

ODPM (2005) *Transitions: Young Adults With Complex Needs.* London: ODPM.

O'Connor, W. and Molloy, D. (2001) *Hidden in Plain Sight: Homelessness Amongst Lesbian and Gay Youth.* London: National Centre for Social Research.

Pannell, J. and Parry, S. (1999) *Implementing 'Joined-Up Thinking': Multi-agency Services for Single Homeless People in Bristol.* Bristol: Policy Press.

Pannell, J., Means, R. and Morbey, H. (2002) *Surviving at the Margins: Older Homeless People and the Organisations that Support Them.* London: Help the Aged.

Pannell, J. and Palmer, G. (2004) *Coming of Age: Opportunities for Older Homeless People Under Supporting People.* London: Homeless Link.

Park, G. (2002) *Someone and Anyone: Assessment Practice in Voluntary Sector Services for Homeless People in London.* London: Homeless Link.

Pearson, E. and Podeschi, R. (1997) Maslow and his Critics. *Adult Education Quarterly.* 234–45.

Perry, R. (2003) Who Wants to Work with the Poor and Homeless? *Journal of Social Work Education.* 39, 321.

Piaget, J. (1926) *The Child's Conception of the World.* London: Routledge and Kegan Paul.

Pilkington, N. and D'Augella, A. (1995) Victimization of Lesbian, Gay and Bisexual Youth in Community Settings. *Journal of Community Psychology,* 23: 34.

Pratt, M. (1992) *Imperial Eyes, Travel Writing and Transculturation.* London: Routledge.

Prime Minister's Strategy Unit (2004) *Alcohol Harm Reduction Strategy for England.* PMSU.

Randall, G. and Brown, S. (1993) *The Rough Sleepers Initiative: An Evaluation.* London: HMSO.

Randall, G. and Brown, S. (1996) *From Street to Home: An Evaluation of Phase 2 of the Rough Sleepers Initiative.* London: HMSO.

Randall, G. and Brown, S. (1999) *Homes for Street Homeless People: An Evaluation of the Rough Sleepers Initiative.* London: DETR.

Randall, G. and Brown, S. (2002) *Helping Rough Sleepers off the Streets.* London: ODPM.

Robinson, L. (1997) Black Adolescent Identity and the Inadequacies of Western Psychology. In Roche, J. and Tucker, S. *Youth in Society.* Buckingham: Open University.

Rogers, N. and McVeigh, J. (1999) *Equality in Housing: Guidance for Tackling Discrimination on the Grounds of Sexual Orientation and Promoting Equality.* London: National Housing Federation.

Rostad, P. and Checinski, K. (1996) *Dual Diagnosis: Facing the Challenge.* Wynne Books.

Rowe, M. (1999) *Crossing the Border: Encounters Between Homeless People and Outreach Workers.* Los Angeles: University of California Press.

Royal College of General Practitioners (2002) *Homelessness.* London: RCGP.

Royal College of General Practitioners (2002) *Meeting Complex Needs: The Future of Social Care.* London: RCGP.

Ryan, C. and Futterman, D. (1998) *Lesbian and Gay Youth: Care and Counselling.* New York: Columbia University Press.

Rybczynski, C. (1986) *Home: the Short History of an Idea.* Oxford: Viking.

Saunders, P. (1988) The Constitution of Home: Towards a Research Agenda. *Housing Studies.* 3: 2, 81–93.

Schön, D. (1987) *Educating the Reflective Practitioner.* San Francisco: Jossey-Bass.

Seal, M. (1999) To Professionalise or not: State of the Debate. *Link,* 3: 22–3.

Seal, M. (2004) *Reflections on Ten Years of Training.* Unpublished.

Seal, M. (2005) *Resettling Homeless People: Theory and Practice.* Lyme Regis: Russell House Publishing.

Seal, M. (2006) *Worker Identities in the Homeless Sector: A Survey of the Demographic Makeup, Working Conditions and Attitudes of Workers Accessing Short Courses.* London: YMCA George Williams College.

Sercombe, H. (2000) *Disciplining Youth Work: The Professionalisation Dilemma.* Paper presented at The Youth Affairs Conference, Pinjarra, Western Australia.

SEU (1998) *Rough Sleeping: A Report by the Social Exclusion Unit.* London: Cabinet Office.

Skills for Care (2004) *The State of the Social Care Workforce.* In Skills Research and Intelligence 2nd Annual Report, April 2005.

Smith, M.K. (1994) *Local Education.* Buckingham: Open University Press.

Smith, M.K. (2002) *Communities of Practice of Informal Educators.* At www.infed.org

Smith, N. and Wright, C. (1992) *Customer Perceptions of Resettlement Units.* London: HMSO.

Snow, D. and Anderson, L. (1987) Identity Work Amongst the Homeless: The Verbal Construction and Avowal of Personal Identities. *American Journal of Sociology.* 92: 1336–71.

Snow, D. and Anderson, L. (1987) *Down on Their Luck: A Study of Homeless Street People.* LA: University of California Press.

Sommerville, P. (1992) Homelessness and the Meaning of Home: Roofless or Rootless? *International Journal of Urban and Regional Research.* 16: 4, 529–39.

Southard, D. (1997) Uneasy Sanctuary: Homeless People Camping on Public Lands. *International Journal of Visual Sociology.* 12: 2, 47–64.

The Housing Corporation and Liverpool Strategic Housing Partnership (2004) *The Housing and Related Experiences of Asylum Seekers and Refugees in Liverpool.* The Housing Corporation and Liverpool Strategic Housing Partnership.

The Refugee Council (2004) *Agenda for Integration.* The Refugee Council.

Taveccihio, L. et al. (1999) Moral Judgement and Delinquency in Homeless Youth. *Journal of Moral Education.* 28: 1, 63–79.

Tucker, S. (2004) *Youth Working: Professional Identities Given, Received or Contested.* In Roshe, J. et al. *Youth in Society.* London: Sage.

UN (1990) *Guidelines for the Prevention of Juvenile Delinquency.* Geneva: UN.

Valesco, I. (2001) *Service User Participation: Concepts, Trends, Practices.* Edinburgh: Scottish Council for the Single Homeless.

Van Doorn, A. and Williamson, D. (2001) *Good Practice Companion for Emergency Accommodation for Homeless People.* London: Homeless Link.

Van Doorn, A. and Kain, M. (2003) *To Boldly Go . . . Where the Homelessness Sector Has Never Gone Before.* Housing Studies Association: on line www.york.ac.uk/inst/chp/hsa/

Wagner, D. (1993) *Checkerboard Square: Culture and Resistance in a Homeless Community.* Boulder: Westview Press.

Watson, S. and Austerberry, H. (1986) *Housing and Homelessness: A Feminist Perspective.* London: Routledge and Kegan Paul.

Weber, Y. (1996) Corporate Cultural Fit and Performance in Mergers and Acquisitions. *Human Relations.* 49: 9, 1181–203.

Widdowfield, R. (2002) *Beggars, Blaggers and Bums: Media Representations of Homeless People.* London: British Academy.

Willcock, K. (2004) *Journeys out of Loneliness, The Views of Older Homeless People.* London: Help the Aged.

Wistow, G. et al. (1994) *Social Care in a Mixed Economy.* Buckingham: Open University Press.

Wyner, R. (1998) *User Involvement in Hostels: A Therapeutic Community-Informed Approach to Work With Homeless People.* www.theraputiccommunities.com

Znaniecki, F. (1934) *The Method of Sociology.* New York: Rinehard.

Zufferey, C. and Kerr, L. (2004) Identity and Everyday Experiences of Homelessness: Some Implications for Social Work. *Australian Social Work.* 57: 4, 343–53.

Websites

www.arhagatep.co.uk African Refugee Housing Action Group (ARHAG)
www.centrepoint.org.uk
www.connections-at-stmartins.org.uk
www.crisis.org.uk
www.hact.org.uk Housing Association Charitable Trust (HACT)
www.ind.homeoffice.gov.uk Home Office Immigration and Nationality Directorate
www.mhp-online.co.uk/metropolitanhousingtrust_html/refugeehousingassociation_ html/RHA/
www.mungos.org/about/mungo
www.nacvs.org.uk National Association of Councils for Voluntary Service
www.nta.nhs.uk/frameset.asp?u = http://www.nta.nhs.uk/programme/guidance/ mocam.html
www.passage.org.uk

www.providencerow.org.uk
www.refugeeaccess.info Refugee Access (website for asylum seekers, refugees and agencies working in Yorkshire, Humberside and Liverpool)
www.refugee-action.org.uk Refugee Action
www.refugeecouncil.org.uk Refugee Council
www.salvationarmy.org.uk
www.shelter.org.uk/sexualexclusion
www.simoncommunity.org.uk
www.society-guardian.co.uk/homelessness/story
www.stonewall.org.uk/stonewall/information_bank/education/section_28
www.stonewall.org.uk/stonewall/information_bank/partnership/civil
www.thamesreachbondway.com
www.torturecare.org.uk Medical Foundation for the Care of Victims of Torture
www.unleash.org.uk/htmdocs/links.htm

Index

agencies
  affect of inconsistencies 166
  need to understand identities 2
  part in construction of identities 9, 165,
    167
  rejection of 24, 139
  stress, not dealing with 139
aggression
  experience of 19, 95
  management of 103–9
  nature of 97, 99–101
  policy 106
ASBOs 19
asylum seekers 58–60
attitudes of workers
  anti-intellectualism 155, 164
  issues of consensus 149–50
  issues of contention 155–7
  minority issues 152–5
  on client capability 154
  record keeping, avoidance of 156
  value of experience 147
autonomy, importance of 161, 168

begging 15, 117–8, 122
body language 107–8
bull ring 117

care sector, opinions of 156
caring, importance of 146–7
couples
  agency discrimination 44, 49
  experience in agencies 49
  lack of understanding of 50
  reactions to services 51
  reasons for discrimination 50
challenging behaviour

agencies contributions to 101–2, 140, 162
  changing perceptions of 93, 163
  definitions 98
  exotic communication 93
  fresh start for 96
  management of 102–3
  mirroring behaviour of 96–7
  recommendations about 109–10
client relationships 145, 150
client responsibilities 153
communication 105–6
conflict 155
criminality 18, 20
culture 9, 161
cultural anchor points of the homeless sector
  126, 130–1, 136, 141
  views and relationships with other agencies
    135, 138
  prioritizing values over expertise 135
  meeting needs with action 134
  need to examine 167
  practical orientation 132, 134, 155, 164,
    168
  seeing clients in terms of housing needs
    133

debriefing 108–9
deceit 97
definitions of homelessness 43
dependency, on services 11, 153
de-skilling of clients 150
detox services 83
dignity, importance of 161, 168
distrust of homeless narratives 11
drinking 17, 22–3, 83
drug use 21–3, 75, 146, 165
dual diagnosis 75–6

empty time 16, 23
equality, fallacy of 164
encounters with homeless people 113–4
    unease about 114–5
    feelings of guilt 115
engagement, disengagement 10
expectations of homeless people 15

finance management 17, 21
funding 87

gender 30
groundswell 52

health services 78–9
home, notions of 119–20, 123
homeless community 51, 168
homelessness
    changing understanding of 132
    as more than just housing 133
homeless strategies 76, 126
homeless sector
    anchor points (see cultural anchor points of
        the homeless sector)
    culture 131
    changes in 128, 132
    existing reports 127
    growth of 140–1
    nature of 129
    need for change 127, 140–1, 164
    negative labels 132–4, 160, 163
hostels, as containment 165

identity
    contesting 2, 26, 162
    importance of 1, 160–1, 168
    lack of rationality 2
    negotiating 20, 26, 162–3
    of workers 155
    redundancy of future 3, 165, 168
    Snow and Anderson 3–4, 122
    positives of street culture4, 160
    rough sleepers 10
institutionalised homelessness 12
interagency working 156

keyworking 137

language 121
Lincolns Inn Fields 117
LGBT homelessness
    agency reactions 33, 35–6, 41
    cycles of rejection 27, 33, 164
    development of identity 27
    double identity 39–40
    under researched 27
    homeless community reactions 34, 36–7
    section 28, 32
    stereotyping 31
    transgender issues 30, 38

managers 138–9
Maslow 1
meaningless exchanges 168
mental health 90, 165
multiple needs
    case studies 90–2
    definition 75
    good practice 87–9
    health services, and 77–9
    holistic treatment of 81–2
    prevalence of 76
    problems with services 77
    services needed 84–5
    young people and 80
myths 113, 118–20, 168
    American dream 119
    Britishness 119–21

needs, models of 3
nimbyism 19–20

ontological insecurity 120
organisational culture 129–30
organisational changes 128
organisational theories 129–31

part-time homelessness 10, 12, 18
pets 52–3
power 151, 153
professionalisation 143, 158–9
professional knowledge 143

qualifications, importance of 146–7

racism 61–2, 67, 114
referral 138
reflective practice 64, 139, 166–7
refugees
    asylum process 64
    benefits 60, 64
    dispersal 63, 68–70
    experiences of flight 63–4
    experiences of loss 63
    lack of agency understanding 61
    NASS 60
    pre-flight experiences 66
    RCO 59
    RSO 59
    support services 62, 70–2
refugee council 59
relationships
    double blind 53
    importance of 47, 162–3, 168
    negativity towards 50–1, 162–3
    protection in 47
    same sex couples 54
    self esteem 48
    taking responsibility in 48
    trust in 48
    ways forward 55–6
repeat homelessness 25–6
resettlement 1, 58, 73
resourcefulness of homeless people 11, 26
risk management 98
romanticisation of homelessness 113
rough sleepers
    abuse 23
    characteristics of 11–2
    friendships 12
    use of night shelters 13
    use of space 13–5

self reliance 23
self belief 71, 150, 168
situated learning 143
social construction of homelessness 18, 20, 24
    distancing from homeless people 115–6

denial of space 116–7
focus on structure and action 135–7
homeless peoples reactions to 121, 123–5
invoking of personal crises 112, 114
invoking of societal crisis 113, 114
lack of reflection 137, 166
media constructions 116, 119
need for changes 124
public constructions 116
rationalisation of homelessness 115
social networks, importance of 164
stereotyping 94–5
structural discrimination 168
supervision, models of 166
supporting people 126–8, 135, 147

teamwork 105
trauma 66, 139, 165, 168
typology of workers
    traditionalist worker 144
    reformist workers 144–5
    individualist trends 158
    post modern trends 158–9

unpredictability 97
user involvement 86, 154, 161–2
utilitarianism 154–5

violence
    against homeless people 20, 113

welfare 21–2
work ethic 120, 122
workers
    attitudes (see attitudes of workers)
    boundaries 139
    cynicism 140
    constructions of homelessness 115
    ex-clients as 145
    factors in being a good worker 145
    lack of training 138, 152
    lack of support 166
    motivations 148
    perceptions of role 150
    responsibilities 151–2
    typologies of (see typology of workers)